THE MIDDLE EAST
A Social Geography

THE MIDDLE EAST

A Social Geography

by

STEPHEN H. LONGRIGG

*Read not to contradict and confute, nor to
believe and take for granted, nor to find
talk and discourse, but to weigh and consider*

Francis Bacon (1561–1626)

ALDINE PUBLISHING COMPANY
CHICAGO

Library of Congress Catalog Card Number 63–21832

First published 1963
ALDINE PUBLISHING COMPANY
64 East Van Buren Street
Chicago 5, Illinois

Gerald Duckworth & Co. Ltd.
London

SECOND PRINTING

Printed in the United States of America

CONTENTS

LIST OF ILLUSTRATIONS

BETWEEN PAGES 32 AND 33.

ACKNOWLEDGMENTS

Photographs have been supplied by kind permission of the following:

BP	British Petroleum Co.	*KOC*	Kuwait Oil Co.
BS	Black Star	*PE*	Persian Embassy
FS	Miss Freya Stark	*PH*	Paul Hartman, Paris
IE	Israeli Embassy	*PP*	Paul Popper
IOP	Iran Oil Participants	*SG*	Sudan Government
IPC	Iraq Petroleum Co.		

No. 57 is reproduced from Asad: *The Road to Mecca* by permission of The Bodley Head Ltd.; Nos. 56 and 60-63 from Stark: *Seen in the Hadhramaut* by permission of John Murray Ltd.; Nos. 9-18 from *Turkey in Pictures* (Duckworth).

MAPS by R. W. FORD

1.   THE MIDDLE EAST: GENERAL, p.12.
2.   EGYPT AND THE SUDAN, p.141.
3.   THE PERSIAN GULF, p.168.
4.   THE MIDDLE EAST: OILFIELDS AND PIPELINES, p.174.

PREFACE

THE pages here following are, in my intention, far from constituting a text-book of Middle Eastern geography or society, or a political analysis of its many problems, or an orderly statistical or economic review; they are, indeed, no nearer to being a substitute for all or any of the many excellent books already published on these subjects than are the sketch-maps to taking the place of the large-scale atlas which, I hope, readers will have open at their elbows. I have felt compelled to pass over important aspects of the Middle Eastern region and its component countries, almost or entirely in silence: among such aspects being those of military resources, prominent personalities, constitutional or legal issues, budgets and balances of trade. And even on matters upon which I have tried to say something fairly specific—topography, races and languages, religions, climates, natural resources and agronomy, industry, communications—too little detailed information can be given in the compass available to satisfy a reader (perhaps, in this case, a student) desirous of a full picture of a given aspect of things in this or that territory. For most of such detail, and not less for an appreciation which may be widely different from mine, he can very easily look elsewhere: the literature of these countries, as of today, is abundant and accessible. My attempt has been to offer an objective but informed account of the different races and social forces found in Middle Eastern environments, urban and rural, in terms of the particular circumstances, problems and hopes of the dozen separate and more or less divided states of the region. It is my hope that the non-specialist reader may from all this learn something true and perhaps suggestive, while the expert may find not too much to offend him. The views expressed are those of one whose personal experience of these countries has been extensive, I hope receptive, and certainly sympathetic. In fully half of the territories covered, and particularly those of the Fertile Crescent, I have, as a long-term resident, had many friends over many years.

At the time of writing, much of the region is, as notably as any in the world, in a continuing state of visible, often revolutionary, change in almost every field—social, cultural, economic, political. Time will, henceforward, greatly modify the conditions here presented. I have intended, therefore, chiefly to emphasize those aspects which, being the least ephemeral, are likely to remain valid for some years, and, I hope, to indicate the areas in which, and the lines on which, change, on indications already visible, is most to be expected. And if in the near future country A acquires or suppresses country B, country C changes its form of government to become a republic or a dictatorship, or discovers oil, and country D becomes a satellite of the U.S.S.R., the reader will at least be informed of the conditions out of which—or because of which—such change occurred.

In the method of spelling oriental names I have, like other orientalists anxious to avoid the appearance of pedantry, tried to compromise between correct and popular spellings—with results which, as usual, will certainly fail to please everybody.

The arrangement of relevant material to the best advantage and the reader's convenience has proved a particularly puzzling problem: was it to be on a regional, or a country-by-country, or a subject-by-subject basis? And how were dullness and repetition to be best avoided? The solution adopted, one of inconsistent compromise, will not suit all tastes; but to the dissatisfied I recommend the use of the two indices provided, whereby they will find, I hope, most of what there is to find.

The kindly individuals and corporations who have made their photographs available for these pages, to an extent which the list thereof will make plain, are hereby most cordially thanked.

S. H. L.

15th November, 1962.

CHAPTER ONE

THE REGION

1. Scale and Orientation

IN a region of the earth where much is dubious, and little undisputed, the content of its very designation, 'Middle East', is the first controversy to be met. The term was invented, half a century ago, by an American admiral, and seemed to fill a need; it gained ground, become respectable, and was accepted, largely thanks to 1939–1945 wartime usage, in official (especially military and political) as well as popular circles. Less generally in the western hemisphere, where 'Near East' still prevails, but very widely now in the eastern, the phrase has taken its place with other convenient titles—Eastern Europe, French Africa, Soviet Bloc, South-East Asia—as meaning something conveniently thus expressed.

But what, and how to be delineated? If on lines of pure geography, one's northern boundaries must be the Caspian, Caucasus, Black Sea and Marmara: the western, the Aegean, eastern Mediterranean, Suez Canal and Red Sea; the southern must be the Arabian Sea and Gulf of Oman: the eastern, perhaps, a line across the horrific desert that covers east-central Persia across most of its narrow waist from the Caspian to the Makran coast. But the area so defined would include Russian Transcaucasia, which nobody claims today as Middle East, and would exclude Turkey-in-Europe, Egypt and the Sudan, and the eastern one-third of Persia. To correct this, therefore, one must add to geographic some cultural and political criteria, on which agreement is no matter of course. Thus guided, we shall omit Transcaucasia: bring in Cyprus, a slightly dubious recruit: enrol obviously Egypt, and less obviously the Sudan, while leaving its southern, pagan, purely African provinces largely out of account, and shut the door, with some hesitation, on Libya, whose Cyrenaican province, up to the great Sirte divide, could well pass as Middle East. All of Persia must come in. It is doubtfully logical to omit, as we do, Afghanistan, but this is more Central Asian: and it is tempting perhaps, but not quite sufficiently, to admit the Islamic, part-Arabian Somalis.

Our area then, in the end, is that of the Egyptian and Sudanese

THE MIDDLE EAST: GENERAL

Republics, the Hashimite Kingdom of Jordan, the State of Israel, the Republics of the Lebanon, Syria, Turkey, 'Iraq and Cyprus, the Kingdom of Persia, that of Sa'udi Arabia, and the Imamate (but since September 1962 the Republic) of the Yemen, the small Arab states and shaikhdoms of the Persian Gulf coast, the Sultanate of Muscat and Oman, and the British protectorate and colony of Aden. We are covering, therefore, some 3,500,000 square miles of land, and some 120,000,000 of human beings. Of all this, nearly 1,000,000 square miles belong to non-Arab states, with 51,000,000 inhabitants; the rest is Arab country.

The region forms, to the eye of the space-traveller (or map reader), a single roughly quadrilateral land-mass, some 2,200 miles from west to east and 2,000 north to south, pierced by two sharply intruding seas on the south, the Red Sea and Persian Gulf, and one on the west, the Mediterranean. The area falls almost entirely between the lines of longitude 25° E to 62° E, and between latitudes 13° N and 42° N; it is all, therefore, outside the tropics except the southern half of Egypt, all the Sudan, and southern Arabia. Typical mileages, to show the scale of the area, are: from the Nile Delta to Khartum, 1,100 miles; Aleppo to Aden, 1,750; the Aegean to the Caspian, 1,250; Lataqiya to Meshhed, 1,425; Istanbul to south-eastern Arabia, 2,250.

These are formidable distances; the territory is wide. It would be more manageable, and its problems diminished, if the natural blocks or major fragments which compose it were to correspond to its political, or national, pattern. But they are far from doing this. Excepting the island-states of Cyprus and Bahrain, and perhaps the detached sea-and-desert-bounded Sultanate of Oman, no single political unit in the Middle East enjoys the security, or the convenience, of natural boundaries. On the contrary, the geographical blocs or units, such as they are, are all composed of more than a single state. The Nile Valley contains Egypt and the Sudan, an area of Libya and Ethiopia, and part of central Africa. Arabia, a broad spacial unity, adds to the Sa'udi Kingdom the important fringe territories of the Yemen, Aden, Oman, the Gulf statelets and, in its northern extension towards the Fertile Crescent, areas also of Jordan, Syria, and 'Iraq. The Levant coast and hinterland—that is, true geographical Syria—contains Jordan, Israel, the Lebanon, Syria, and the Hatay province of Turkey. In Asia Minor, which contains all Turkey except its small European residue, there are none but the most blurred or arbitrary of boundaries against the U.S.S.R., Persia, 'Iraq and Syria.

The Tigris–Euphrates Valley, all 'Iraqi, is flanked by a quite dis-similar but equally 'Iraqi area of mountainous Kurdistan, and by a Persian province (Khuzistan) which is strictly southern-'Iraqi in character. Persia has no natural frontier on its north-western or north-eastern front, nor on the east; indeed, the land-block of which it forms part includes also Afghanistan and part of Pakistan.

Any who follow today's controversies in the region—Nile waters, Euphrates and Jordan waters, Kurdish unrests and ambitions, Perso-'Iraqi bickering, Yemeni claims to Aden, 'Iraqi demands for Kuwait, Sa'udi for Buraimi, and many more—will realize how much happier an area—or possibly less happy, with its most favoured occupation gone?—the Middle East would be if each of its states enjoyed a territory demarkated on something like natural or logical lines; yet nothing could be less likely than the achievement of any such goal.

Looking outward from within the area, one sees how various, and fraught with what implications in war or peace, are its avenues of approach or egress. In the east, Persia lies open to Afghanistan and Pakistan, which are highways to central Asia and the Indian sub-continent; in the extreme north-east, it offers the most open of frontiers to the Soviet Socialist Republic of the Turkmen. In the north-west, beside the Caspian (itself a Russian lake) Persian Azar-baijan looks across no barrier on to the Soviet states of (Russian) Azarbaijan and Armenia, as north-eastern Turkey looks equally at Georgia—these being all territories, south of the Caucasus, which were Persian or Turkish before the Russian conquests of the nine-teenth century. The north-western frontier of the Turks is an arbi-tary, defenceless line as against Bulgaria and Greece and all south-eastern Europe behind these. The whole western border of Egypt and the northern Sudan with the Kingdom of Libya is open desert; to the south, the Sudan's neighbours (remote indeed from any Middle Eastern character) are the ex-French independent republics of Chad and Centrafrica (formerly Oubangui-Chari), the ex-Belgian Congo, Uganda, Kenya and Ethiopia. From no one of all these directions have the Middle Eastern peoples, throughout history, failed to derive immigrant elements of their population, culture, or political or dynastic fortunes; and, among the many examples which this consideration, thoughtfully pursued, will evoke—to and from central Asia and India, across the Caucasus, into and out of Europe, up and down the Nile—the sea-ways, and above all those of the

Mediterranean and Aegean, will provide a store not less rich than the routes and bypaths of the mainland.

2. Content and Circumstance

Although its formative and dominant features extend beyond it to west and east, a rough classification of our region into three zones is convenient and, since these zones differ so widely in their potential as human habitations, is not uninstructive. The most northerly, a sector of the inter-continental folded zone stretching from the Alps to the Himalayas, covers Asia Minor and Persia; it is marked by long parallel, but sometimes diverging, mountain ranges, whose irregular emergence under powerful pressures of the earth's crust has been further diversified through the ages by more local movements, varying resistances, uneven weathering and other factors. In fact, it is not today a single tidy ridge which reflects in our region these millions of years of geological stresses, with successive earlier and later, stronger and feebler, movements all contributing; it is a wide, deformed and tangled belt of mountainous country, enclosing valleys and lakes, a few rapid unnavigable rivers, depressions rendered salty and repulsive by inward drainage, and high inter-mountain plateaux of which both Turkey and Persia have major examples or of which, indeed, these countries largely consist.

South of this mountain zone lies another, extending from the Sinai peninsula around north Arabia (but south of Taurus) and covering the Euphrates–Tigris lowlands, and the southern shores of the Persian Gulf. Of this area the western flank (Syria, Lebanon, Jordan, Israel) shows faulted, north–south ranges running parallel to the Mediterranean coast; the eastern two-thirds represents the unfolded surviving area of the great Persian Gulf geosyncline deep in the sediments of an ancient sea and modern rivers—and, as we shall see, by far the greatest storehouse of liquid petroleum in the world. This intermediate region is thus less uniform, less clearly characterized, than the other two, yet is more livable and more productive than either.

Our third zone, by far the widest and most uniform, stretching from north and east Africa across almost all Arabia, is that of the African-Arabian Shield. It is characterized by its horizontal masses of ancient and strongly resistant rocks, little disturbed except by the deep (but geologically recent) fissure of the Red Sea, and by volcanic action and lava-flows closely following the fissure line. The

Shield, tilted in Arabia to slope gently downwards towards the east, has been at different geological periods depressed at its edges below sea level, with resulting deposit of sedimentary rocks, not generally comparable in depth with those of synclinal areas but enough to account for Libyan and Algerian oil. The local mountain systems of Oman and the Yemen must be somehow fitted in to the general scheme or schemes of western Asian land-folding, according to the taste of debating geologists.

Partly from these structural differences, partly from others of rock and soil, rainfall and aspect, latitude and temperature, there results in the Middle East an astonishing variety of topographic or land-surface character; the European who has lived in Egypt, or shopped in Beirut, or crossed a desert, or passed months somewhere in an Embassy, cantonment or college, little realizes the widely varied scenic resources, the diversity of settings, which the region can afford. What, and where, are these?

True desert (distinct from lightly-vegetated steppe) is seen by few outsiders, and crossed by fewer. It can be sandy—with or without dunes—or marly, gravelly or stony, for each variety of which local dialects have their word: waterless, or with stretches of salt-marsh: flat or broken or hilly or, as in Sinai, mountainous. Passable always in favourable months by lightly-riding camel-parties, the true desert today offers relatively little resistance to the motor-car, none to aircraft; and one age-long horror is, or need be, no more. Typical middle-eastern deserts, far smaller than the Sahara, are those to east and west of the middle Nile, the Nafud of northern Arabia and the greater Ruba' al-Khali (Empty Quarter) of southern, and the deserts of east-central Persia, the Dasht-i-Kavir and Dasht-i-Lut. Many others would qualify for inclusion. In spite of dust storms and mirage, hideous aridity and wearying surface, the true desert has its attraction, even its beauty; and there are men of quick intelligence and humour to whom it is, if not home, at least familiar and not uncongenial.

The lightest steppe is but one remove from sheer desert, with the basic difference that its scanty, scrubby, thorny, and in rarer places grassy, vegetation can provide, at least in the spring months of a favoured year, some sort of grazing for the camel-herds of the true *badu* who lead in isolation their comfortless, precarious life from waterhole to waterhole. Such steppe country is found, characteristically, on the southern face of the Fertile Crescent, and in partly-vegetated, partly-desertic stretches of Arabia. Less arid but still normally uncultivable steppe is the normal grazing-ground of inlying camel-herds and of the sheep- and goat-owning sections of settled tribes. This is the countryside which, found in southernmost Turkey, western 'Iraq, eastern Syria and Jordan, and wide areas of Persia, can after spring rains turn into a sea of light, ephemeral grass and flowers of wonderful beauty, only to revert weeks later into forbidding brown-grey waste. Steppe life, with all its rigours and poverty, is healthy, strenuous, and full of the tradition and pride of tribalism undebased by the labours of the plough. It is a type of country and of life unknown in western Europe.

Both in utter desert and in all the varieties of steppe-land the oasis is a much-romanticized, yet truly a life-saving, feature. It is marked always by some supply of permanent water, a few dwellings —or in some major settlements, a fair-sized town, as in the oases of central Arabia—probably date-gardens and possibly other limited cultivation, and provision made, by merchant and shopkeeper, for the needs of buying-parties from the steppe-dwelling folk. No country which offers desert or semi-desert areas lacks some examples of oasis life, which modern transport and amenities are daily removing farther from their old remoteness.

A different world is that of the higher, often too the lower, mountain zone with its watered valley cultivation—sometimes immemorially terraced, as in Lebanon or the Yemen—its movement of migratory herdsmen between upper and lower pastures, its clinging hillside villages and intermontane small towns, its planted groves on the lower slopes and the wild scrub or (infrequently) genuine forest on the upper, and in places—the highest peaks of eastern Taurus and of Zagros and Elburz, with Ararat and Demavend outstanding—crowned with perpetual snow. Major stretches of exploitable forest have not, on the whole, survived in the Middle East into the modern age; there is no forest way of life. But otherwise in the wide and wild mountain zones of the region there is room for every type of urban, village, farming and pastoral life, led by peasants, herdsmen and tribes of many races against backgrounds of sometimes grim, sometimes friendly land-surface, at all levels both of physical altitude and of human evolution.

Contrast all this with the lives of the fishing or coast-wise sailing folk of the Black Sea (with its tropical south-eastern shore), or Caspian or Aegean; or the normal Mediterranean seafaring from the delectable villages and port-towns of Syria and Lebanon which face the bluest and clearest of tideless seas; or the reed- and shoal-

and lagoon-fringed Nile Delta, or the featureless sparsely-inhabited shores of the Red and Arabian Seas and the Persian Gulf. No single country of the Middle East lacks a sea-outlet, even 'Iraq with its one river-estuary, even Jordan with only 'Aqaba.

Agriculture, the occupation of far the greater part of Middle Eastern populations, covers in one of its many forms all cultivable areas, tiny percentage as these are of the whole land-surface. Most of western and northern Turkey and part of southern, is agricultural country of a sort, and so is Cyprus, and much of Persia outside the desert regions, and the broad dry-farming lands of the Fertile Crescent as well as the irrigated lands of central and lower 'Iraq, Syria, the Egyptian Delta, the Yemen, and the greater Arabian oases; and later pages of this book may show how various are the scenes and methods, the potentialities of planting and crop-growing in the dozen countries. These are the settled, most favoured areas of many thousands of regionally characteristic villages, locally varying in type, scale, appearance and amenities; of populations sometimes dangerously too dense, sometimes inadequately scanty; of dependence on uncertain rains, or of security assured by irrigation; of primeval method and low yield, or of modern mechanization and pretension. These, in all, are the regions which contain the greatest human activity and wealth production, dull and almost empty as much of them can appear, to the consternation of western visitors, in the seasons when no crops are standing, and where half the land may be fallow. And it is true that few Middle Eastern scenes offer the luxurious greenness of grass and scrub and soft verdant hill and valley, which are the delight of Europe.

These more smiling regions of farmland or easy pasture are those which contain most of the great modern and ancient cities of the Middle East, names too famous to need repeating here; the renowned sites of antiquity, from Persepolis or Babylon to the upper Nile, and the famous still-flourishing shrines of the Islamic and Christian middle ages, from Isfahan and Meshhed to Konya, from Cairo, Damascus and Jerusalam to the Holy Cities of Arabia and 'Iraq.

Of the Middle Eastern landscape, the widest areas present today a picture nearly identical to that of previous centuries, perhaps millennia. Yet a revisiting ghost from antiquity or the Middle Age would still notice changes, not indeed in the face of desert or ocean, but in the course of rivers, the silting at their mouths, the extent of marshes; in human works of drainage, barrage-building, and flood dykes, with irrigation canals and perhaps hydro-electric stations dependent on these. He would see cultivation extended today to limits familiar, perhaps, to our *revenant* from antiquity but far wider than those of the earlier centuries of modern times. He would be shown how thousands of miles of modern roads and railways, with scores of massive river-bridges and hill-cuttings, have shortened distance and sophisticated the scene. A glimpse of seaport installations, giant oil pipelines, industrial workshops, power and telegraph lines crossing desert and mountain, would puzzle and amaze him. In fact, not only in the partly-modernized face of the cities (and hundreds of the villages) has modern effort attacked the whole aspect of the scene, but in the countryside also it is, within limits, ever changing; yet far more is unchangeable, at least until unknown agencies bring about a basic variation of climate. As to this, it has been widely believed that climatic conditions, thought to be cyclical, have varied in the course of human history, and may vary again. Dry water-courses in Arabia, long abandoned, Roman tanks in Jordan, legends of ancient fertility in 'Iraq, and the visible fact of giant canals aligned in now waterless tracts, the imposing scale of steppe-country oases in Persia and Syria, are adduced to prove that, in earlier ages of our race, the Middle East was better watered. This is not proved; it is more probable that the days of greater humidity were those of pre-human ages—the Pleistocene, perhaps; and that, since man's appearance, the phenomena noticed can be well enough explained by a diminished population, a lowered water-table, some deforestation, much soil-erosion and scouring of river-beds, with the abandonment of once-inhabited sites for political or security reasons. In older human times, it rather seems, the conditions of life were substantially as they are today, with the same problems and disabilities, the same balance between agricultural and pastoral life, the same routes and halting-places.

Our region is, almost uniformly, one of hot summers and cold or cool winters, and the range of variation between July–August and January–February is unusually wide. The heat of mid-summer, its severity due to cloudless skies, scanty vegetation and (except near coasts) 'continental' conditions, runs in most Middle Eastern capitals to an average daily maximum in July of 82° to 92° F, but higher—93° to 100°—in Aleppo, Damascus, Teheran, Cairo and Aden, and well beyond 100°, up to extremes little short of 130°, in the cities of 'Iraq, inland southern Persia, and penisular Arabia. In mid-winter, the greatest cold occurs in eastern Asia Minor and parts of northern Persia, where a February average night minimum can be

—15° F, with an extreme of —35° or less. Aden is never less than warm in winter, Egypt cool (45°–50°), 'Iraq cooler (32°–42°), with northern Persia chilly (around 25°), Ankara cold (17°). Snow in winter, habitual in the north and the mountains, is not unknown throughout the region, except in the farthest south. Streams can freeze anywhere north of a line Jerusalem–Basra, and sea-water in the Black Sea. The greatest night–day variations occur far inland, and at high altitudes; here they are a marked feature, and restorative cool nights are the greatest of blessings in scorched 'Iraq and elsewhere. Air humidity is extremely low in 'continental' areas, where great dryness helps the endurance of intense heat; it is greater, or great, in seaside areas—the Mediterranean, Red Sea and Persian Gulf coasts—where, expecially in summer, it is highly uncomfortable. Fog is uncommon, but by no means unknown. The high dust-laden winds of summer, notably in 'Iraq and north Africa (the *sharqi* or *sharji*, and the *khamsin*) are a sore trial during their three or four days' duration; 'Iraq's northerly, date-ripening *shamal* is a corresponding relief.

The whole region would be transformed both in aspect and in economic potential if its rainfall were more plentiful and better distributed. Except in north-eastern Turkey, Caspian Persia, and parts of the Yemen, rain is nearly everywhere inadequate and in most cases gravely deficient. It falls, almost universally, in winter and spring only, with very minor or freakish falls in autumn; but its precise timing, a vital matter to the growth of the rain-dependent spring grains, can vary tragically, and in not infrequent years it can fall to half or less of its normal deposit: that is, well below minimum crop requirements. This does not preclude showers of great violence when they occur, giving, over small areas, an inch of rain in an hour —with effects on traffic which can be imagined. Most of Arabia and Egypt are habitually rainless, the Fertile Crescent and most of Iran ill-supplied with a bare 6 to 14 inches a year, western Turkey and the Levant coast fairly adequately with 20 to 30 inches; but the deficiency of statistics, and the caprices of the weather itself, make precision impossible. Both local and annual variations are extreme, yet of immense importance to immediate human needs.

Are human needs, then, in general well served or not by Middle Eastern conditions? In spite of travellers' tales and some admittedly adverse features, and in so far as one may generalize over so wide and heterogeneous an area, conditions must be pronounced favourable. If temperatures can be extreme, they are never unbearable, and neither physical well-being nor morale need suffer. Cool and clear summer nights are normal. Winds can be high—as they can be in Europe; rains can fail—not in the Middle East alone. Air is pure, often highly invigorating. Every season has its charm, if rarely quite unalloyed. Contrasts of temperature should be welcomed. With a reasonable personal régime and intelligent adaptation to conditions, excellent health can be enjoyed; the indifferent physique of too many Middle Easterners is due mainly to causes other than their natural environment. Indeed, considering the dangers to health consequent on a central position in the world, and numerous centres of thronged pilgrimage, and widely low standards of living, endemic disease is less menacing than might well be expected, and can without great difficulty be almost entirely avoided by the careful and the competent. Malaria is widely prevalent, in its usual haunts, but is easily treated and is being yearly circumscribed. Yellow fever, known in the Sudan, is rare in the Middle East. Typhus occurs epidemically, but is never widespread. Cholera, never endemic, is now uncommon. Dysentery is a known danger to foreigners, but can be kept at bay by due precautions. Bilharzia is common in Egypt and in 'Iraq; hookworm (ankylostomiasis) is similar. Eye diseases, especially trachoma, are common and distressing but, under treatment, now fast diminishing. The same is true of the painless but disfiguring 'Baghdad boil' or 'Aleppo button'. Of all of these and other diseases, dirt, poverty and ignorance are the firm allies, in whose absence they can be, indeed to an encouraging extent are being, overcome. Sheer malnutrition, reflecting a too generally low level of wealth and resources, is by far the greatest enemy of health and vigour, and its progressive correction, significant of all-round improvement in standards of life, must remain the supreme task of governments and peoples.

3. Does it matter?

This is the moment, perhaps, for pausing to ask and answer two questions which a critical reader may have been formulating. The first is—has this region, upon the many diversities of which we have been insisting, any *unity* at all?—is it authentically a Region? and secondly, is it, or ought it to be, of any genuine or particular *interest* to the present-day citizen of the world?

There is no geological and little topographical unity, racial homogeneity only in a generalized sense, linguistic not at all, political too evidently imperfect. Yet, apart from the sheer propinquity and con-

tinuity of the Middle Eastern territories one with another, their overlapping physical circumstance, and considerable cultural and religious
(that is, Islamic) unity, there are also undeniably similar features of
character among most of the populations concerned, familar elements
of common regional history, not dissimilar phases of national emergence and aspiration—and shared antipathies!—and, with all this,
much modern inter-territory social admixture, mutual familarity,
visiting, intermarriage. It is, on the whole, a Region.

As to its degree of significance to the world outside, it could
indeed be, and has been, argued that for some centuries the region
has made no first-class, acclaimed contribution to the world's learning, culture or outstanding performance: that it has long fallen away
from, and is not yet restored to, the main currents of human progress:
that it lacks any broadly based social or intellectual contact with the
West. On another plane, it may be felt that the uneasy bickering and
inconstancy of its political attitudes, its alleged immaturity or irre-
sponsibility in international affairs, its tiresome egocentricities, its
failures in democratic government, are neither admirable nor re-
assuring. Economically, it is known to possess no single important
resource, save only petroleum; it is an area of poverty and want,
backward in its traditional agriculture, and but a beginner, and of no
more than mediocre promise, in modern industry. These are harsh
charges; they are, to be sure, not wholly true nor wholly false; and,
either way, there is much more than this to be said.

This region indeed, which seems, by its continuous prominence in
the world's headlines, to be thought interesting by mankind at large,
has high claims to our close attention, and to our sympathy. In the
field of sentiment, it offers a great and often beautiful variety of
scene, a persistent survival of the romantic, and the spectacle of
societies, themselves most varied, of attractive human beings in
many environments and at diverse stages of their evolution from
earlier to the most modern phases of development. There are everywhere links with the early days of the great religions of Islam,
Christianity and Judaism, all of which are still abundantly alive in
the area. To the missionary and educator, the field has long been
one of outstanding attraction and major effort. To the archaeologist
and historian, it is a region of unique appeal for its ancient and
medieval civilizations, for the world's earliest recorded ways of life
and cities and empires, with all that these involve and offer. To the
orientalist it is the greatest of storehouses. And to thousands of
families in the West it is the scene of two world wars in our own

century, whereby thousands of their kinsmen found graves in 'some corner of a foreign field' within these territories.

In the sphere of economics, the presence in the Middle East of the greatest petroleum deposits in the world must outweigh its comparative lack of other indigenous wealth, and must be of outstanding interest to the producing countries themselves (who own the oil-fields), to the great international companies entrusted by them with operation, and to the world at large whose adequate supply of this most indispensable of substances depends on the Middle Eastern sources. Apart from this, the agriculture, the stock-breeding, and the increasing industry of the territories themselves are, and can be, on a scale by no means unimportant; the populations can offer markets which will inevitably increase in scale; and they call for assistance in the execution of their own development plans, which the nations of the West do not find uninteresting. Nor is the economic future of Middle Eastern countries, on their national scale, other than an engrossing study.

Strategically, this three-continental region has all the importance of its unique central position, its immemorial east–west routes between Europe and Africa and central and southern Asia, its endless available airfields, its almost unavoidable (but nationalistically sacrosanct) inter-continental corridors of air-route. It contains narrow but vital strategic sea-ways—Bosphorus, Dardanelles, Suez Canal, and the straits at the base of the Red Sea and Persian Gulf —and harbours, repair bases, and bunkering stations. It seems indeed to be recognized that to wage global war without holding at least a favourable position in the Middle East, the wasp-waist of the Old World, would be barely a possibility. Of its value as a counter-attack area against northern enemies there may, in the age of atomic warfare, be less certainty; in a conventional war, it would be at least considerable.

As to the present politics of the region, these, in terms of the internal stresses and intrigues, the personalities and the fragile institutions of each single territory, are a study perhaps fascinating, often depressing, certainly instructive; and if today most of the Middle Eastern countries are of no great moment in the balance of world affairs, some few are of more significance and higher potential, while nearly all offer the far from banal spectacle of political entities yearly developing their public and economic life and passing, as they hope, from backward obscurity into a place and an individuality of their own on the world stage. This aspect, the emergence of communities from colonial or provincial or mandated status into sovereign rank, affords interesting examples of a movement common in twentieth-century Asia and Africa, and among the most significant of our times. Its immediate interest is all the keener since most of the nations concerned, once made members of United Nations, take their place among the officially uncommitted or unaligned, and, linked with sister nations of Africa, can by their votes exercise an influence wholly disproportionate to their own strength, wealth or population.

But this is still not the whole content of their international interest. Because the Middle East contains the sacred homelands of Islam, and the State of Israel, and the birthplace and home of Christianity's Founder, it follows that Muslims, Christians and Jews throughout the world take a keener interest in its vicissitudes, as these affect their religion and their co-religionists there, than in the fortunes of any other region on earth save those of their own residence. Muslims of Indonesia, Pakistan, Morocco, Senegal; Jews in New York, South Africa, London; Christians throughout Europe, America, Australia; all or any of these can be moved by actual or threatened events in the Middle East, and by their own government's attitude towards them, in the direction of political gestures or pressures at home which these governments cannot ignore. Thus Middle Eastern antipathies and hopes can cast their shadow into far-off lands, and can remind distant governments and publics of the unique and too easily dangerous sensitiveness attaching to the region of which we write.

CHAPTER TWO

ANTIQUITY

1. *Before the Dawn*

DOUBTS as to whether a Social Geography should pay heed to ages of past history in the region concerned can be dispelled by some cogent considerations. The early origins of the inhabitants, most imperfectly ascertainable, may throw but scanty light on their present idiosyncracies, but can hardly be uninteresting; their successive stages of cultural history have all contributed to what they now are, their racial admixtures show at least with what sort of human blends we have to deal, and the mere growth in scale of human groupings—village, canton, city-state, nation—reveals the power or impotence of contemporary society to face new problems. The effect of foreign contacts, by action and reaction, through trade or mere cultural borrowing, can be assessed. The influences of environment on the march of local history can hardly escape the observer, and may sway his present judgments, since they are sure to persist. The occasions of the introduction or evolution of new conceptions and inventions in the region may have significance. And in the recorded, or often enough the invented, achievements of their alleged forebears, a modern nation may find inspiration or political predilection still today operative.

We pass perforce, therefore, to a consideration of the races of men found originally and later in our region, and their early and subsequent history, until we see them in our own century taking form as the familiar nation-states of today.

In terms of population, we are limited to very few original elements. They belong, as do practically all later accretions that we shall note, to the Caucasiform group of humanity: that is, roughly, to the European-like, largely or mainly 'white', wavy-haired, narrow and salient-nosed, thin-lipped part of the human race so classified. The student of Middle Eastern affairs is almost never concerned with Negroes or Mongols, but only with our own main family. And, even within this, many sub-groups have no place on our stage; except for uncertain or slightest admixtures, the scene belongs to Alpine, Mediterranean and Nordic man.

Nordic man does not appear in the Middle East till historical times. He belongs by origin to the great central Asian grass-lands, but with gradual specialization to northern conditions in Asia and then in Europe. The body is slender, extremities long, skull and other bones rugged, face and nose narrow, cheekbones fairly prominent, colour blond. The variations of stature and skull-form (mainly long-shaped) show in historical times much admixture with the original 'pure' type (whenever and wherever evolved and dispersed) of other breeds encountered during millennia of movement.

Primeval Alpine man is of darker colouring, abundant body-hair, lightish eyes, medium height and strong build, with short or roundish head, high curved occiput, short narrow nose, broad face. The special Alpine type which, all agree, has contributed so largely to Middle Eastern populations (especially in Asia Minor, parts of Persia and 'Iraq, and the Syrian mountain-country) is the Armenoid, with a characteristic flat occiput, receding forehead, strong brow-ridges and cheekbones, long face, and a high-bridged nose with depressed tip and curved wings—the so-called 'Jewish' nose. It is likely that these Alpine types were, from some unknown place of origin, very early entrants into western Asia. They have dominated mountain areas ever since, but have penetrated far less into Africa or Arabia.

Mediterranean man is today found (never 'pure', but nearest to purity in Arabia and North Africa) all round the Mediterranean coasts, in non-mountainous 'Iraq and Persia, in Palestine and Egypt. In what is effectively a complex of similar types there is always discernible a dolichocephalic skull and a sallow pigment. In western Asia the type is of generally medium to tall stature, with prominent cheekbones, oval face, narrow skull, and a large, fairly broad nose, straight or convex and placed high on the face. The area in which this extremely prevalent breed, Mediterranean man, may have originated cannot be discovered; indeed, not only the unknown, probably unknowable, provenance of all human families must be emphasized, but the fact also that purity of type had been lost millennia before any race emerged into history; not only are all men mongrels, but they have been so for many thousands of years. It is apparent, however, for our present purpose that the first occupation of our region by *homo sapiens* was at a very remote palaeolithic period, when, after the retreat of the last glaciers, human societies penetrated the area: societies of physical types which, blended and adapted through the centuries to many environments, have in

Europe and Asia persisted and progressed more, in terms of valuable achievement, than other branches of the human family. And
the same processes of migration, penetration, settlement, and reblend-
ing have, as Middle Eastern history repeatedly illustrates, continued
from prehistoric times without interruption to our own.

In the days when the earliest artifacts, as discovered in many
parts of the Middle East, were fashioned by fumbling human or
near-human fingers, there was already a wide diversity of communities in many settings—hunting, food-gathering, fishing, or busy
with the earliest agriculture and animal husbandry—incorporating
the basic Alpines and Mediterraneans we have described, and keenly
conscious of village, tribal or (later) city identity. Among these, the
prehistoric Egyptians of, let us say, 5000 B.C., seem to have been
brunette Mediterranean types with almost certainly some darker-
skinned admixture from the south, with a strain also of Arabian
from across the Red Sea, and probably already some contribution of
Alpine immigrants from the Syrian hills. They lived in villages,
farmed, fished and hunted, used pots and baskets and flint-knives in
neatly-built houses, knew weaving and leatherwork, obeyed half-
priestly head-men, worshipped gods. The earliest Syrians were
Alpines in the coastal ridges, mixed already with Mediterraneans
from the flat Fertile Crescent hinterland where the latter prevailed.
These Neolithic folk were, like the Egyptians, very far from savagery;
they had their homes, furniture and implements, their way of life
varying between steppe, valley and sea-coast. The use of copper
came in about 4000 B.C. Cyprus was perhaps first occupied by
emigrants from western Asia, with a mixture of very early Aegean
settlers. In Asia Minor one would expect Armenoid types, perhaps
already diluted by the inward movement of undiscoverable non-
Alpine strains from south-east Europe or south Russia by way of the
Caucasus. Civilization, well begun by the fifth millennium B.C., varied
here as between the fringes of the central plateau, the two plains
south of Taurus, and the Aegean-type valleys of western Anatolia;
but in them all civilized village life was already developed. Persia,
not yet Aryanized, held a diffused, intelligent, village-dwelling Neolithic population, presumably Alpine and Mediterranean. Only in
the south, the future Khuzistan, does it seem that some alien strain
(just possibly north Indian or Dravidian) had penetrated. It had
created the highly developed civilization of Elam, already grouped in
large villages or even cities under priest-kingly control, with skilled
agriculture, fully articulate religion, and foreign trade.

The same picture holds good for central and southern 'Iraq. The Sumerians, small, dark and round-headed, and speaking an agglutinative language, remain mysterious, but, whoever they were, they had welded aboriginal elements into a new type of community, grouped in highly organized and competitive city-states directed by able, sophisticated men. Elsewhere in 'Iraq, Mediterraneans, with Alpine types in the (later) Kurdish mountains, were dominant. The open plains of northern 'Iraq and eastern Syria had held from remote ages settled and half-settled communities, less advanced than those we have mentioned but already providing the means of communication between Asia Minor, Syria, and the Euphrates Valley. In Arabia the population was probably less impure Mediterranean, but had experienced at some period an incursion of round-headed large-nosed Alpines from the northern mountain-zone to such territory there, in the deep south, as suited them. Arabia indeed, potentially the most isolated of our areas, was no doubt already developing its own migratory and, in the extreme south-west, settled ways: was reaching the limits of population it could sustain, and cradling the original Semitic stock—a population, that is, substantially uniform in type and speaking some basic variety of the later modified and localized Semitic language-family.

All this involves much vagueness and doubt; and even the terms and classifications we use have little enough of precise content. It is certain, however, that the more favoured areas of the region were inhabited by man from his earliest ages, and that he had by 5000 B.C. passed through the stages of acquiring speech and clothing, domestic comfort, settled residence, and relatively advanced notions of social organization, during millennia when his presence is still but faintly discernible to the archaeologist. And of what other area of all the world could this be said with so much confidence?

We proceed next to ask what, after a great leap through centuries, was to be the Middle Eastern picture by—to take a date almost at random—2500 B.C.

2. *Earliest History*

The emergence of our region into a faint light of history was by 2500 B.C. far from complete; we depend still on the archaeology which, in the hands of patient experts of a dozen nations, at scores of buried sites, has in the last century and a half made the Middle East the paradise of the scholar-digger.

But the pace of change was by that date already accelerating far beyond the nearly-static tempo of past millennia. The use of metals —copper, then bronze, then iron—was spreading into the fields of ornament, utensil and weapon; clothing, housing, specialization of function, were all developed and developing. Agriculture, and especially controlled irrigation, the lifeblood of Egypt and 'Iraq, had made strides of progress. Early forms of writing, not yet alphabetic, were in use in Sumer, Babylonia, Elam, Egypt, in the hands of priests, traders and account-book-minded landlords. The arts had reached a high perfection, royal and public building attained unknown levels and used materials brought from far afield. The worship of local (city and tribal) gods was ever more elaborated, and merged with the pretensions of local rulers more and more theocratic. Egyptian sovereigns had from about 4000 B.C. onwards built the greatest of the pyramids, the Sumerians their *ziggurats*, and by both Nile and Euphrates the sciences of measurement, astronomy and mathematics had been much more than initiated. The grouping of villages and the countryside into larger units was in train; the chiefs of Elam successively but ephemerally mastered each other; in 'Iraq the Sumerian cities formed short-lived empires within their world, which was gaining space physically year by year, as it still is, by riverain silt-deposit on the Gulf shores. The title 'Lord of Sumer and Akkad' was claimed by the priest-king of one city after another, with varying fortunes. In Egypt the Nile-side villages were drawn closer together and, after intermediate stages of unifying, the legendary Menes at last created, in the First Dynasty, a single Egyptian Kingdom destined to set the not-always-maintained standard of country-wide unity. What forms, if any, of grouping were in hand elsewhere, in Persia, Anatolia or Syria, we cannot know; but probably some nucleus of consolidated power in Cappadocia was already forming, and some city-king of Cyprus could briefly claim the whole island's allegiance.

Intercommunication between the various territories, highly significant for their later fortunes, was by this time increasing. There are suggestions of an inroad of Asiatic (Syrian or Arabian) tribes into Egypt, perhaps in the third millennium. There was trade and raiding out of Egypt towards Sinai, Syria, Nubia, and intercourse between Syria, Cilicia and 'Iraq. The Tigris–Euphrates Valley was, as ever, exposed to incursions from the surrounding mountain country to the east and north, and this could not remain one-sided. Already the traditional function of hungry Arabia, as a reservoir of potentially emigrant tribesmen, had begun to operate; Semitic-speaking tribes, probably in slow persistent trickles with occasional denser waves, had by 2500 moved into eastern Syria, perhaps abortively down into Egypt, certainly into central and western 'Iraq. Here, the area immediately north of Sumer had become largely Semitized (while retaining or borrowing Sumerian ways) and recently under a great leader 'Sargon of Akkad' had raided far afield into Syria and Lebanon and the Persian hill-country. This was a one-man exploit; Sargon neither founded nor conceived an empire and did not long disturb the balances of city power even in Sumer and Akkad. But from now onwards the Semites were, with great persistence, to repeat their gradual yet pervasive entry, every few centuries, deep into the Fertile Crescent—yet were never to penetrate into Anatolia or Persia or, save briefly, into Egypt. The 'Iraq city-states of this period traded widely with neighbouring lands, enriching their material life and techniques, and their knowledge of the world.

A thousand years later, in 1500 B.C., the picture has changed in a score of ways. Far to the north-west, Greece and the Aegean had begun to receive waves of Nordic Greek-speaking immigrants, and these were developing an amazing civilization based first on Crete and spreading soon to the mainland, to the islands, and to the western approaches of Anatolia. In Asia Minor, associated waves of Nordic immigration, by way of the Bosphorus and possibly the Caucasus, had entered the territory, provided a new dynamism and a ruling class, and fashioned, *inter alia*, the strong continental power of the Kheta, or Hittites of Cappadocia. This by 1500 had gained control of most of Anatolia, had occupied Cilicia and northern Syria and the great trade-routes, and had raided Babylon. At home it evolved an efficient government, as then conceived, with a careful diplomatic service, an established law, a complicated polytheism, and its own social system. The Hittite State, using metals (though not yet iron) and based on a well-adapted agriculture, had already attained a high standard of life under its ruling dynasties and provincial governors.

In Syria, the year 1500 opened upon a scene where an extensive political unity had never been attained; the country, from Sinai to Cilicia, was too open, too vulnerable to stronger neighbours on north, north-east and south. It had developed instead a highly civilized system of city-states, which had by now absorbed and learnt from Semitic invaders of the great Amorite migration-wave, had sustained strong influences from Egypt and from 'Iraq, and was subjected to Hittite aggression from behind the Taurus. The cities of all parts of

Syria had multiplied their mutual and their foreign connections, had corresponded with a score of distant potentates and merchants, and had perfected the system of writing imported from Babylonia. On the coast, the Phoenicians developed on lines of their own, with a wide sea-borne trade and close contacts with other east Mediterranean seafarers; they were wealthy, self-contained, and devoid of imperial ambitions. The Canaanitish amalgam in southern Syria, who consisted of earlier Palestinian stocks with a now dominant Semitic element, still awaited the Hebrew invasion.

Egypt had suffered much and achieved much in the last thousand years. The Pharaonic dynasties had succeeded, with some lapses, in retaining Egyptian unity against the sometimes successful pretensions of regional kinglets and priestly ambition, and with each century had rendered the prevailing theocratic system, with its ancestor-worship, its colossal burial places, its powerful priestly interest, its divine omnipotent Pharaohs, more rigid and conservative. Trading and military and naval expeditions had around the nineteenth century extended Egyptian influence in coastal Syria almost to the point of empire; the aggressive Libyans were kept at bay, Nubia was colonized, lost and reoccupied, the land of Punt (perhaps Somalia) was visited for its tropical products. In the eighteenth to the sixteenth centuries a confused period of dynastic weakness was followed by an Asia invasion and partial occupation, that of the mysterious Hyksos, under whom weakness and regionalism again prevailed. Traditionally 'shepherd kings'—which seems to mean nomadic tribesmen from the Arabian steppes—the Hyksos are thought by other scholars to be some intrusive northern element, or even a mixed force of mercenaries collected in Syria itself. Nobody knows. The eighteenth dynasty, however, arose and expelled the intruders in the mid-sixteenth century, restored Egyptian unity, and reasserted full imperial power over Syria and the upper Nile. This, at home and abroad, was Egypt's greatest period; it began about 1525 B.C.

In 'Iraq the exploits of Sargon of Akkad were followed by an obscure period in which the city-states, under each its dynasty, could preserve their own now complicated and refined manner of life, but suffered also, it seems, from incursions of hill-tribesmen from the east, and even more, from the current waves of ex-Arabian Semitic invasion and immigration. This was operative equally in northern 'Iraq, where it transmuted the old population into a new, Semitized and formidable type—the disciplined, militarist Assyrian devoted to the truculent service of his (Semitic) god, Asshur. In

south and central 'Iraq it led to the establishment of the new,
dynamic state of Babel or Babylon, in which by 1800 B.C. their great
king Hammurabi ('Amraphael, King of Shinar' in the Bible) had
fashioned an 'Iraqi empire, raided his neighbours, and gained im-
mortal fame by his code of laws. Babylon, greatest name in ancient
'Iraq, held thenceforth for more than a thousand years a unique
status by its wealth, culture and dominion. But for the moment it
was to fall, soon after Hammurabi's death, by natural causes and
by the effects of a long-range Hittite raid, to the obscurity of a
centuries-long occupation by a Kassu (or Kassite) dynasty, imposed,
it seems, by tribesmen from the Persian mountains, and capable of
acquiring civilization from its new subjects, the Sumerian and
Akkadian cities. 'Iraq has little history known to us from 1750 onwards till fully three centuries later. Culturally its ways of life,
sciences, writings, and political forms remained remarkably uniform
and constant, and closely parallel to those of the contemporary Nile
Valley. Elam at this period preserved its independence, and even
gave rulers, for a time, to some of the Sumerian cities. A major part
of 'Iraq's extreme south formed its own Chaldaean State of 'the
Sea-land'.

The Kassu, with all their own mystery, are significant of great
events elsewhere. They were in all probability forerunners of a
great movement of peoples from the central grasslands of Asia, a
movement which was reaching and overspilling the Persian plateau
towards the second quarter, or the middle, of the second millennium
B.C.—and related, therefore, to the contemporary descent of Nordic
peoples into the Aegean world and Anatolia. These people, whose
cousins were simultaneously invading India, spoke Aryan or Indo-
European languages, were of generally Mediterranean type and, with
their vigour and mobility, their fresh conceptions, their horses (now
seen in western Asia for the first time), were to provide the Middle
East with a contribution in blood and character to counterbalance
that of the Semites. The first phase of this process was to furnish a
ruling caste to widely separated communities in various parts of
Persia. In the north and north-west 'Iraq and north-east Syria,
around the same period, populous communities hitherto obscure
turned into considerable states under dominant Indo-European clans
or families; the Hurri formed one such, the Mitanni, spread out in
the long-settled upper Khabur flat-lands, were another, while around
Lake Van, deep in the mountains, was a third, the little-known State
of Urartu.

1. Pipelines crossing the hills in the Agha Jari area, Persia

2. Abadan refinery and the Shatt al-ʿArab

3. Tabriz: new and old bridge across the Aji Chai river

4. Digging their fields near Isfahan.

5. The great Square in Isfahan

6. Southern Zagros: oil-field country

7. Teheran: a side street

8. Mount Demavend in the Elbu

The Golden Horn, Istanbul (*above*)

The Place de la Nation, Ankara (*top right*)

General view of Ankara (*right*)

The tombs of Osman and Orkhan, Brusa (*below*)

Turkey:

13. Camel convoy with reed mats

14. Village transport, with olive trees

15. Turkish village market

16. Antalya, Northern Turkey: small boat harbour

Open space and rket, Kayseri, rkey

18. City and castle: Mardin, Turkey

19. Haifa, the harbour area

20. Beginnings of a colony (Nahariya), Israel

21. Kadhimiyah Mosque, Baghdad

22. South Gate, Baghdad

23. Date-gardener of Southern 'Iraq

24
Northern
'Iraq: the
city of
Arbil

25. Government afforestation scheme, Northern 'Iraq

26. Ruwanduz: 'Iraqi Kurdistan

27. Damascus: the street called Strait

28. Damascus: modern residential quarter

29. Damascus: Barudi square

30. Village of Central Syria, near Homs

31. Ruins at Palmyra, Syria

32. A schooner captain, Rawad Island

33. Beirut, Lebanon

34. A street in Tripoli, Lebanon

35. View of Juniya (Joumie) Lebanon coast

36. Beirut, Lebanon:
cliffs and flats

37. Sidon, Lebanon:
harbour and Crusader Castle

38. Lebanon: the cedars

39. A view of Limassol, Cyprus

40. Kyrenia: castle and harbour

41. Cyprus: Nicosia–Limassol road

42. Jerusalem, Jordanian sector: the Via Dolorosa

43. Jordan: ruins at Jarash

44. Jerusalem: Jordanian pottery-maker

45. Cairo, from t[he]
Ibn Tulun mosqu[e]

46. Cairo: Liberation Square

47. Cairo: the new Corniche road

48. Archimedes' screw: primitive water-lift on the Nile banks

49. Egypt: a village market at Bardis, near Baliana

50. Railway construction: Central Sudan

51. Village agricultural show, Sudan: dancers and drums

52. Cotton growers, Gezira

53. Ferry across the Blue Nile, Khartum

54. The harbour, Aden

55. The refinery, Little Aden

56. The Hadhramaut: part of Shibam town

57. (*Facing page*) Mecca: the Ka'ba

58. Abu Dhabi: Liwa sand-dunes

59. Trucial coast: Camel train, Abu Dhabi

60–63. Four types in the Hadhramaut: village woman,
basket-maker, retired seafarer, mercenary soldier, Shibam

64. Trucial coast: a guide

65. Abu Dhabi policeman

66. School children: Abu Dhabi

67. Abu Dhabi: one
of Sheikh Zaid's
retainers with falcon

68. Trucial coast:
Dibai creek

69.
The new
Kuwait

3. *Crowded Millennium*

The thousand years stretching from 1500 to 500 B.C. were filled with great events in our region—movements of peoples, rise and fall of empires, disruption and coalescence, significant innovation—which have visibly and invisibly marked the course of all later periods. It was an age of large-scale political experiment, of developed international relations, of a new confrontation of Asia and Europe, as well as of scientific and political discovery—of the solar calendar, human records, alphabetic writing, coinage—which we directly inherit. And for every notable event known to history, a score of items were occurring unseen and unrecorded yet integrally part of, and perhaps in aggregate profoundly affecting, the whole march of affairs and the future.

The Egyptian monarchy, with its background of a culturally static population, a privileged priesthood, and strong cross-currents of internal ambition and subversion, failed in these centuries to maintain its imperial position. In spite of repeated military expeditions northwards into Syria, and bloody battles there against confederate Amorite cities and their allies, in spite also of an ever-active diplomacy and royal intermarriages with Hittite rulers and Mitanni, the mastery over Syria—at best a mere overlordship over tributary communities—was weakened, regained, and lost. The strain of control, so far from the homeland and among vigorous and alien city-states, proved too much for the Nilotic power, and this was further weakened in the thirteenth to twelfth centuries by attempted foreign invasion of its own frontiers, on land by incursion of Libyans, and by sea from northern Mediterranean forces, mainly Greek and presumably all-'European'—the Sea Peoples of contemporary inscriptions. These trials were survived; but from 1050 onwards national weakness was more apparent, the kingdom itself was divided and reunited, all military dependence was on mercenaries, the throne fell to Pharaohs of foreign origin, and an occasional expedition despatched into Palestine could do no more than sack a city (as Jerusalem in 930) and return. Egypt with all its immemorial and strangely specialized culture, law-codes, science, medicine, arts, and complete mastery of its unique environment, was no longer a great power. Its rulers were glad to welcome Greek colonies in the Delta, and were forced, in the mid-seventh century, to bow to the invading Assyrian power of Asshur-bani-pal, to pay him tribute and accept his garrisons. A national revival under a new Greek-aided dynasty followed the fall of Assyria, and Egypt could enjoy a century of revived prosperity and a resolute but finally abortive attempt to refound its empire in Asia. But Egyptian forces were defeated by Babylonia (Carchemish, 605), and less than a century later (525) the country fell helplessly to the new, all-conquering, Persian Empire.

In Anatolia, the fortunes of the Hittite State in the seventeenth and sixteenth centuries are unknown to us; thereafter, stronger than ever, it established relations with resurgent Egypt, could interfere decisively in Mitanni affairs, ally itself with rising Assyria, and keep its place in Syria until, after the extinction of the Mitanni principality, it could dominate it. The Hittites absorbed a further incursion of Nordic tribes from the north-east, intrigued and bullied among the Amorite and Phoenician city-states of Syria, and played the role of paramount power in the Levant whenever Egyptian control weakened; Hittite-Egyptian fighting was indecisive, and a régime of formal treaty and royal intermarriage suited both parties better. In Anatolia itself, Hittite predominance did not exclude a number of other independent, if intermittently tributary, states on fringes of the plateau —Lycians, Carians, Lydians and others. The seemingly sudden end of the Hittite State in its own homelands, around 1230 B.C., is best explained by further and stronger Nordic incursions from eastern Europe—perhaps of the Phrygians (who proceeded to found a rich, progressive state in western Anatolia), and certainly as part of the massive restlessness of the Mediterranean-Aegean world in the thirteenth to twelfth centuries. Similar blows were to fall again on the plateaux and valleys of Anatolia in the early seventh century when an invasion of northern tribesmen from the grasslands beyond the Caucasus—fierce, horse-mounted Kimmerians, and Scythians the scourge of the settled populations—poured into the land, and made a place for itself there partly by founding small mountain principalities under their own ruling caste, and partly by slow absorption or dispersal, as one more digested, invisible element in the population. But the Hittite name, and much of its prestige and culture, survived in 'Hittite' cities of north Syria (known as such to the Assyrians and in the Bible) in the ninth and eighth centuries. The Hittite blood and tradition, as of a race of imperial conquerors, were a legacy to successors in Anatolia.

In Syria, political unity was never achieved. The cities of Phoenicia —Ugarit, Byblos, Tyre and Sidon amongst them—persisted in their far-flung maritime trade, were familiar with all parts of the Mediterranean, founded colonies in north Africa (Carthage and Utica) and

Spain (Cadiz), and benefited by the collapse of the Cretan sea-power, about 1400. The strong and highly civilized city-states of the hinterland could sometimes combine—notably but vainly against Egyptian, Hittite or Assyrian pretensions—but more often pursued their bickering separatism even in times of foreign overlordship. Their struggles partly conceal from our sight a major event common to all Syria in this period, the gradual but pervasive incursion of yet another major wave of Semitic-speakers from the eastern and southern steppe-country, this time the Aramaean. The newcomers acquired no empire, the cities founded by them claimed no major place in the teeming political life of the Levant; but within three centuries (fourteenth to eleventh) the Aramaeans not only became full Syrians but, by intermixture and intermarriage, by the almost universal spread of their Aramaic (north-west Semitic) speech—soon to be the *lingua franca* of a great part of the Middle East south of the Taurus—and by merging their culture in that of the pre-existing population, they became easily the dominant element in the territory.

With the rest, they suffered in these centuries the aggression or butchery of Assyrian armies, and found themselves at most times tributary to Nineveh or Babylon. First in the thirteenth and twelfth centuries, and later in the ninth and thereafter, the kings of Assyria with their bloodthirsty armies entered the territory to destroy and loot, and to claim every privilege of ruthless conquest. Not always successful, since their communications were long and the military effort immense, their king could in the eighth and seventh centuries undertake repeatedly the conquest of the Syrian principalities, including those of Palestine and the Hebrews. Esarhaddon's invasion of Egypt, by way of Syria, in 670 was the last appearance of this detested power on the Mediterranean coasts.

In southern Syria—Canaan, or Palestine—the entry of the Hebrew tribes, subject of so much curious legend and later intense world-interest, took place slowly over many decades about the thirteenth century. Overcoming by degrees the resistance of Transjordan tribes and fortresses and those of Canaan itself, the new Hebrew or Israeli community was important in Palestine by the twelfth century, and dominant, though still locally resisted, by the eleventh; its half-anarchic period of 'the Judges' gave way to a central monarchy by 1000 B.C., as recorded in the Bible stories of Saul, David, Solomon and their quarrelsome successors. These rulers, and especially the last-named, were able effectively to create one more among the many petty states of the Levant; they traded widely, organized a close national life, and found peaceful or violent contact with Egypt, Phoenicia and the Amorite and Aramaean cities. They overcame after long struggles their enemies, the doughty yet highly civilized Philistines, a community of European immigrants (p. 33) now settled on the coast of Palestine, and they developed, with sublime poetry and sonorous 'prophecy', the worship of their vengeful tribal god Jahweh, or Jehovah; a religion destined to develop, in the hands and hearts of a gifted race, into a broad monotheism with a moral content rare if not unique in that period, side by side with an exclusive nationalism which prevented its wide diffusion. Meanwhile, the two yet smaller kingdoms into which the Hebrew State divided, those of Israel and Judah, both fell victims, like all their neighbours, to the armies of foreign empires. Both were invaded and became tributary to the Assyrian tyrants. Thousands of Israelis were carried off to captivity in Media in 721, while Assyrian colonists, brought to Palestine, settled and intermarried there to form the Samaritan community. The kingdom of Judah and Jerusalem, after a further century of strain, threat, and invasion, fell in spite of an Egyptian alliance to the arms of revived Babylon (p. 37) in 586, and the 'Babylonish captivity' of its people began. This ended in 538 with the gradual return of part of the exiles, under the Persian Empire; a larger part declined to leave their new homes.

In lower 'Iraq, the supremacy of rich, luxurious, learned Babylon, once freed from its unwanted Kassite rulers (c. 1200), was never in doubt until the end of the period we are reviewing. The old Sumerian states were slowly losing their traditional character and contributing little new; the Sea Lands, like them, were undergoing population changes, probably by Arabian immigration, but managed to keep their near-independence. Babel itself, with a revived vigour and sense of mission, organized its own central area of 'Iraq, raided mountain and desert neighbours, and until 612 maintained with its formidable northern neighbour relations varying from war and mutual destruction to peaceful ceremonial exchanges. This neighbour was, from the fourteenth century onwards, the aggressive and brutal, but efficient and not uncultured state and later Empire of Assyria. With its successive capitals at Asshur, Nimrud, Khorsabad and Nineveh, the Assyrian kings, who included such great names as Tiglath-Pileser, Asshur-Nasir-Pal, Shalmaneser, Sargon, Sennacherib, Esarhaddon, inspired terror in a wide circle of territories by their military prowess and innovations, which included the use of horse-chariots. Apart from Syrian and Egyptian campaigns, which enforced obedience and tribute, the Assyrian invaded also Asia Minor, outlasted the Mitanni and the Hittites, clashed with King Midas of Phrygia, put an end to Elamite independence, practised long-drawn diplomacy with Pharaoh, and pressed hard on Babylonia. Assyrian merchants settled in north-western Persia, in and beyond the Taurus, in Elam and southern 'Iraq. The state was for five centuries (twelfth to seventh) a major power of the Middle East, and for the last three of these was harshly dominant. When Nineveh, exhausted by incessant warfare, fell in 612 to a newly risen Iranian power, that of the Medes, it left vast records in stone and marble, but little in humanity or the arts of living. The succession fell, as we shall see, first in part to the Medes, in part to Babylon (whose last century of independence under a Sea Land dynasty was one of power, wealth and foreign campaigns), and later all to the Persian Empire.

In Persia the appearance of a great power, emerging from the new country-wide demographic conditions there which followed the Indo-European (or Indo-Iranian) mass immigration (p. 32), was long delayed: partly, no doubt, because this inward flood was a continuing and restless process needing time for absorption, habituation and community-building, and partly also through the jealous power of neighbouring Assyria which was forced, for its own security, to deal hard blows at such hopeful new Iranian groupings—in the Azarbaijan region, for instance (Urartu, p. 32), and in western and southern Iran. But the Aryan ruling caste, which penetrated both throughout Persia (except in certain aboriginal enclaves) and deeply also into Asia Minor, but never into 'Iraq or Arabia, contained newness of thought and potential, and some remarkable characters, one of whom was soon to emerge. We cannot now know the course of alliances, intrigues, expansions or hostilities among malcontent neighbours of Assyria in the twelfth to eighth centuries; but a Median nation, across the Zagros from 'Iraq, came into existence in that period, resisted Assyrian raids, and produced (or was produced by) a strong ruling family. By the end of the seventh century Nineveh was exhausted and degenerate, and the Assyrian power fell in a day and for ever (612 B.C.). Babylon resumed its independent sway in 'Iraq, while the vigorous rising state of Media took the place of Assyria in all the northern and eastern dominions of its empire.

The Median State lasted a bare half-century, time to establish new forms of rule in Iran itself and to press new foreign campaigns, notably against Urartu and the Lydian State in Anatolia. Power

then passed to a south Persian nation, of closely similar racial mixture. It was led by Cyrus (or Kurush or Khusrau), of the so-called
Achaemenid family. From this followed immediately the world-
famed Persian Empire, whose armies in the next few years took
Sardis, destroyed Lydia, subdued the Greek cities of the Aegean
coast of Asia Minor, overthrew Babylon and absorbed its dominions,
lorded it on the Syrian coast and hinterland, and invaded the eastern
regions of Persia itself and far beyond them. Later kings, successors of Cyrus (Cambyses, the great, Darius, Xerxes, Artaxerxes)
invaded and ruled Egypt, visited Nubia or Kush (the Egyptianized,
independent kingdom of the middle Nile), and overcame a Greek
revolt in Ionia (499).

The life, more than two centuries long, of this immensely extended,
highly organized and, at its best and by comparison with previous
empires, humanely administered Persian Empire, stretching with
close intercommunication between its score of satrapies from central
Asia into Europe and Africa, was to witness, along with all the age-
long phenomena of royal intrigue, provincial and tribal revolt and
racial separatism, great changes also in political and administrative
conceptions, with new standards and currents of thought flowing
westwards into western Asia. A seriously attempted central control
was accompanied, in the Empire's first and best period, by much
local freedom, reasonable taxation, fair justice, and willingness to
acquire culture and ideas from others. It was an Empire of Indo-
European, or Indo-Iranian, leadership in succession to two thousand
years of Semitic; and it was destined to be succeeded by other rulers
of Indo-European mind and orientation—Greek, Roman, Byzantine
—for nine full centuries, until the coming of the Arabs and Islam.

4. Persia, Greece, Rome

Something approaching the political unity of western Asia was
achieved during the two-century period of Persian dominance,
thanks to its organization and prestige, its formidable military
machine, its sporadic unformidable opponents. The Great King
failed, indeed, to subdue by his arms the brilliant, restless Greeks,
who at first resolutely held their own but later vied with each other,
Greek against Greek, in intrigues with the nearest satrap: Greeks at
their most wonderful period of questing intelligence, love of personal
freedom, devotion to art, science and philosophy, but cursed with
endemic disunion and instability in their politics. The Persians

retained Egypt, though with a régime highly unpopular and intermittently rejected. Fragmented Syria took generally the line of non-resistance, and Phoenicia that at first of devotion and valued naval co-operation, followed by a revolt which Artaxerxes bloodily repressed. Asia Minor was for the most part Persian-governed, but increasingly in the fifth and fourth centuries 'native kingdoms', and anarchic tribal groups in the mountainous or coastal fringes, began to re-arise from their now multifarious population elements, and paid minimal regard to the behests of harassed satraps, many of whom schemed themselves for independence. In 'Iraq, the status of a subject province was accepted after initial revolts, and its age-long civilization greatly influenced that of its imperial masters. The Persian homeland, where lay three out of the Great King's four capitals, was habitually unquiet in its open eastern frontier regions and in outlying areas elsewhere, but the régime was generally unthreatened; in spite, however, of the official and general adoption of the worship of the supreme god Ahuramazda (that is, Zoroastrianism) and his vast number of lesser, satellite deities, the loosening of administrative and social standards, with deterioration in the royal family and general corruption and loss of impetus, weakened the Empire more and more from the mid-fifth century onward, until it was bound to fall at the next serious blow.

This came from the west. In twelve years, 331–323, Alexander of Macedon—young, brilliant, impulsive, visionary—conquered Egypt and north Africa and the whole of western and far into central Asia, ostentatiously adopted Persian ways and those of oriental kingship, and installed a rough but comprehensive administration, with dozens of Greek cities, settlements and garrisons, and thousands of Greek officials, traders and colonists.

Almost in a day the whole balance of world civilization (west-east, Greek-oriental) appeared to be shifted; and indeed these conquests, this new Empire, heralded a tremendous influx of Greek or Hellenistic influences, of culture, speech and religion, deep into the Middle East: influences destined to last, though far from uniformly, for nine centuries until displaced by Islam. This penetration was on a scale at least comparable to that which the west again undertook, but this time not militarily, in the nineteenth and twentieth centuries of our era. Two features of post-Alexandrine Middle Eastern Hellenism, which were to continue or increase throughout Roman and Byzantine times, may in passing be indicated: the one, that it was generally limited to urban and educated circles, extending little to the countryside, the tribes, or the poor; the other, that it was not by any means uniformly beneficent, since through defects both in itself and in its vehicles, and through its unselective, too ready acceptance in the east, what it in the end contributed was far below the best that the west had (or had had, a century earlier) to offer. This aspect too, it may be felt, was destined to repeat itself in the Middle East two millennia later.

Alexander's Empire, after his early death, immediately fell apart into the hands of his Macedonian generals, the self-appointed Successors.

In Egypt, the line of Ptolemy managed to maintain itself for three centuries, though after more than a hundred years of quarrels and campaigns it lost to its Seleucid rivals most of its Levantine territories and pretensions. Cyprus, which had belonged to Achaemenid Persia, was lost but later recovered for Ptolemy. Many thousands of Greeks were settled in Egypt, the city of Ptolemais was founded, Greek privilege emphasized, and an inevitably re-emerging Egyptian nationalism was kept in check. The régime of the Successor was in Egypt on the whole unhappy, 'race relations' distressingly poor, the ruling house itself divided by faction and intrigue; and in the first century B.C. the Ptolemaic power could survive only under Roman patronage. Its end came in 31 B.C., after the lost battle of Actium and the romantic suicide of Queen Cleopatra. Egypt, by now a strange cultural and demographic blend of old and new, Egyptian and Greek, became a Roman province with special status; Alexandria survived as the greatest centre of contemporary Hellenism and learning.

Syria, at first divided between the successor-states of Ptolemy and Seleucus, fell in time solely to the latter. His policy of thorough-going Hellenization was fairly acceptable in most areas, where indeed it was no novelty; but in largely Jewish Palestine, despite the willing modernism of the more evolved classes, it provoked a determined uprising, that of Judas Maccabaeus and his line, which founded and maintained an independent state destined, in spite of rival policies and factions within it, to survive into Roman times. (Its successor was the Hellenized, or Romanized, puppet state of the Herods, till A.D. 6). Other areas of Syria and its hopeful city-states assumed at the same time a near-independence, among them those of the half-Arab Nabataeans around Petra in southern Transjordan, and the ancient coastal cities of Phoenicia. The reduced, distracted Seleucid Empire, at last confined to Syria, with its capital at Antioch, finally yielded to the power of Rome. In 64 B.C. it was made by Pompey a province, later two provinces, of the Republic: provinces which still contained semi-independent enclaves and privileged local rulers, and strong cross-currents of diverse culture, religion, and temporal interest.

In Asia Minor under the Successors each of the three main claimants strove initially for mastery. But within a century only Seleucid pretensions remained, and these only in the south-east; the central and main block of the territory had split or relapsed into independent kingdoms—those of Cilicia, Cappadocia, Pontus, Paphlagonia and Armenia. Part of the centre had been occupied, about 280, by an irruption—once again!—of northern tribesmen from Europe across the Bosphorus, this time the (Celtic) Galatians, who founded a state around Ancyra (later Angora or Ankara); the west belonged to monarchies of Pergamon, Rhodes, Bithynia, Phrygia and a number of smaller units. In them all the processes of westernization proceeded apace. The advance of the Roman power eastward led first to diplomatic relations, then to invasions and campaigns, then to the creation in 133 of a Roman province of 'Asia', and finally after 63 B.C. to comprehensive settlements in each Anatolian area. These gave provincial, or dependent, or allied, or independent status to successive regions and states, among which those of Pontus (Mithridates) and Armenia (Tigranes or Dikran) were to prove the longest to survive. The whole region now lay open to Greco-Roman penetration, colonization, and influences of every kind, opposed only by Persian counter-influences and coercion.

The latter country and 'Iraq formed the eastern half of the Seleucid inheritance, in which the Indian and central Asian conquests of Alexander were soon abandoned, the rest treated at first to a resolute régime of Greek and Macedonian colonization and favour to the Greek cities (including a new capital, Seleucia, founded on the middle Tigris), but later, and in spite of this early discrimination, to the ultimate coalescence of most of the native Persian and new Greek populations. No Persian resistance on national lines was encountered, and religious tolerance was practised; nevertheless, the open eastern frontiers were often ill at ease and, as the dynasty declined, outbreaks of sporadic insurgence called for efforts of suppression not always successful. The Seleucid frontiers gradually contracted. Only in the mid-second century B.C. did a major rival appear to the uneasy Seleucid power in the east; it was the increasing strength of a Parthian, that is north-east Persian, or Perso-Scythian, tribe-group or nation, formed by the descendants of one Arsaces, who had begun a slow rise to power a century earlier. This Arsacid or Parthian Empire had by 130 B.C. firmly established itself in eastern, northern and western Persia, and in 'Iraq as far as the Euphrates. 'Iraq as well as Persia was thus lost to the Seleucids. The latter were, moreover, further embarrassed by growing Parthian relations, often those of suzerainty, with the ambitious potentates of eastern Anatolia. The new Empire was, however, never truly robust; tribal and nomadic in origin, its organization was sketchy, its feudal structure unsure, its armies little trained. Adopting Zoroastrianism and a strong strain of Iranian national feeling and anti-western prejudicies, the Arsacids were still far from closing the doors to Hellenic practices, arts, pleasures and influences, though these became politically unfashionable with the ruling class; instead, Persia was being little by little re-persianized. The interesting Greek kingdom of Bactria, a relic of Alexander, was swamped by Scythians in 140 B.C.

The Parthian Empire, such as it was, lasted for three centuries. The succession, after its last feeble decades, fell to a national and nationalist all-Persian dynasty of the Sassanians, true successors, as they could justly claim, of the Achaemenids, and devoted or even fanatical Zoroastrians and traditionalists. The Sassanian period, which endured until the Arab invasion (A.D. 637), was perhaps Persia's most secure and brilliant era, during which it enjoyed a good administration and legal system, a renaissance of its own art and culture, strong priestly influences (now facing the rival claims of Christianity and Manichaeism), and witnessed at the same time the almost total eclipse of Hellenism and the Greek language. Of its foreign relations we shall speak later.

The rest of the Middle East, from Bosphorus and Nile to Euphrates, found itself, as the Christian era opened, under the Empire of the Roman Caesars, an Empire exercised largely by direct provincial rule, partly by a system of subordinate, client states (as for a time in Palestine, and for much longer in eastern Anatolia) and partly by alliances and spheres of influence beyond the frontiers, as in Armenia. The gift of Rome to this eastern world was its Pax Romana, security from outside aggression and from other than temporary and local domestic disorder, and a wide, almost a world-wide, field for its subjects in trade, travel and literary and official ambition. The distinction of Roman or non-Roman became blunted as the centuries paased and the franchise was extended; local and municipal self-government was allowed, when not abused; large numbers of Roman cities were founded and Roman conceptions of order, the rule of law, civil dignity and personality had every chance to take root, even though in practice Roman rule was too often corrupt, oppressive and disliked. With all its pockets of surviving local devotion and its shadowy areas of backwardness, the social and public tone of the Empire was European, Roman-Hellenistic, and later Byzantine. The west had made, it seemed, a vast inroad into the east, and the distinctions of which Periclean Greece had proclaimed itself so conscious were out of sight—for ever, a thoughtful contemporary must have thought! Dozens of the best writers, scholars, and artists of the Roman and Byzantine worlds (including Christian saints, hermits, Fathers, heresiarchs) were of Middle Eastern birth; and the rapid rise and spread of Christianity (the official religion of the Roman Empire from A.D. 313 onwards), in spite of its own many and bitter doctrinal disputes, was another welding element between west and east, another potent force in society—yet was also, because standing for personal, anti-imperial values, another force added to the revival of local, nationalistic, foci of loyalty. In these years, save only in remote regions of mountain or desert, the great majority of the Middle Eastern population became Christian as well as European. Judaism had meanwhile sustained a severe blow by the destruction of Jerusalem by the Romans in A.D. 70, and the diaspora of the Palestinian Jews.

Externally, the dominant feature of the times was the struggle between Rome-Byzantium and Arsacid-Sassanian Persia for the allegiance of the eastern Anatolian states by rival diplomacies of threat, inducement and fomented internal dissidence, and for possession of the Mesopotamian flat-lands, now Persia's western province, by direct force of arms. These needless and weakening struggles, essential to neither Empire and destructive of both, contributed to their later, easy conquest by the Arabs; and it would be tedious to describe their intricate, swaying fortunes, which involved the greatest rulers and generals on both sides, and the flower of their armies, for seven hundred years. They were marked by fierce battles, and by deep massive raids—to the Mediterranean, into Anatolia, even into Egypt—and the wholesale removal of captive populations. Other features were occasional calm interludes, broken treaties, the encouragement of embarrassing pretenders, and the head-on confrontation of rival religions. But, as the seventh century opened, a total transformation of the whole Middle Eastern scene was at hand, from the most unexpected of directions.

5. *Some features of Middle Eastern antiquity*

A few moments of reflection, even at this mid-point of history which our survey has now reached, and even after no more than hasty a scramble through four millennia, may be instructive. We have seen the high state of civilization in which certain, very limited, communities (Sumer, Elam, Egypt, Crete) emerged from the darkness of prehistory; civilizations built up by unknown hands at a slow but increasing tempo, and resulting from we know not what changing environments and racial mixtures. And we have noted the, thereafter, comparative rapidity of social and political change, and the ever-growing scale of political units into groups, states, nations, empires. There has been endless movement of peoples into and within the region, each bringing unascertainable contributions of character, technique and habitude; there has been coalescence of the new elements, or their disappearance, or their successful establishment of a ruler or ruling class. There have existed, concurrently, areas of continued aboriginal backwardness, of which parts of Persia and Anatolia furnish examples; areas also of remoteness from, non-participation in, the field of Middle Eastern development, such as southern Arabia or the Sudan. With new blood, and often without it, have arrived, repeatedly, new cultures, and the flow of these has been (an aspect now half forgotten) east–west as well as west–east, as is testified by early days in the eastern Mediterranean and by Greek borrowings from Babylonian and Egyptian science. The conception, incidentally, of an 'unchanging East', dear to our own nineteenth century, is revealed as clear absurdity.

The record has shown the effect of a secluded or protected geographical location on the possibilities of early empire-building which, achieved by Assyria, Egypt and Persia, proved impossible to fragmented Greece as also to the Syrian communities on their much-trodden land-bridge; but not even the isolation of Hittites or Iranians or (the most striking case) of Egyptians could in fact protect them finally from invasion and overthrow. (Modern transport and modern armaments have, of course, now destroyed all hope of safety through inaccessibility.) Meanwhile, no profundity of study is likely to reveal, to anything like our satisfaction, why success, power and progress came to one ancient emergent nation rather than to another; varying answers lie somewhere, no doubt, in the field of favouring environment, exceptional leadership, a strong ruling caste, some fortunate blend of aboriginal and immigrant, some timely discovery or import of technique, weapon or concept, or a sudden acquisition of wealth by raid or warfare, or a catastrophe befalling neighbours. Nor are we able to assign reasons for this or that notorious 'national character', if such authentically exists. There is less, or no, mystery about the mere impulse of early rulers to acquire wealth and empire, since it conforms to the deepest and worst instincts of our kind, not least when these are confronted with the familiar dichotomy of 'us' and 'them'—*our* community against the foreigner, Hellene versus barbarian, Jew against the uncircumcized—in which latter-day conceptions of European and Asiatic, or white and coloured, have come to take their maleficent place. Nor indeed is there much mysterious about the inability of early empires to endure; this is easily traceable to their uneasy heterogeneity, to the normal lack of intelligent loyalty to the imperial centre, to failure by the latter in sympathetic devolution or even in acceptable tolerance, and to the great distances which must be destructive of control, because beyond the range (in spite of Achaemenid and Roman improvements in communication) of contemporary transport.

At all periods we have had occasion to observe the strong influence of religion, ranging from ceremonially worshipped city-gods and deified rulers to—to us more acceptable—monotheisms. This influence was rarely beneficent; it created, at least in its public manifestations, a lust for divinely approved conquest (as in Assyria), or a jealous nationalism (as in Israel), or an anti-social privileged class (as in Zoroastrian Persia, and in Egypt), far more than it inspired to morality or gentleness.

One more feature, prominent in later history, had already shown itself in these pre-Islamic times: the eager adoption of national legends as emotional rallying-points. Based often on more than half-mythical figures of heroic dimensions, as in Greece or Sassanid Persia, or on alleged divine discrimination, as in Hebrew history, such legends could too easily be a powerful force inspiring peoples to self-glorification and aggression.

CHAPTER THREE

NINE CENTURIES OF ISLAM

1. *The Impact*

THE Prophet Muhammad, son of 'Abdullah, was born about A.D. 570 and bred in a leading family of Mecca, then a considerable and highly civilized city, caravan centre, and sanctuary of western Arabia. He passed there most of his life of trading, meditating and preaching, lawgiving and organizing; and his new creed of Islam was finally adopted, thanks to its own force and content and to his burning sincerity, by nearly all the townsfolk of Mecca and Medina and by most of the primitive and chronically lawless and divided tribesmen of Arabia, before his early and sudden death in 632.

The faith of Islam, which means 'submission' (to the will of Allah), however rigid and positive in its monotheism, was yet with no great difficulty livable in terms of contemporary Arabian life, by reason of its easy intelligibility, its attractive concessions and promises, and its wise adaptation to Arabian conditions: conditions which themselves, climate and terrain apart, reflected a centuries-long past of earlier civilization in the west (and particularly the fertile, settled south-west) of the peninsula, adopted in varying degrees by its quick-witted, impatient, unstable sons in city and desert. The religion as it took form in the utterances of Muhammad—he was illiterate—and even more in the later-compiled Qur'an (Koran) and the collections of his Sayings, was not, like Judaism, that of a nationalistic community, but had universal appeal. Developing monotheistic ideas which (a fact often under-emphasized) were endemic in Arabia, and drawing, often naïvely and with imperfect understanding, on Christian and Jewish sources available in many Arabian communities as well as in Syria, Islam as it took independent shape insisted above all on the uniqueness and the eternal, universal power —but also the lofty compassion—of Allah; on the status of Allah's Prophet as that solely of a man and a messenger, the last and best of a long line of prophets but without personal claim to divinity; on belief in angels and devils and the Last Judgment; on the holy books of previous revelations and the new divinely-dictated Law, on public prayer, fasting and almsgiving, and the annual Mecca pilgrimage; on Holy War against the pagan; and on certain rigidly defined improprieties, such as the use of wine and pork, usury and gambling, and images which might lead to misplaced worship. Slavery and polygamy were both accepted as natural institutions, but with a new emphasis on the duty of restraint and kindly treatment. Many pre-Islamic elements of custom and ritual, and some of belief, were indulgently incorporated. It is, indeed, idle to look in the Qur'an or the Traditions for a developed, satisfying system of theology; what was offered, and is offered today, was a single, complete law and guide to human life, claimed as divinely revealed, as adequate to every activity and situation, and as the sole pathway to eternal bliss.

No close series of historical events in the Middle East has ever produced results so immediate, yet so profound and lasting, as those which followed the unbelievably rapid, unexpected and complete conquest by the earliest Muslims, under the first Successors (or Caliphs) of the Prophet, of practically all the territories of western Asia (except Anatolia) and of north Africa. These conquests, dating from the fourth decade of the seventh century of the Christian era, represented in one, but a quite incomplete, sense another great outpouring from the human reservoir of Arabia; they proved final and irreversible, yet were orderly, unmarked by ruin or massacre, and were preliminary not to a violent but rather to a peaceful revolution, visible and invisible, in society and policies and men's minds throughout the region, and far beyond it. The changes which henceforth supervened in these ex-Roman and Persian provinces led them, as we now see, from antiquity to the Middle Ages, and introduced modes of living and thinking which were viewed for centuries as those which most distinguished Asiatic from European societies. The substantial reorientation of the whole Middle East gave new importance to hitherto neglected regions, notably Arabia itself; it obliterated long-standing boundaries, and made the Arabs for centuries the most considered people in the region, instead of the least. The social structures within each conquered territory changed overnight, with a new aristocracy and plutocracy, new land-ownership, new privileges which incoming and settling Arab Muslims were in no hurry to share with the growing crowds of converts.

From the camps and settlements, and soon from the cities, spread the new, Arabian fashions in dress, speech, manners and private and public way of life; and this, the highly characteristic, dignified, self-contained Muslim fashion of living, was accompanied, as it spread more widely, by the general adoption of Muslim conceptions of society and the universe. Conversely, the early Muslim material contribution to wealth or economics was negligible, unless in the form of an abrupt redistribution of possessions.

The Muslim reconquest or restabilization of Arabia, necessitated by the death of the Prophet, was complete by 634; the invasion and occupation of 'Iraq, Persia, Egypt and Syria were achieved within the next decade. These truly remarkable victories and permanent acquisitions were carried out by sparse, ill-equipped and untrained 'troops', under commanders hitherto unknown and untried. Reasons for this ease of conquest lay in the exhaustion of the Sassanid and Byzantine Empires, the scanty loyalties they had inspired, the divisions caused by heresy, and the general resentment at oppression and over-taxation. Nevertheless, every detail of the campaigns, every episode and leader, every authentic or imagined conversation, became thenceforward part of the basic Arab, and Muslim, tradition and heritage; with the Prophet's own life, it was their heroic age, their lasting inspiration; and, leading back to the speech and words, the poetry and fable, of pre-Islamic ages in Arabia, it helped to seal the close and persisting, yet not easily definable, bond between the Arabs and Islam.

The wide territories thus acquired for Islam and Arabism had been strangers hitherto to Arabian cultural or spiritual influences, even though receptive at times, as we have seen, of mass immigration from the peninsula. They now became in a short span of years predominantly Arabic in speech, by the rapid spread of that tongue to primacy over all others; Islamic in religion, through the gradual, unforced, progressive adoption of that faith by populations little devoted to their corrupted or worldly Byzantine Christianity or to the national creed of Persia, and eager to qualify for the social as well as fiscal benefits reserved for Muslims; and sharers in the prestige, the sense of compact superiority found in the single, highly conscious Muslim community which was at once a nation and a supernational social and religious entity, and which was held firmly together as such, in spite of all dynastic or doctrinal quarrels, however bitter, by the bonds of the sacred Law and the Tradition, and the shared sense of prized distinctness from all non-Muslim communities. The time required to render the conquered territories substantially Islamic varied locally from a dozen years to half a century; certain pockets of resistance—often recognizable as the

Christian minorities of later days—declined Islamization, and were tolerated without oppression. The Islamic conquests were never ethnic, since the numbers involved, even including the later immigrants who for centuries thereafter moved up in small or greater bodies from Arabia, were never such as obviously to modify existing physical types; all were absorbed, as later arrivals in the area (Turks, Mongols, Tartars) were in due course to be absorbed. Some departments in culture, in trade and craftsmanship, in government itself, remained for centuries as unresentedly non-Muslim. Indeed, a great part of the governmental systems of the occupied countries —not including, of course, the courts of justice, or law-codes, or military establishments—stayed for a considerable time unmodified, with administration in the hands of the former officials and with the old currencies and taxation and irrigation systems still in operation. Central and western Anatolia, against which with its Byzantine emperors and armies, its high level of cultured development and prosperity, the Muslims matched themselves in vain, resisted Islamization for more than four centuries, and in the end were never Arabized.

Apart from this latter territory, to which Islam penetrated only from the later eleventh century onwards, the strength of the hold of the new Faith, and (as we shall see) the local dilutions or admixtures which it was to undergo, varied widely; it produced everywhere, however, a specifically Islamic civilization with much in common which was outwardly apparent and much that was inwardly fundamental, while it was subject also to the strong influences of pre-existing populations, environments and cultures. It followed that Muslim society differed perceptibly though unessentially in Egypt, Arabia, Syria and 'Iraq, though all were Arabic-speaking and in close intercommunication. In Persia the Arabic language failed, in the end, to displace the Persian, and Persian national pride and idiosyncracy, art and subtlety, so far prevailed over the incoming Arab contribution that, two or more centuries after the conquest, Persia, though deeply Islamized in its own heterodox fashion, had still its language and its culture intact.

2. *Golden Age*

The six centuries of the western Asian record, from A.D. 632 to 1258, were those of the early, the mature, and the final periods of medieval Islamic civilization. They formed the era of the Caliphate at its greatest (indeed its only) reality, and witnessed the succession of phases of power and decline, state-building and invasion, among the Middle Eastern peoples which gradually moved towards the setting of the stage, in the wasteful, disorderly fashion of human history, for the groupings and nations of our own time.

The political history of the period, detail of which cannot be included in these pages, falls into stages which it is possible to delimit only by over-simplifying the course of events and ignoring a world of activity, intrigue and disorder which produced them. The succession of the first, the 'well-directed' Caliphs, four in number, lasted for a bare generation (632–661) after the death of the Prophet; strife and jealousy were already stirring, and the third and fourth Caliphs were both murdered. Then while Islamic—at this stage Arab—rule was settling down in the new-conquered provinces, the Empire's centre of gravity shifted in 661 from the Hijaz to Syria, and for a century the Caliph, deriving now from another branch the Prophet's own tribe, the Quraish, ruled from Damascus by his viceroys and governors a still expanding Empire. The dominion of these Umayyid Caliphs was firm, efficient, worldly; but even their greatest rulers—Mu'awiya, 'Abdul Malik, al-Walid—are today little remembered by the world at large. A second major shift of power, from Syria to 'Iraq, marked the replacement of the Umayyid by the 'Abbasid dynasty when the supreme power was seized by descendants of the Prophet's uncle, al-'Abbas. These retained it, in changing and sadly diminishing form, from 750 until 1258, based still on the new capital of the Islamic world, Baghdad, founded by them in 762. This was the ever-famous Caliphate of the 'Abbasids, the earlier period of which, in the eighth and ninth centuries of our era, was by far its finest in practical, as distinct from cultural, achievement. The long line of these Caliphs, succeeding always by family claim to an Empire which in temporal terms was later to diminish almost to vanishing point, contained great names—al-Mansur the founder of Baghdad, Harun al-Rashid, al-Ma'mun—as well as a host of obscure sanctified puppets. The political unity of the Empire was broken increasingly and beyond hope of repair, from the mid-ninth century onwards, by the establishment of a score of effectively independent states within nominally Caliphate territory; these offered the Commander of the Faithful a merely formal allegiance or none at all, while of many temporal dynasties, from the tenth century onwards, he was, otherwise than in Islamic prestige, the mere dependant. With the extinction of the 'Abbasids by Mongol hordes in 1258 ends, save in Egypt and Syria, most of what still remained of the glories of medieval Islam.

Certain features of this six-century period need little emphasis here, though they fill its long-drawn record with pages of intrigue, violence, and bloodshed. Such were the bitter quarrels between individuals and families, with high office—and the Caliphate itself —as the prize, followed by war and the execution, or the mere murder, often of persons with high claims to Islamic reverence; these included the Prophet's own son-in-law, 'Ali, his grandson Husain, many of his staunchest original supporters, and many later Caliphs. Strife between pretenders to power, between rival dynasts, against ambitious provincial rulers, against seceding or aggressive mobs turned into fighting forces (Carmathians and Kharijite heretics, rebellious slave-armies, or the followings of upstart 'prophets'), was exemplified in every decade; and for the first four centuries of the period large-scale and reprisal-provoking expeditions against the still Christian-held territories of 'Rum' (Asia Minor) were almost annual events, and caused a ruinous drain of blood and treasure.

The Caliphate itself, an institution never closely formulated but conceived as rather constitutional and temporal than spiritual, changed essentially during the period. From being, as it was at first, entrusted to the fittest person in age, piety, efficacy and general acceptability to act as official head of the Islamic world (and therefore as chief enforcer of the sacred Law), the position became an object of keen temporal rivalry and soon, as the Umayyids and early 'Abbasids had made it, a hereditary kingship of almost normal oriental type. This status was modified again when in Baghdad the Caliph's own mercenary bodyguard could exercise a tyrannous and humiliating control, and even drive him from his capital or take his life; and again, when with the Abode of Peace occupied by the thrones and armies of upstart Persian or Turkish princes (p. 54), the 'Abbasid was no more than their outwardly venerated pensioner, and giver of empty, formal recognition to their authority.

The Arab Empire of the early Caliphs lasted as a single sphere of government, with minor but serious local usurpations, for three centuries. During this period the Arab ruling class saw itself decreasingly differentiated from the upper strata, and then the main body, of the Caliph's multi-racial subjects, as indeed were, with passing years, the further incoming contingents of Arab tribesmen from the far south. In the administration of the Empire, Arabs played first little, then a limited, and finally a large part as they acquired the needed experience and skills; Arabic became the official language of government, Arab coins were minted, and Arab conceptions of law, conduct and justice prevailed, while in the fields of finance, diplomacy and economy they made their contribution even though the far more sophisticated and adapted methods of Constantinople and of Persia, familiarized by long usage in the now occupied territories, were generally adopted in more or less Arabized form. Thus, variously derived, a full provincial and central administration for the Empire was evolved and, with some admitted inconsistency and discontinuity, applied.

Even in the early-middle ninth century, however, the slightness of Arab control in Persia began to appear, where that country's own national life was still vigorous though in part concealed; and Persian influence in Baghdad itself was, from the beginning of the century, considerable. Henceforward, officers of the Caliphate government, members of outstanding local or transplanted Arab families, successful generals, or scions of central Asian noble families, managed to found dynasties of their own in different areas of Persia and to transmit power to their sons and grandsons. Such were the Tahirids (820–926), Dulafids (825–896), 'Alids (864–926) and Saffarids (867–903), and these were partly contemporary with, partly succeeded by, the more formidable states of the Samanids (874–999) of eastern Persia and Turkistan, and then by the various branches of the Buyids or Buwaihids (932–1035), one of which entered Baghdad itself, occupied most of 'Iraq, and deprived the Caliph of all but his prestige. Nor was this all; lesser Persian statelets continued to form—Ziyarids (928–1042), Hasanwaihids (959–1015), Kakwaihids (1007–1051), and in 'Iraq itself and to the westward, tribally-based Arab dynasties had arisen, each for a brief life of sovereignty. Such were the Hamdanids (929–1003), 'Uqailids (996–1906), Mirdasids (1028–1079), Mazyadids (1012–1150), and the Kurdish Marwanids (990–1096). At the same period in Egypt, and with it usually most of Syria, after more than two centuries of resented and resisted rule by the viceroys of the 'Abbasids, effectively independent dynasties founded by ex-Caliphate officers had flourished for a generation or more (Tulunids 865–905, Ikhshidids 935–969) before the more formidable and longer-lasting State of the Fatimids moved in from North Africa in 969, and founded Cairo. They were to remain in unchallenged dominion for two centuries, a period of wealth, luxury, and cultural achievement, some pretensions to empire (in Syria and Arabia), frequent warfare with Byzantium, and wide trading relations with Europe. In Arabia, the shift of Islamic power to the north—to Damascus, then to Baghdad—led to a world of disgruntled Hijazi intrigue and armed reaction, with violent interruptions of Caliphate rule. The extravagant impieties of the Carmathian sectarians were especially outrageous in and around Mecca, until the Fatimid power could restore tolerable conditions. Later, at the end of the tenth century, families of Sharifs (descended, therefore, from the Prophet) managed to conduct a precarious government in Mecca, while in the Yemen a succession of similar city-dynasties maintained an isolated independence, theocratic in tone and heedless of the far-off Caliph.

The Arab Empire was thus already fragmented before as well as after its capital had been occupied by secular, and mostly non-Arab, forces and rulers; the Middle East had become once again—though now with the important new element of a shared religion, law and sense of community—a group of independent though similar states. Of the latter, it is noticeable that they could emerge from very different origins, racial, social and personal; no suggestion of nationality as a basis for unity or separation existed, while the notion of rule by the consent of the subjects, or even of their welfare, was inconceivable; and even adherence to a heterodox form of Islam seemed to matter little, since both Buwaihids and Fatimids were Shi'i. Rule, while it lasted, was transmitted from father to son, the Caliph's formal brevet being usually but not always asked and forthcoming. The princes issued their own coinages, though their scale of empire varied from a few valleys to a considerable state, and their effective authority differed correspondingly. A single family or clan often split dynastically into branches, each assuming rule in a separate province or city or area; their natural enemies and probable successors were each other, or some new local aspirant like themselves, or the jealous relations of the ruler himself, or the resentful Caliph. The type of government provided by these now forgotten medieval Muslim states, which covered so great areas of time and territory, was, if one can generalize, formal and orderly, studiously Islamic in law and conduct, and often favourable to art and culture.

3. *Turks and Moguls*

The second millennium of the Christian era opened, then, with the Caliphate helpless if tolerated and by some revered, Persian and Arab secular dynasties lording it from central Asia to the Mediterranean, Arabia governed precariously under petty if holy city-

princes, sayids or sharifs, or by the new Shi'i masters of Egypt—or
enjoying congenial anarchy. Egypt, with most of Syria, was ruled
from Cairo by the Fatimids. Muslim conquest and government, so
early divorced from the Baghdad Caliphate, had long since been
carried beyond Middle Eastern frontiers into Central Asia and
northern India, along the north African littoral as far as the Atlantic,
and into Spain and Sicily. Eastern and south-eastern Anatolia was
Muslim under Hamdanids and Buwaihids; its western marches were
still part of the dominions of Rum under its Byzantine emperors,
often invaded but never conquered.

But a moment of major change was at hand; a new character was
to enter upon the western Asian scene, in the guise of an eager
immigrant and conqueror, but with new gifts and qualities: the
Turk.

The words Turk or Turkish stand, ethnically, for no definite
human type or group. The term is linguistic, covering the speakers of
Turkish dialects, and is racial only as a vague designation of interconnected groups who emerged from central Asia as nomadic tribes
in the early Middle Ages; these represent steppe peoples not unlike
the earlier Aryan-speaking communities of similar provenance,
except in their different language-structure and their greater measure
of contact, in blood and culture, with Mongol stocks farther east.
The Turks were also, as compared with the Aryan-speakers, in
general more warlike and enduring, less artistic and intellectual.

The Seljuq Turks (so called from the name of an earlier chief)
entered the Middle Eastern world from inner Asia at a time with the
Caliphate was fragmented and decadent, Islam itself no longer simple
or uniform, the Byzantine Empire intact and still capable of aggression, and western Europe soon to launch the Crusades. An advance-
guard of Turks was indeed already known, since the early ninth
century, in Persia, 'Iraq and farther west as slaves, mercenaries, and
hired officers of the Caliphate. The Seljuq incursion, that of whole
communities recently converted to orthodox Islam and led by virile
and ambitious chiefs, entered Persia in the first years of the eleventh
century, swept away the power in that territory of the doughty
Ghaznavid State of Afghanistan and north India—and with it some
lesser Persian statelets—unified its own community and command,
and assumed rule in all parts of Persia. Tughril Beg after occupying
Hamadan, Rayh, and Isfahan in 1041 entered Baghdad (1055), dismissed the last Buwaihid, re-established Sunni orthodoxy and
'protected' the Caliph, and died (1063) sole master of a loosely united

Seljuq Empire stretching from east Persia to the fringes of Syria and the Taurus. The original invaders were thereafter reinforced periodically by fresh Turkish contingents from the east, in sufficient force to impress that language and character on wide areas of the Middle East, notably Azarbaijan and northern 'Iraq (and later, obviously, Anatolia), as well as profoundly to affect its political history. The Arab states of the Fertile Crescent did not long survive the Seljuq flood, though Fatimid Egypt, with much of Syria, could still maintain itself secure and prosperous.

A nominal though always imperfectly unified Seljuq Empire continued in being until the mid-twelfth century. Its great rulers were Alp Arslan (1063–1072), Malik Shah (1072–1092), and Sinjar (1117–1157); but, as ever, local offshoots ruled by sons and nephews managed to establish, in the twelfth century, separate if connected dynasties in Persia, Syria, 'Iraq and Kurdistan. A further, yet largely contemporary, phase was reached in the appearance, all over the Middle Eastern map, of dynasties founded by ex-slaves or captains or ministers of these Seljuq princes. These were the Atabegs, and such dynasties, with varying lives and fortunes, flourished from the early twelfth to the mid-thirteenth century in northern 'Iraq (Baghdad, Mosul, Arbil) and the Jazira (Diyarbakr, Mardin, Sinjar), in northern Syria (Aleppo), and in Armenia and Persia (Azarbaijan, Fars, Luristan, Kirman). They fell in the end, one by one, to ambitious rivals, or to each other, or to one of those major thirteenth-century cataclysms shortly to be mentioned. Some pockets of local, pre-Seljuq, power—notably that of the heretical, dreaded Assassins of Alamut in the north Persian mountains—managed to survive till Mongol times. The epoch of the Seljuq emperors and their diverse, widespread Turkish successors, in spite of its full share of violence and egotistical brutality, gave the Middle East two centuries of relatively stable, unprogressive Islamic rule, and contributed much to the substance, and to later conceptions, of medieval Muslim life.

The 'Abbasid Caliph survived in the teeming, immensely wealthy and cultured city of Baghdad, still bestower of the formal brevets of princedom, still titular head of the whole Islamic community. In Arabia, one princely or sanctified family after another ruled the few cities of the Hijaz and Yemen, with occasional acknowledgment, to suit their purposes, of the overlordship of Cairo or Baghdad; the Arabian tribes were as ever ungoverned save by their own customs and some diluted Islamic notions. South-eastern Arabia (Oman) became a semi-heretical Imamate of the 'Ibadi sect, in almost complete isolation. In Egypt, Fatimid rule after two centuries gave way in 1169 to that of the famous Kurdish-born Saladin (Salah al-Din), an outstanding officer of the Zangid Atabeg of Syria. He died in 1193. His dynasty of the Ayyubids, orthodox Muslims unlike the Fatimids, held power in Egypt, with most of Syria and part of western Arabia, for a century; he himself is best remembered for his powerful but chivalrous opposition to, and reconquest of, the Crusader-founded Latin Kingdom of Jerusalem (1099–1187), in campaigns of which the earlier phases (in the First Crusade, 1097–1100 and the Second, 1147–1149) had witnessed the Islamic prowess of the Syrian Atabegs. The whole episode of the Crusades, abounding in picturesque if not always edifying episode, and still to Muslims an example of western 'unprovoked aggression', left finally no more than minimal effects on the contemporary society or policies of the Middle East, and bequeathed, even to Syria, and even after so close a confrontation, almost nothing of western thought or achievement.

The impact of the Seljuq Turks, profoundly important throughout the Middle East, was in no direction more decisive than in Anatolia, where it entirely altered a position and frontiers uneasily maintained, between the Cross and the Crescent, for more than four centuries. As part of almost the first phase of the Seljuq onslaught, forces and, with them, considerable civil population elements, swept by order of Tughril Beg, about 1050, from the northern Jazira deep into Asia Minor. In 1071 at the fateful battle of Manzikert the Roman Emperor was defeated and captured, Seljuq Turks spread over wide areas of Anatolia and could establish a considerable state in the central and some western areas. Its capital was for a time at Nicaea (Iznik) and it soon assumed a degree of paramouncy over the other Turkish prince-doms which formed, such as the Danishmendids of Sivas (Sebastia) and Kayseri (Caesarea). Throughout the twelfth century and there-after, more and more miscellaneous Turkish or Turkoman bands and parties, armed and unarmed, entered Asia Minor, nomadic and predatory in habit, feudal in organization, innocent of culture, crude and ill-instructed in their Islam. The first-born state, that of 'Seljuqs of Rum', was forced a century later to retire from much of its western territory when the Latin forces of the Fourth Crusade occupied Constantinople, and the Greek emperors withdrew to Iznik (1204–1252), displacing the Turks. Konya (Iconium) then became the latters' capital, and from it, profiting by the weak disunity of the forces and statecraft of Rum, they could extend their power to the south-west, south, and east: a process accompanied by the ruin of the countryside, the retrogression of government and civilized tranquillity, and the loss of much, or nearly all, of the long-collected heritage of Greece and Rome. But they had come to stay, and on their own destructive terms.

A catastrophe more sudden and far more bloody than the Seljuq invasion of the mid-eleventh century was now to ensue in the mid-thirteenth. Mongol hordes, moving from the farther East early in the twelfth century, first consolidated a wide empire of many peoples in central Asia under the single rule of Chinghiz Khan, then destroyed the power of the Shahs of Khwarizm (or Khiva)—a power centred at Khiva but extending, in the first quarter of the thirteenth century, over nearly all Persia and 'Iraq—then entered north Persia with Azarbaijan and Transcaucasia. Chinghiz Khan, proverbial for ruthlessness, died in 1227. Of his vast empire which, part directly administered and part entrusted to terrified vassals, remained for three centuries undivided under a supreme ruler, a major fraction fell in 1256 to his grandson Hulagu. This succession ended, with tragic finality, the terrors and hopes alike of a dozen Atabeg states, and those also of the last of the 'Abbasid Caliphs, who had struggled back to a final Indian summer of local power in 'Iraq; Hulagu's armies, or hordes, swept over the rest of Persia, took and sacked Baghdad, destroyed all that was destructible in 'Iraq (including its priceless canal-system), advanced victoriously into Asia Minor and there displaced the Seljuq ruler and the lesser amirates. They met successful resistance only in Syria. Hulagu now, paying but a faint feudal homage to his suzerain the far-off Great Khan in China, ruled from India to the Black Sea and almost to the Mediterranean. The Caliphate, except for an obscure 'Abbasid pensioner maintained at the court of Cairo, was no more; the states and dynasties of Persia, or 'Iraq and the Jazira—Turkish, Persian, Arab—had gone for ever. And even in the Egyptian-Syrian State, where the Mongols met their match and made no headway, a change of rule had preceded, by a few years, the Mongol inrush; the Ayyubids, founded by Saladin, had given way in 1250 to a dynasty of Turkish or Circassian exslaves, or Mamluks, whose origins were in the picked bodyguards and fief-holding officers of the Ayyubid rulers.

4. Darkest Age

The period of two centuries and a half which separates the Mongol invasion under Hulagu from the establishment of the Ottoman Turks

as the paramount power of western Asia is among the darkest known
to our region. Subjected to despotic, warring rulers of no more than
ephemeral interest, under overlords without local roots or devotion,
without aspiration to progress or enlightenment save in rarest individuals, and suffering materially from the destruction wrought by
the Mongols and the resulting poverty or despair, the populations
were helpless witnesses or victims of strangers' struggles for power.
In the provision either of new racial elements or of practical or
cultural contributions the Mongol-Tartar period was far inferior to
that of the Seljuqs and their Atabegs (1037–1258). At best it permitted, by its very miseries, the slow regrowth in Persia of a national
spirit never wholly extinguished, and, in the Arabic-speaking countries, the assurance of no more than a feeble resistance to the
powerful imperialism from without which was, early in the sixteenth
century, to submerge them all.

Persia and 'Iraq were in this period governed for seventy years
after the death of Hulagu (1265–1335) by his descendants in the Il
Khan dynasty, with its centre at Tabriz. Its frontiers marched with
those of the central Asian Mongol Empire, those of the Egypto-
Syrian State of the Mamluks, and, until 1453, those of the shrunken
dominions of the eastern Roman emperors. A dozen Il Khan rulers
succeeded Hulagu, in a now Muslim government undistinguished
and alien but no longer barbarous, until the usual processes of
intrigue and violence destroyed it. Three lesser principalities succeeded: that of the Jal'airs in 'Iraq and north-western Persia (1336–
1411), the Mudhaffarids in Fars and Kirman (1313–1393), and the
Sarbadarids in Khurasan (1337–1381). The latter two fell at the end
of the fourteenth century to the forces of Timur the Lame, the
Jal'airs to those of a dynasty of Turkoman chieftains of the Black
Sheep tribe-group who from 1378 to 1469 managed, with interruptions due to Timur's irresistible raids, to maintain a state stretching
from Armenia and Azarbaijan to southern 'Iraq. The Black Sheep,
who were of Shi'i faith, gave way in turn, about 1470, to the similar
Turkoman dynasty of the White Sheep, who were Sunni; their
centres of power were in Azarbaijan and the Jazira.

A far more imposing figure and shaper of eastern destinies was
Timur, a high-born relation of Chinghiz Khan. Timur, from his
base in central Asia, launched from 1380 onwards a series of cam-
paigns which conquered all Persia with a ferocity rare even in the
Mongol-Tartar world. He took and sacked Baghdad in 1393, overran
'Iraq and the Jazira, invaded Asia Minor to defeat and capture the

Ottoman Sultan (p. 60) in 1401–1402, and after brilliant successes in Syria received formal homage (but nothing more) from the Mamluk ruler. He died in 1405. The Timurid Empire, for a few years extraordinarily extensive, could not endure; many of Timur's conquests were revealed as little more than destructive raids which bequeathed not empire but anarchy. This empire maintained itself, under the great Shahrukh and his successors in Persia, for a century of decreasing power. (The Timurid dynasty of Babar, which became that of the Moghul emperors of India, does not here concern us.) In Asia Minor and Syria the Timurid tide swiftly retreated, and soon little or nothing of Mongol power remained. In 'Iraq and Kurdistan, Azarbaijan and the Jazira, the principalities of Black Sheep and White regained their thrones, and the last-named was still in power when in 1502 the great national revival of Safawi Persia swept it away.

The history of Asia Minor in this period moved fast, and to significant ends. The first Mongol incursion (1243), and Hulagu's vice-regal governor who stayed behind, destroyed most of what remained of Seljuq power; this made it the easier for a dozen, if not a score, of local small-scale principalities to establish themselves in the ex-Seljuq territories, and beyond them. Their rulers, mostly ex-vassals of the Seljuq but with loyal heterogeneous followings of their own, were by race Turks or Turkomans, Greeks, Kurds, Armenians, or a variety of mixtures; their power dated from around 1300, by which date the Seljuq rulers were far gone in enfeeblement, but was precarious and unequal. One amongst them, established as a separate unit located near the Byzantine frontier at about that date, and led by a succession of outstanding chieftains, now rapidly expanded. It absorbed its nearer neighbours, occupied Bursa (Brusa), sent forces across into Europe, and by 1370, under a great ruler, Murad I, had conquered wide areas of Balkan territory. Such was the genesis and youth of the Ottoman (Osmanli) Turks, named from Osman their founder; though the Turkish, or Turkoman, element among them physically was in fact minimal, it was to this constituent in their leaders and population that their pride and consciousness were directed. Indeed, Asia Minor had by now long ceased to be Greek; it had become a racial and cultural amalgam known as 'Turkish', speaking that language and proud of its far-off half-mystical origins.

The Ottoman power, on varying terms—but at least those of equals—with Constantinople and the major cities of south-east Europe, and pushing its conquests far into Thessaly and northern

Greece, had by 1400 absorbed most of the post-Seljuq amirates of
Asia Minor. The invasion of Timur inflicted a severe set-back, from
which however in a dozen years recovery was complete. The Anatolian amirs restored by Timur were again dethroned; a widespread
rebellion was put down. Europe was next raided or conquered to
the Danube; and in 1453 Constantinople itself, greatest of all prizes,
fell to Ottoman arms and became their capital: a capital which later
history was to show as fatally misplaced for a power whose roots
and strength were in truth Asiatic. Wars with Serbia, Hungary and
Venice continued, the Empire grew fast; a new power not only by
Middle Eastern but by world standards had arrived, and was fast
developing its own novel institutions and seeking new frontiers. Its
Islam, or that at least of its rulers, was orthodox, its ambition and
sense of destiny immense, its superiority complex limitless; and its
hereditary monarchy was still producing great rulers. The upper
strata in Ottoman-Turkish society, including its rulers, had by now
widely intermarried with Anatolian and European Greeks, and was
already composite in its culture and far from its barbarous origins.
So opened the sixteenth century.

The island of Cyprus, ruled from Constantinople from the year
400 onwards with only brief interruptions by Arab invaders after
650, passed in 1192, after short interludes of other rule—Richard I
of England seized it from the Greeks in 1191 and sold it to the
Knights Templars, who resold it to Guy de Lusignan—to French
ex-Crusader kings. These were to hold it for three centuries, with but
one (Genoese) interruption. It fell next to the Venetians, in 1498,
and was so held for a further eighty years, till the Ottoman conquest.

The Mamluk dynasties of Egypt—these were two, the Bahri
(1250–1390), and the Burji (1382–1517)—in spite of periods of mur-
derous violence among themselves which led to short uneasy reigns,
were destined to pass their power from master to slave, or father to
son, for more than 250 years. On the whole they provided Egypt,
and normally most of Syria, with an effective if restless government,
distinguished by its achievements in art and, mainly religious, architecture. The Mamluks could boast also in Baibars, Qala'un, Nasir,
and half a dozen more of their slave-kings, some rulers of outstanding merit, who performed doughty services to Islam in arms
not only against the last remnants of the Crusaders, but in resistance
also to the Mongol hordes of Timur himself. They little expected, as
the sixteenth century opened, the quarter from which their end as
rulers would come.

5. *Islamic Civilization*

Since this over-compressed and doubtless distorted narrative has now reached a period less than a half-millennium from our own, and since the main contribution of Islam to Middle Eastern (as well as much wider) society had by now been made—a contribution of transcendent and lasting significance—a page may well be devoted at this stage to assessing something of the nature of the Islamic civilization and communities from which is so directly derived the modern Middle East, in many countries of which this medieval period (both the true and the idealized) is the pride and boast of their modern nationalism.

Racially, no profound change occurred in the content of the Middle Eastern populations between A.D. 600 and 1500; when there were internal population movements, or such from outside the region, they were in general soon absorbed and contributed little (though considerably more than nothing) to existing racial composition. The single-community pretension of Islam, and a single dominant language, encouraged far more internal migration—by Persians, for example, or North Africans, or, later, by European Muslims—within Dar al-Islam than that of previous centuries, and many families of such migrants were to be known in new homes by a reminiscent surname. More Arab tribes moved from Arabia into the Fertile Crescent and into and beyond Egypt—and, exceptionally, into Persia—and with these, encouraged by Islamic usage, more negro slaves. At the same time an increase in nomadism was to turn back to grazing lands where settled populations had long dwelt, as in 'Iraq between the rivers and in north Syria. The infiltration, then the large-scale incursion, of central Asian Turks—pre-Seljuq, Seljuq and post-Seljuq—involved a more significant addition, which left some visible influences everywhere, with enclaves of Turkish-speaking population in a few localities; and, as we have seen, it transformed completely the culture and very life of Anatolia.

The Mongol or Tartar contribution, politically of the highest distinctive importance, was racially as well as culturally almost negligible, so small were the population elements of Mongolian type left behind when their warriors withdrew. The contribution of the infinitely mixed, Greek-speaking hotch-potch which was the Anatolian population when this first became accessible to Islam, was at first limited to Asia Minor itself (so soon to become Turkey-in-Asia), until Ottoman dominance of nearly the whole Middle East brought Anatolians, now Turks, in hundreds, as soldiers and officials, to every subject territory.

The Muslim civilization of these centuries was, with all its palpable unity, both complex and variegated. If differed obviously, as between the great cities and royal or viceregal courts, and the open country. In the latter, it is safe to imagine, life was but little altered in most essentials from that of earlier, pre-Islamic, ages, and a replacement of the old language and tax-gatherers with new could scarcely modify a hard and changeless environment. Indeed rural life, as that also of the great nomadic tribes (unchanged in every respect since the Times of Ignorance), received little from Islam and contributed little to it; and even the traditional picture of high fertility, marvellous gardens and abundant crop-yields in the fabulous days of the Caliphs owe, it is probable, as much to legend and idealization as to fact.

The true and indeed glorious Islamic civilization of the cities varied as between different regions. The incoming Muslim Arabs were few in number, and brought with them no more than a scanty and scarcely transplantable civilization of their own, above all in the material and artistic fields; it was inevitable, therefore, that the mixed culture which developed in Egypt, or Syria, or Persia should incorporate much, in tone and feature, of what these countries had already long since achieved, accepted and lived. Differences between countries in dress, dialect, social usage or taboo resulted, and such are still observable today. It may be asked, indeed, how these few Arabs of Arabia, so poor and inexperienced, could impose themselves at all upon far more populous and extensive, richer, more sophisticated territories so as to justify the phrase 'an Arab civilization'. Yet the term is not unjustified; the Arab Muslims brought rare gifts and qualities, their initial simplicities were of short duration, and, intellectually and culturally, they could soon hold their own with any. They brought from Arabia, and it kept them united amid diverse peoples, their own conscious solidarity, a fresh, confident approach, a burning enthusiasm for the Faith, and that Faith's drive and restraints. They brought the language of the Prophet himself, his Qur'an and Traditions, the divinely-given Law, and the pride and the folk-tales of the Prophet's own country and age-long way of life. In Islam, for centuries the focal point of all thought, law and living, Arabic was the sole, and the divine, key to knowledge and acceptable doctrine, of which the earliest exponents were Arabs to a man. It followed that in medieval Islam the Arab enjoyed a scarcely contested moral superiority.

But the contributions from other sources to their evolving and evolved civilization were essential to it, and made it what it became. That of Persia, where indeed the masses were never deeply Arabized, was subtle and pervasive in all fields of literature, science, theology —and luxurious living; not their own national myths or claims, but their *finesse*, their metaphysical teaching, their artistic and literary gifts, their craftsmanship, left a deep imprint in Baghdad and other great cities of and beyond the Caliphate. From the west and north came, into the cultural pool, a major contribution of Byzantine art and architecture, governmental procedure, coinage, and (as from Persia also) words into the Arabic tongue. From such direct contacts with Europe as existed—through traders to and from Egypt and Syria, Holy Land pilgrims, frontier neighbours with Greek-held territory in Asia Minor, scholars, war captives, Crusaders at work and play—came glimpses of a wide, impious, unknown world beyond Islam. From or through the Christian communities, from Egypt to Persia, came conceptions and usages which reflected not only Christian, and not only Judaic, thought and speculation and custom, but the whole body of Hellenistic literature and learning with which Islam had somehow to come to terms: and behind that, the classic philosophers, scientists, and doctors of old, with Plato and Aristotle at their head.

The 'Arab civilization', which, after its first post-conquest decades of acclimatization and acquisition, took gradually from the ninth century onwards a characteristic and a dynamic form, was indeed a remarkable phenomenon. Imposing in appearance, great in achievement, rich in the products—which became and are still the legacies —of hand and mind, it can claim, in spite of all political distractions, to have contributed one of the great periods of human history. Not only in or near the seat of the Caliphate, but in cities throughout the Middle East as well as north Africa, Spain, central Asia and India, it produced orderly and gracious cities, mosques and palaces, barracks and offices, caravanserais, libraries, public baths, pools and fountains. Many or most of these were of unusual, sometimes outstanding, architectural beauty, both of outline and in each meticulous detail. Delightful gardens abounded, bridges and streets were maintained, paved and cleaned, water supplies were provided, security was assured (doubtless with no infrequent lapses) for residents, pilgrims and travellers. A comprehensive civil service saw to the conduct of government, markets were regulated, craftsmen multiplied, trade flowed across every frontier. The Law was upheld and administered, and justice the first objective of the better rulers. Taxation, in normal conditions, was moderate, great works of irrigation and flood-protection were carried out.

Benevolence towards art, study and literature was rather the rule than the exception among Muslim princes, and these activities could not but flourish in conditions which provided wealth and leisure, and inexhaustible human and cultural material both religious and secular, in a region-wide society which blended, as we have seen, many diverse contributions and racial and environmental varieties. From Egypt and Syria to the Hijaz and farthest Persia the period from the mid-ninth century onwards produced artistic work which was, within the fairly narrow Islamic limits, of high merit in textiles and brocades, carpets, glassware, leather and woodwork, jewellery, metalwork, paper-making and illumination, tilework and design. The period produced an abundant literary output—some reflecting an Arab, some a Persian, some a Hellenistic background, and much that was blended from varied sources—in poetry, music, history, philosophy, geography; in physical science and medicine, astronomy and mathematics; and in the wide field of religious, religio-legal, and metaphysical speculation or exposition. In these few lines we must dismiss, reluctantly, a copious and remarkable literature, which included also, with profound results on human cultural history, the translation (and thereby, for centuries, the rescue) of works of the greatest Greek thinkers.

Islam itself, as a religion and way of life, underwent profound changes in these centuries, changes whose course and ramifications cannot be followed in detail here. As the size and the geographic, racial and historical variety of the region precluded the possibility that the Caliphate could long survive as a single state, so the same features—and with them the restless individualism of minds, and pre-existing religious-philosophical tendencies—were bound to destroy much of the unity of Islam itself, and admit deep clefts and varieties within it. Primitive Islam was too simple, too little thought-out, too vulnerable to survive unmodified and undeveloped; and, with far subtler Hellenic and Hellenistic strands of thought entering the Islamic world, and Zoroastrian elements from Persia, and Christian and Jewish contributions (not unknown, already, in the Qur'an itself, though unadmitted as such) brought in by eager converts, and relics of animism or ancient local beliefs from many quarters, there was copious material for speculation and new thinking, or for sheer heresy, within Islam. Differing religious interpretations—of the rights of succession to the Caliphate, for instance—were soon adduced as political and dynastic arguments, and led to the great split between the Sunna (traditional orthodoxy) and Shi'a, the sect of the followers (almost the deifiers) of 'Ali. Repeatedly a movement of political or popular secession or rebellion was presented as a religious issue, by the Carmathians, the Kharijis or the Assassins; the names of highly unspiritual leaders became those of major sects of Islam; and a new regional religious attitude, for example in western Arabia, could be determined by its political misfortunes. The adoption by this or that Caliph or prince of a new pseudo-Islamic conception could instantly affect his friends and foes in the dynastic or political field.

The picture of an Islam divided by walls of mutual disapprobation, perhaps hostility, between communities was much intensified, from the tenth century onwards, by the proliferation of the new Ways of a host of variously orientated Sufi or mystic sects, varying from the unorthodox to the heretical or barely Islamic, and led by thinkers, saints or mystics, or charlatans to whom, and to whose followers, orthodox Islam had ceased to appeal. These Sufi orders, often incorporating emotional non-Islamic conceptions and devoted to individual teachers, shrines, incantations, and ceremonies, became a major element in the body of Islam; an element which departed far, very far, from the Prophet's teaching, but which attracted and held within its Faith thousands of the simple, the impressionable, the deprived. At the opposite end of the Islamic range stood, and stand, the Men of Learning (the *'ulama*) of sober, traditional, established Sunni orthodoxy, rigid guardians of the Faith unpolluted.

CHAPTER FOUR

MODERN TIMES

1. Sultan and Shah

THE story of the world-famous Ottoman Empire, from its half-concealed, intrusive, gallant beginnings to its shabby and helpless decline is, in outline, well known. Since it covered, with various degrees of effectiveness, all the Middle East which is here our subject, except Persia and the farthest fringes of Arabia, and since Turkish influence on Arab society thus imposed was and remains profound, the story closely concerns us; but it can be told only in briefest outline.

The main eastward and south-eastward expansion of Ottoman power occurred half a century after the fall of Constantinople to their arms (1453), and their completion of the conquest of the Balkans and south Russia. It was Salim I—the Grim!—who, now secure in the possession of all Asia Minor, including the territories of a Greek survival in Trabzon (Trebizond), those of the White Sheep, and those of minor Anatolian valley-dynasties, led his army eastward, met and beat at Chadiran (1514) the forces of newly-arisen Safawi Persia (pp. 59, 69), acquired Kurdistan and Cilicia, and effectively parrie dthe danger of Persian (and therefore Shi'i) westward penetration. The Grim Sultan proceeded next to defeat the Mamluks of Egypt, make the Nile Valley an Ottoman province, acquire the Hijaz and its Holy Cities, and take with him from Cairo to Istanbul (as Constantinople had now become) the robes and trinkets of the 'Abbasid Caliph, which honorific rank the Sultan shrewdly assumed. His yet greater son, Sultan Sulaiman Qanuni (the Lawgiver, called in Europe the Magnificent) (1520–1566), took Erzurum, suppressed serious sectarian troubles in Anatolia, and in rapid campaigns added Tabriz (temporarily) and then Baghdad, with most of 'Iraq, to the Empire. Repeated wars with Persia ended with a peace treaty in 1555; Baghdad and much more was retained, Tabriz was surrendered. Turkish fleets dominated the Mediterranean, and in the Red Sea established footholds in the Yemen. Cyprus was acquired from the Venetians in 1571, the year of Lepanto.

The sixteenth century in Turkey was one in which external

triumphs (not unaccompanied, however, by reverses) were mixed with much internal disorder created by lawless nomadic elements—the old, essential Turks—by extremists' and heretics' religious movements, by revolts of provincial Pashas and ambitious robber-barons, and by the gross indiscipline of the Turkish soldiery, notably the famous Janissaries. These conditions made possible the Persian recovery of Azarbaijan and 'Iraq, where Baghdad fell to them in 1623. The position was outwardly restored by the prowess of Sultan Murad IV, who disciplined the provinces and sects of Asia Minor, punished the Janissaries and purged the civil service. He then strongly engaged the Persian power, recovered Azarbaijan, 'Iraq and Kurdistan, and by the Treaty of Qasr-i-Shirin (1639) established an eastern boundary (which left Tabriz and Azarbaijan to Persia) nearly identical to that of today.

From 1640 onwards, after three centuries of success, began three more of humiliating decline. Except for the addition of Crete (1645) no new territory was to fall to Ottoman arms, while the loss of province after province, especially in Europe, marked the ensuing years. The well-known Turkish system of recruiting both their fighting forces and their whole civil service from trained and devoted ex-Christian slave-boys, of many Asiatic and European races, had worked well, by Turkish standards, for two centuries; but from the eighteenth century onwards it was an obsessive anachronism, and was finally abandoned. No progress, because no new conception capable of shaking an almost morbid conservatism, could be achieved in the body politic. Corruption and venality spread to the point of universality. Control and security fell to the lowest levels and the remoter provinces and their governors rendered an ever diminishing obedience to the Padishah and his viziers. High office was everywhere for sale, the purchase price recoverable from the public. The Islamic religion, retained with full rigid orthodoxy by the Sultanate and the 'Ulama, who provided almost the only Muslim educated class, was throughout much of the Empire defiled with all sorts of heresy and barely-Muslim contamination. The administration of the provinces was capricious and venal, habitually combining truculence with weakness, injustice with high pretension. By any standards the rule of Law, even of the Shari'a Law to which there was conceived neither rival nor replacement, did not prevail. Taxation was oppressive and monstrously ill-regulated. No economic conceptions existed save those dictated by immediate, blind self-interest. The important Christian and Jewish minority communities, in part self-governing under the *millet* system, were, while still regarded as politically innocuous, treated with tolerance; commerce and nearly all foreign social contacts (at least until the late eighteenth century) were the near-monopoly of these non-Muslims. Turkish Muslim society was ceremonious, ultra-polite, archaically stratified, strongly tinged with religiosity. The political or military power of the Sultan-Caliph ceased to be the terror and, in spite of the enormous popular prestige of his throne within Turkey and the fabled luxury of his Court, was later to be the scorn, of Europe and the world. The line of rulers themselves, once outstandingly able, was too often corrupted by extravagance, vice and harem influences into ignominy. The defeat of Turkish arms in Europe at St. Gothard (1664), Choczim (1673), and Lemberg (1675), the fatal siege of Vienna (1682), the fiasco at Mohácz and loss of all Hungary, the invasions of Turkish territory by Austrians and Venetians, the battle of Zenta (1697) and treaties of Carlovitz (1699) and Passarovitz (1718), were followed by successful Russian counter-invasions from 1736 onwards. By the end of the eighteenth century the Ottoman Empire was far gone in humiliation, feebleness and misery.

Egypt in the same period passed through three centuries of disorderly government, little as this, one may suppose, affected nine-tenths of the public. The Sultan's viceroys could not for long prevail over the entrenched local authority, and the far stronger forces, of the Mamluk beys; insubordination, murder and massacre, overt rebellion and large-scale armed quarrels between Mamluk cliques and candidates for power not only reduced Ottoman authority to a flickering shadow but involved the self-made rulers, or irremovable officials, in Syria also. Egyptian Islamic civilization, by now a peculiar blend of Nilotic, Mediterranean, Arab and Turkish, remained highly distinctive and by no means without attraction.

Western Arabia, claimed as belonging to the Ottoman dominions, increased its (largely involuntary) contacts with the western world; Portuguese, English, Dutch and French shipping and traders intermittently appeared on its coasts. The attempts of Istanbul to exert authority, whether in the Hijaz or the Yemen, were successful only locally, temporarily, intermittently; the indigenous lines of sharifs and amirs, with their wealth of local contacts and intrigues, could more than hold their own. It resulted that the Hijaz for short, and the Yemen for long, periods were left alone by their nominal overlord the Sultan-Caliph; of Turkish direct administration, and indeed of social or cultural influence, there was little or none. So passed three centuries of intense, sophisticated, self-seeking intrigue in the historic and holy Arabian cities, surrounded by purest non-government in the tribes and oases. In central Arabia the Wahhabi movement, a strong puritan Muslim revival, arose in one of the small Najdi amirates about 1740; its founder and adherents gained converts and strength, raided and conquered, carried terror into 'Iraq and the Hijaz, alarmed the Sharifs of Mecca, and was reported to Istanbul as a new threat or indignity; and indeed of these Wahhabis, and of their original backers of the House of Sa'ud, much was later to be heard. Eastern Arabia—Oman and the Trucial Coast, Bahrain and the al-Hasa coast-strip—had little visible history; its contacts were with the Gulf itself and India, its isolation from the Ottoman power complete, while its fierce local struggles for power, from one of which a new (the present) dynasty arose in Oman in 1741, mattered nothing to the world outside. The tiny state of Kuwait was founded about 1750 by a party of 'Aniza tribesmen from the desert hinterland.

'Iraq and Syria, Arab countries but nominally Turkish since the sixteenth century, endured as best they could the long Ottoman domination and all the characteristic features of its provincial administration. Their distaste at an oppressive, alien and incalculable government was tempered in some measure by its not inconsiderable short-term shrewdness, its prowess in 'divide and rule', and the unique prestige, felt by every Sunni, of the Sultan-Caliph. Local despots and dynasties could rise and fall in the Kurdish mountains, the deserts and marshes of lower 'Iraq, the coasts of southern Syria, the deep valleys of Lebanon; governors-general and their elaborate entourages, military commanders and judges, could come and go; the Sultan's government somehow survived, with all its weaknesses, shame and absurdities. The constant seventeenth- and eighteenth-century wars with the rulers of rival and incompatible Persia disrupted it no more than did its own habitual impotence to impose its will, keep order among its tribes, or guarantee an ordinary bestowal or use or continuity of power. The society and manners of the period were of medieval-Islamic type, artistic or cultural output was negligible, security poor or non-existent, poverty extreme.

Persia herself, a few years before the great eastward Ottoman expansion, produced suddenly a unifying, all-Persian, Shi'a-inspired revival, conceived and led by a religious aristocrat, Isma'il Shah the Safawi (or, to our Elizabethans, the Sophy) who inspired and rallied his country, exalted the Shi'i branch of Islam, and posed at least potentially a major threat to the Turks. The Safawi dynasty, at its height a match for the Ottoman power, ruled Persia without a rival for 225 years, built and adorned cities, notably Isfahan, and treated and traded with the powers of Europe. Shah 'Abbas the Great was its outstanding figure (1587–1629). Afghanistan broke off from the Safawi Empire in 1747, under a separate Sunni dynasty, and has never been reunited. The Safawis were succeeded by a brief Afghan usurpation (1722), and then, after a decade of anarchy, by the dominant figure of Turkish-descended Nadir Shah (1736–1747) the Afshari—statesman, great soldier and conqueror, but brutal despot— and after him by the mild and civilized rule of Karim Khan Zend (1750–1779), with the capital at Shiraz. This too-short phase ended with the enthronement of the bloodthirsty tyrant Agha Muhammad (1779), first of the Qajar dynasty, of Turkish tribal origins. He was succeeded in 1797 by Fath 'Ali Shah. Persia throughout these three centuries was politically independent and reasonably secure. Notably backward in conceptions of government, it was polished and sophisti-cated in social forms, highly cultured on traditional lines of art and writing in its small educated élite, yet in the country at large almost untouched by modern or western influences; the lot of the poorer worker, villager or herdsman had changed little since antiquity.

2. *The Nineteenth Century*

Immense, yet almost nowhere spectacular, changes occurred in Middle Eastern society and policies between 1800 and 1914. These were at their least in Arabia and Persia, at their most striking in Turkey and its provinces.

The Ottoman Empire with its Sultan-Caliph remained in existence until 1914, though it had lost most of its territory in Europe—Greece (1830), Rumania (1866), Serbia, Montenegro, Bulgaria, Thessaly, Bosnia, Herzegovina (all in 1878) and, in 1912, almost all the rest north-west of Marmara—and in Africa (Algeria 1830, Tunis 1881, Libya 1912). In Asia the Sultan lost Cyprus to Great Britain in 1878 and an area of eastern Anatolia, to Russia, in the same year. Every-where else, though with widely varying degrees of real control, or intermittent interference, or merely nominal suzerainty, the Ottoman power persisted, its progressively modified—and, in general, im-proved—governmental machine somehow operated, its peculiar social and religious mystique prevailed. Except in Arabia and Egypt, for reasons which will appear, the discontinuous half-hearted struggles of the Ottoman power to modernize and revivify itself, to catch up with the nineteenth century, to gain the respect or at least the tolerance of Europe without losing that of its own subjects, were visible in every province, from Basra or Sinai to the Bosphorus.

The reforming movement, deeply important both socially and governmentally, began with well-meant but abortive projects late in the eighteenth century (Salim III, 1789–1807), and had more to show under Mahmud II (1808–1839), to whom was due the destruction of the Janissaries, the formation of a new Prussian-trained army, schools and medical and military academies, increased foreign trade, and the multiplication (for better or worse) of resident foreigners in Istanbul and elsewhere. In the period 1839–1876 two major attempts at fundamental constitutional-legal reform were made (1839 and 1856), largely under European pressure; both produced considerable though inadequate results, both were followed by a wave of educational, administrative, economic, and even, within limits, political development, only to give place again to the thirty-year absolutism, secretive, corrupt, obscurantist, despotic, of 'Abdul Hamid II: a ruler who, detested by all progressive elements, and known in Europe as the butcher of the Armenians, was sincerely lamented, as an exemplary Muslim and as Caliph, by millions in his shabby and backward Empire. As the climax of a long-maturing plan by progressive army officers with wide backing, the Sultan was dethroned and replaced, by a complacent nonentity, in 1909. In the period 1909–1914 Turkey, with a restored but little respected parliamentary constitution, was in practice run by a clique of officers devoted, in foreign affairs, to Panturanianism and to Germany, and in internal policy to single-party power—that of its own Committee of Union and Progress—to a purging of the administration, and to insistence on national unity as Turks, even though three-fifths of the Empire was in fact linguistically and self-consciously Arab. The years immediately preceding 1914 were scarcely less unhappy and distracted than former decades; but by dint of nearly a century of attempted reform, and by greatly increased foreign contacts through improved land and sea communications, international posts and telegraphs, a railway network in Anatolia, foreign missions, increasing travel to and from Europe, the foundation of schools and colleges, modernized law codes and procedures, the beginnings of industrial development, the presence of European military and naval experts, the Turkish scene and urban society at all its higher levels—and, scarcely less, that of the 'Iraqi and Syrian cities—was far removed from its aspect of a century earlier. However superficially, indis-

criminately, imperfectly, long stages of modernization had been somehow accomplished, new and irreversible conceptions had been
admitted.

In the 'Arab provinces' the aspect of life in the cities was not
dissimilar from that of Asia Minor; in the tribes and villages it was
still traditional in form and spirit, except in new-fashioned official
nomenclature and system and in greater signs of governmental
activity. In 'Iraq—that is, the three *vilayets* of Mosul, Baghdad and
Basra, later to become 'Iraq—the new era began in 1830 with the fall
of the century-old dynasty of slave-Pashas, followed by the progressive introduction of all that could substantially or nominally be
made available of the codes and departments, the troops and police,
the modern communications (roads, bridges, railways, river-
steamers), the attempts at land-settlement, and, in general, standards
and procedures less archaic than those of earlier days. And in society,
urban or tribal alike, new ideas, a new awareness of the world outside,
some suggestions of western manners and fashions, had become
gradually visible. In Syria—that is, the *vilayets* of Aleppo, Damascus
and Beirut and their sub-districts, with the two 'independent
sanjaqs' of Dair al-Zaur (Deir ez Zor) and Jerusalem and the tiny
internationally guaranteed 'autonomous Lebanon' dating from 1860
—the case was similar or perhaps indeed more marked as foreign
(notably French and American) contacts were closer. The short-lived
emergence of local, almost independent rulers—Ahmad al-Jazzar of
Acre and Damascus, the Amir Bashir of Lebanon—and the Egyptian
viceroyalty of Syria for a decade, belong to the earlier years of the
century, as do the Maronite-Druze clashes to the middle; the last
half-century of our period, in Syria as in 'Iraq, was mostly peaceful
and (except for the Hamidian stagnation) not wholly unprogressive.
In both territories an Arab nationalist or home-rule movement came,
slowly and uncertainly, into existence with its tentative, but later
bolder, propaganda and its secret societies and conferences; but it
failed to make much headway against either the jealous autocracy of
'Abdul Hamid or Young Turk intransigence. Some small-scale but
interesting colonies of European (mainly Russian) Jews in these
years were being founded, with 'Zionist' as well as pre-Zionist funds
and initiative, in the south Syrian *sanjaqs* of 'Akka (Acre), Nablus
and al-Quds (Jerusalem).

Egypt, invaded and evacuated by Napoleon in 1798–1801, and
thereafter subject to the increasing and finally dominant authority of
Muhammad 'Ali Pasha, an Albanian captain, emerged at the end of

the first decade of the nineteenth century from bitter and bloody struggles for power involving Turks, Albanians, Mamluk Begs and foreign (French and British) armies, to find itself destined to be governed for the next thirty years by Muhammad 'Ali, under a merely nominal Turkish suzerainty. The Pasha, after restoring order and massacring almost the whole body of the Mamluks, sent forces on his suzerain's behalf to Arabia to deal with the Wahhabis, conquered and occupied most of the Sudan, and created an Egyptian fleet and army. His establishment of local industries was generally a failure, his brutal use of forced labour was deplorable, his fiscal oppression almost intolerable; nevertheless, he introduced cotton cultivation, carried out large irrigation works, and after his armies' successful campaigns in Asia Minor and Syria he could count his rule as permanent and hereditary—as it proved to be. Under his successors, considerable progress achieved in modernized public services, and the opening of the Suez Canal (1869), was accompanied by foolish extravagance and reckless borrowing. This led, on behalf of the European lenders, to an enforced Anglo-French control of Egyptian expenditure. A nationalist or anti-dynastic revolt, that of Ahmad 'Arabi in 1881, led next to British armed intervention to support the Khedive, and thereafter to an effective British occupation and government of Egypt, whereby, in the event, an immensely improved administration and a reasonable financial régime were by degrees achieved. The Sudan, grossly misgoverned for half a century, was the scene in 1882 of the fanatical Mahdist rebellion; this led to the total loss of Egyptian control, chaotic conditions and general depopulation for sixteen years, until its reconquest by Kitchener (1898) and the establishment of an enlightened administration in the formal guise of an Anglo-Egyptian condominium. The government and people of Egypt entered the twentieth century nationally solvent, intelligently governed, forward-looking, prosperous; but they were still faced by serious problems and among the intelligentsia and the politicians were, ever increasingly, resentful at their effectively subordinate status in their own country. The territory contained great potentialities, a small upper class conspicuous for their wealth and culture, a mass of peasantry in great poverty, and all the attractions of a vast tourist centre.

In western Arabia, officially the *vilayets* of Hijaz and the Yemen, the intermittent, half-hearted yet bitter struggle between Turkish pretension and local independence continued; one or other branch of the Sharifian family in Mecca, and the Zaidi (dissident Shi'i)

Imamate of San'a in the Yemen highlands, claimed and could for long periods exercise substantial autonomy; but, in the nineteenth century, first Egyptian and then Turkish governors did their best to diminish this and to assert imperial authority. This clash involved constant, fluctuating trouble—intrigues, interventions, expulsions, violence, and decades of treacherous diplomacy—while the Yemen in particular became the dreaded graveyard of Turkish armies. From the mid-century, Ottoman rule became somewhat more real, though still interrupted by frequent revolts; the Yemen highlands were penetrated, and a new small state of 'Asir, north of the Imamate, was recognized under a ruling family of Sayids. In 1908 was completed, as far south as Medina, the Hijaz Railway from Damascus, intended to serve pilgrims and to endear the Sultan-Caliph; but the Prophet-descended Sharif of Mecca abated none of his pretensions. On the Arabian south coast Great Britain occupied Aden in 1839, Perim Island in 1857, and began to exercise a vague protectorate (under the government of Bombay) over the Hadhramaut hinterland, the future Aden Protectorate.

The British were active also in eastern Arabia. Here they discouraged and finally suppressed piracy, the slave-trade and gun-running, kept political watch over the area, charted the Gulf waters and entered into agreements and 'truces' with the ruler of Muscat and Oman (then as now an independent state) and with the small and weak coastal shaikhdoms of the so-called Trucial Coast, and Qatar, Bahrain and Kuwait. None of these was colonized, all under their own shaikhly dynasties were protected. Kuwait was, like most of Arabia, the subject of a Turkish claim to suzerainty, which existed solely on paper. Central Arabia, meanwhile, saw in the early years of the nineteenth century the further expansion of the Wahhabi power under the Sa'ud family; this was followed, however, by its almost complete suppression by a military expedition ordered by Istanbul but executed by the Pasha of Egypt (1817–1819). The Sa'udi power later revived, showed aggression by raids and tax-collecting forays towards the east and south-east of the peninsula, but was again diminished by a Turkish-fostered rival Amirate, that of Ha'il in the Jabal Shammar, and by a brief Turkish occupation (1870–1913) of the al-Hasa coast of the Gulf. The Najdi amir of the Wahhabis, however, after a period of defeat and banishment (from 1891) re-occupied his homeland and oases in 1901 and, regaining al-Hasa in 1913, re-established his government of the Najd deserts while submitting, as 'Wali of Najd', to a purely nominal Turkish suzerainty.

Arabia as a whole began during the nineteenth century to attract the interest of the West; much of it was penetrated and described by successive European travellers, diplomats and scholars.

Persia in this century fared but poorly. Campaigns with Russia in the early years, ending in 1828 with the Treaty of Turkoman Chai, deprived her of a wide Transcaucasian area and secured privileges for the Russians. Wars with Afghanistan, in one case involving a brief British intervention (1856), followed in mid-century. Russian expansion in central Asia menaced the Shah, but a safe frontier was established in 1884. Throughout the century, and not least during the long reign (1848-1896) of Nasir al-Din Shah, the society and economics of the country were stagnant and medieval, its government despotic and illiberal, the Shah extravagant and greedy, the small but would-be progressive western-educated intelligentsia unheeded. Districts of Persia remote from the capital (Teheran, since 1788) enjoyed no government worth the name, or were the tacitly admitted private empires of land-owning notables or tribal princelings; insecurity was general, corruption universal, progress in any direction nugatory. Only in 1906 did popular discontent and mob action succeed in obtaining the grant of a constitution; but, opposed by the Shah, it was barely operative, disorder continued widespread, Russian penetration was resolute and, in north Persia, authoritarian and threatening. Spheres of permissible economic activity in Persia were delimited as between Russia and Great Britain by the 1907 agreement, the text of which emphasized the intention of both (sincere as far as regarded Great Britain) to respect the independence and integrity of the country. Oil was discovered in the Khuzistan province of south-western Persia by a British concessionary company in 1907, and was at once developed; it was destined to become Persia's greatest single asset. The export of oil began in 1912.

3. The last half-century

The fifty years stretching from 1913 to 1962 saw striking alterations in the political map of the Middle East. They saw the emergence of new sovereign states from the shrinkage of the Ottoman domain, and the enhanced status of once subordinate territories. Of the states which today (1962) constitute the Middle East, very few correspond in their geographical boundaries or their international status with their counterparts of the period before the First World War; such few, indeed, include no more than Persia, Oman, Aden and its

Protectorate, and some Arabian shaikhdoms. The territory of historic and geographic Syria—three provinces of the Ottoman Empire (p. 72)—was divided into four states; those of the restricted Syrian Republic, of an enlarged artificial Great Lebanon, of southern Syria now to be known as Palestine and later as Israel, and of the desertic region east of Jordan, to be known at first as Transjordan, later as the Kingdom of Jordan. The three *vilayets* of the Tigris-Euphrates Valley became the Kingdom, later the Republic, of 'Iraq. The mid-desert Wahhabi principality of the House of Sa'ud became a kingdom stretching from the Red Sea to the Persian Gulf. Egypt attained full independence as a sultanate, then a kingdom, then a republic. Cyprus emerged in 1959 as a bi-racial sovereign republic. In Turkey itself the ancient monarchy made way for a modern-type republic, ruling, however, less than half of the former Turkish territory.

Nor, for the rest, do even these visible changes of name or status or frontiers equal in importance the profounder movement in social and governmental conceptions and progress in these countries, and in their material development. The whole region has in our day assumed a new importance from a variety of aspects (p. 21 ff), and occupies a place of greatly enhanced significance in the world. If the famous Eastern Question of Victorian times (which concerned the impending demise of the decrepit Ottoman Empire, and aspirants to its succession) has been settled by the then unforeseeable course of history, the new Middle Eastern Question, or questions, remain with us for solution; they concern the stability, viability and attitudes of the new states in the region, and their interrelations and foreign policies. The pages here following can attempt no more than to give, in the fewest words, a sketch of the stages by which the present-day political map came to be drawn; other aspects of the territories in their new form will occupy subsequent chapters of this book.

TURKEY, left defeated and apparently prostrated after the War of 1914–1918, yet emerged from its astonishing aftermath, by her own efforts, more united, compact and progressive than ever before. If her condition late in 1918 appeared desperate, in the subsequent six years her statesmen, with Mustafa Kamal Pasha (later Kemal Atatürk) towering above them, defied the Allies, successfully resisted the imposed partition of his country, evicted the invading Greeks from Asia Minor, rejected the damaging Treaty of Sèvres, and renounced for ever the Arab provinces of the Empire. Kemal after brilliant successes established a republic, dethroned the Sultan, and inaugurated a remarkable series of modernizing, westernizing, laicizing reforms. The capital was moved from Istanbul to Ankara in the heart of Anatolia. Islam was disestablished and even discouraged, women were unveiled by law. European clothes (and hats) were *de rigueur*, Roman script was substituted for Arabic, new codes of law were introduced and a republican constitution proclaimed, and the administration was overhauled and amended at every level. The new régime and most of its frontiers were internationally established by the Treaty of Lausanne (July 1924); Turkey, now relatively small and for the first time mainly homogeneous, had turned into a modern, constitutional state. It was free thereafter to press on with reform, to suppress its rebellious Kurds, to extend education (including adult education), to experiment cautiously with party and parliamentary systems, to fix its frontiers—accepting the loss of the Mosul *vilayet* to 'Iraq in 1926, but acquiring Alexandretta-Antioch from Syria in 1939—and to join the League of Nations (1932).

Kemal died in 1938. Throughout the Second War the country, courted by both sides, preserved its neutrality. After it, Turkey was a founder of United Nations, successfully resisted Russian pressure, ranged itself openly with the West, joined NATO, and enjoyed copious western material aid for its never robust economy and its armed forces. Its internal policies were uneasy, with deep and bitter interparty differences and democratic institutions operative only with many shortcomings. In May 1960 a military *coup* installed a National Unity Committee (in effect a clique of army officers) in place of the dismissed Grand National Assembly; adherents of the outgoing régime and party were subsequently tried and sentenced in scores, and a new constitution was drafted and accepted (far from unanimously) by referendum. The mainly military committee, with various modifications, retained power until the permitted revival of political parties and the general election of early 1962. The results revealed deep disunity, and gave little promise of a stable parliamentary régime.

CYPRUS, declared a British Crown colony in August 1914, remained as such with a normal colonial administration until the establishment in 1960 of the Republic of Cyprus, which was accepted as a member of United Nations; the intervening half-century had been filled, intermittently in the 1930s but continuously after 1945, with a violent campaign by Greek Cypriots in favour of Enosis, or union of the island with Greece. This was led after 1950 by Archbishop Makarios, but opposed no less whole-heartedly by the Turkish element, and by the Turkish Government.

The campaign, conducted with great bitterness, violence and bloodshed, ended, after many tragic episodes, with an Anglo-Greeko-Turkish agreement (1959) for full Cypriot independence (not, after all, Enosis), which, with the establishment of a bi-national Republic of Cyprus, accepted in 1961 as a member of the British Common-wealth, permitted the retention of a British military base on the island. Thereafter, development works were pressed forward, but local politics, and especially Turko-Greek relations, showed small promise of tranquillity; nor by some had Enosis as a still outstanding objective been forgotten. Membership of the House of Representatives, and of all ranks in the public service, was fixed at 70 per cent Greek, 30 per cent Turkish. Each community has its own communal Chamber, with control of religious, educational and cultural affairs. The Archbishop became President in 1960, and the first elections were held in that year.

Unlike those former provinces of the Turkish Empire which are now sovereign states, PERSIA, for all the complications and abiding problems of her existence, had by 1962 changed but little in funda-mentals since 1914. During the First War her condition was highly confused and almost anarchic, with warlike operations waged on her soil by Russian, Turkish, British and (her own) tribal forces, followed by an abortive Anglo-Persian treaty in 1919 designed to assist her in rehabilitation and government, and by a Russo-Persian treaty in 1921. The rise to ministerial power, and then in 1925 to the throne of Persia, of the uneducated but ruthlessly capable army officer who became Riza Shah Pahlavi, in supercession of the effete Qajar dynasty, inaugurated a half-generation of despotic government and sweeping reforms. The tribes and local rulers were disciplined as never before, communications and government-initiated industry were vastly ex-tended, rough but effective government intruded actively in every sphere. The state finances were re-established with enforced taxation and wide-stretching government monopolies, local crafts were fostered, new law-codes adopted. The representatives of old-fashioned religion were terrorized, women (in law and regulation at least) were emancipated and social manners in the cities increasingly westernized. But the avarice and cruelty of the ruler destroyed his popularity, and his obstinately Germanophile policies, in the early days of the Second War, led to his abdication in 1941. Trans-Persian routes to aid Russia were thereafter widely used by the Allies, including the United States, in 1941–1944. After the War, determined Russian attempts to pene-trate and dominate Persia were with difficulty—and incompletely—

frustrated by the Persian Government, with western help. The post-war history of the country has been one of restless, violent and some-times grotesque policies (those notably of Dr. Musaddiq in 1950–1954), with riot and assassination, and with still unended struggles between the forces of liberalism, conservatism, communism, religion, the landlords, the intelligentsia and the monarchy. These struggles have been marked by army intervention, student demonstrations, suspension and restarting of the unreal and barely operative parlia-mentary machine. Persia is, under its constitution of 1906, later amended, a constitutional monarchy with a 200-member elected Majlis (National Assembly) and a part-nominated Senate of 60. But government by decree, in the absence of these bodies, is far from uncommon, and the main political, as well as social, issues in the country are still unsolved.

The 'IRAQI and the LEVANTINE provinces of the old Sultan's Empire entered, after the First War, a wholly new phase of their existence; from being shabby and neglected dependencies, they be-came sovereign countries central to, and highly important in, the new Middle Eastern picture. Liberated from the Turks in 1914–1918 by British forces, and entirely divorced from Turkish authority, they became in the post-war settlement the separate governments of 'Iraq, Syria, the Lebanon, Palestine, and Transjordan. All of these were in 1920 recognized by the principal Allied Powers, with the later confirmation of the League of Nations, as potentially indepen-dent states in need, temporarily, of assistance. They were accordingly placed under Mandate—the new form of international trusteeship, well described as 'imperialism in reverse', designed to meet such cases: 'Iraq, Palestine and Transjordan under Great Britain, Syria and Lebanon under France. Their history from 1921 onwards was one of territories under Mandate, until the Mandatory Powers, responsible as they were to the League of Nations, in due (or undue) course surrendered their trusteeship powers, and the territories be-came fully sovereign states.

'IRAQ, where King Faisal, of the revered Sharifian family of Mecca, was installed as constitutional ruler in 1921, made immense progress towards modernization, good government and stability under British guidance until 1932. At that date the Mandate was surrendered, the country becoming a fully independent member of the League of Nations; its frontiers had been stabilized, its security and public services developed, its officials and army trained, its legal and constitutional systems installed and operative. Once 'free', the government of 'Iraq was afflicted between 1932 and 1941 by a series of military *coups d'état*. The Second War period was one of stress and wartime difficulties, but peaceful except for one brief, abortive Nazi-favouring military movement; and from 1945 to 1958 policies and administration of normal Middle Eastern type continued, with the new oil-wealth (p. 255) making possible great projects and improvements. The régime and the hitherto popular monarchy were, however, violently overthrown and destroyed by a sudden military *coup* in July 1958, following which, under the name of a republic, a military dictatorship under General 'Abdul Karim Qasim (Kassim), conducted a strictly repressive régime, far less liberal or representative than that of the monarchy. There was no indication, at the time of writing (late 1962), when the normal institutions of government—an elected President, a responsible cabinet, a representative parliament—would be permitted to resume working. The pre-1958 constitution was annulled in July of that year, and the new 'Provisional Constitution' proclaimed made no provision for democratic institutions.

Geographical SYRIA was after 1918 detached permanently from Turkey and divided, as we have indicated, into four separate states. The French Mandate covered the thenceforward restricted Syria as one unit, and an enlarged LEBANON (the old mainly Christian autonomous sanjaq of Mount Lebanon of 1860, but with the addition of important Muslim districts) as another. The mandatory régime, to which France devoted much effort and expense, lasted from 1920 till its somewhat inglorious end in 1943–1945. During its course, important benefits accrued to both territories in the fields of administration, law, the armed forces, communications and the public services, and much was done visibly and invisibly to prepare the two states for an ultimate independent constitutional and international life of their own. The political aspects of the period were less happy, and French handling of the important minorities, and of impatient nationalist aspirations, was often so far ill-judged as to lead to seriously impaired security and to widespread (never universal) political discontent, which was increased by French reluctance to terminate the Mandate and depart. The problems of society and government in the two republics, since their achievement of sovereignty at the end of the Second War, were (and indeed are) both specifically different and yet generally similar. Lebanon since 1946 has been repeatedly torn by intercommunity (mainly Muslim-Christian) as well as by normal political faction, and passed through a crisis of these in 1958; thereafter it resumed normal government under its elected President, its single-chamber parliament, and its cabinet composed of ministers representing the communities in strict proportion. Syria was in 1949–1954 subjected to successive military régimes, and from 1954 to 1958 returned to uneasy party warfare and brief, unstable governments. In February 1958 Syro-Egyptian coalescence, in the form of an integrated United Arab Republic, was announced; this was to remain in fairly stable but (in Syria) largely resented existence until late in 1961. It was then, on Syrian initiative, dissolved, and the country relapsed again into its own type of frustrated and frustrating party-politics, with military intervention as an imminent probability, and relations with Egypt highly acrimonious. The form of constitution which, with restored normality, would take the place of the provisional régime of September 1961, was not apparent at the time of writing.

Both Syria and Lebanon, as independent republics, became founder-members of the Arab League (1945), and members of United Nations.

The southern districts of the Turkish *vilayet* of Damascus east of Jordan—those of Hawran (in part) and Karak—were, in the early post-war days of 1919–1921, a no-man's-land of rudimentary government, under vague British control. In the latter year the territory, restyled as the Amirate of TRANSJORDAN, was entrusted, under a British Mandate separate from that of Palestine, to the Amir 'Abdullah, son of King Husain of the Hijaz and brother of Faisal of 'Iraq. Its history from 1921 to 1946 was generally peaceful and, on a humble scale, progressive, with minimum and acceptable British guidance. In 1946 the country, already a member of the Arab League, became independent, and in 1948, renamed the Hashimite Kingdom of JORDAN, acceded to full sovereignty and membership of United Nations. The parts of Palestine not occupied in 1948 by the forces of Israel (p. 134) were incorporated in Jordan, in which also much of the evicted and fugitive Palestinian Arab population took the refuge of homeless and hungry exiles. King 'Abdullah was assassinated in July 1951. He was succeeded by his mentally afflicted son Tallal, and a year later by his grandson Husain. The largely desertic and barely (or non-) viable kingdom has since then been the victim, for political reasons, of fierce propaganda attacks by Egypt and sometimes by Syria, of brutal 'reprisal' raids from Israel, as well as of serious weaknesses in its own constitutional, political and economic life. It formed part of a short-lived Arab Confederacy with 'Iraq in 1958 (an intended counter-move to the United Arab Republic) until this ended with the revolution in Baghdad of that year. The official régime in Jordan is in 1962 that of a constitutional monarchy and two-chamber parliament, the one elected, the other nominated. The Cabinet is responsible to parliament. In practice, the Royal power is paramount and ubiquitous.

No phenomenon in the modern Middle East, indeed in the world, is more remarkable than that of the establishment of the State of ISRAEL. An undertaking was given by the British Government in 1917 to a leading Jewish personality to 'view with favour the establishment in Palestine of a National Home for the Jewish people . . . it being clearly understood that nothing shall be done which may prejudice the civil and religious rights of existing non-Jewish communities in Palestine . . .'. This guarded and limited undertaking, seized with eagerness by a world Jewry in which political Zionism had constantly gained ground, was incorporated (with the same specific safeguards for the Arab population) in the British Mandate for Palestine, and, with the installation there of a Jewish Agency, was the charter for large-scale but still controlled Jewish immigration in the period 1920–1947. This movement, alarming to the Arabs of Palestine (a 90 per cent majority of the population in 1920), and to Arabs everywhere, could not but lead, with the pronounced favour shown to the Jewish minority and the background of powerful Jewish influences in the world outside, to the disappearance of all possibility of self-determination for the Palestinian population. Frequent disorder, due to Arab resentment and fears for their future, marked the years 1919–1946; conferences, missions, restatements and counter-statements of policy, and representations made by Arab states, all equally failed to find a solution for the dilemma as between immigrant Jew and native Arab—a solution which, as long as the safeguards prescribed in the Balfour Declaration and the Mandate were in practice ignored, not only did not, but could not, exist. The abominable treatment of European Jewry by Hitler's Germany during the Second War greatly increased Jewish pressures to be admitted to Palestine; the government of the United States, for whatever reasons, adopted a powerful—in the event, an irresistible—pro-Zionist attitude in 1945–1948; and British abandonment of the Mandate, in despair of an agreed 'solution', was followed by the proclamation at Tel Aviv of a State of Israel, early in 1948, in the heart of a territory as unquestionably Arab as any in the world. The ill-managed, futile Arab-launched campaigns that followed, the exodus from their homes and lands of hundreds of thousands of Palestinian Arab townsmen and peasants, the extension of Jewish frontiers far beyond those authorized by United Nations, the consolidation of Israel as a vigorous, modern, progressive state, able to refuse all compensation or restitution, to supply its financial needs from governments and its co-religionists outside, and to defend its frontiers: of all this nothing need here be said, these events being recent and familiar. The State of Israel, a single-chamber constitutional republic and member of United Nations, had by 1962 existed for fourteen years, as the greatest of all single causes in the Middle East of regional unease and Arab ill-will towards the West.

EGYPT, on the outbreak of war in 1914, was immediately and for ever severed from her long but now meaningless Turkish connection, and became a Sultanate under declared British protection, a status which Egyptian politicians strongly resented. After the war period, in which Egypt served as an important Allied base and entrepôt, its future status became in 1919–1922 a burning question which led to a series of demands and refusals, demonstrations and imprisonments, diplomatic missions and outbreaks of violence. Finally in 1922 a unilateral declaration by Great Britain confirmed the country's formal independence, as a constitutional monarchy; but four 'reserved subjects', as between Egypt and Great Britain, remained for solution later. Sixteen uneasy but (with sad lapses) non-violent years followed, in which the problem of Anglo-Egyptian relations, viewed from two widely different angles, remained uncomfortable and seemingly unsoluble; in 1936, however, under threat of Italian aggression in East Africa, a Treaty was concluded whereunder Britain retained only minimal rights, in the fields of defence and communications. The internal struggles between a corrupt and reactionary Palace and successive Prime Ministers continued, as it was destined to do, till 1952. In the Second World War Egypt took no part save that, again, of Allied base, a role which, in self-defence, compelled the British (King Faruq being, like his father, Italophile) to a measure of interference in Egyptian affairs. After the war Anglo-Egyptian negotiations for an improved Treaty were renewed, to be constantly broken off—usually on the Sudan issue, or that of the Suez base—and once more restarted, with uniformly unproductive results. Finally, the 1936 Treaty itself was unilaterally abrogated by the Egyptian parliament in 1951, and the integral union of the Sudan with Egypt under a single crown was proclaimed. The British-occupied Canal Zone, the subject already of prolonged negotiations,

became now a scene of active hostilities, and serious riots took place
in Cairo (January 1952).

The Egyptian revolution of July 1952 overthrew the long-detested
monarchy and installed a committee of army officers as the provisional government. This, ten years later, still filled the same role,
and still under its President, Col. Gamal 'Abdul Nasir—the 'Nasser'
of the western publics. (A brief tenure of the Presidency by General
Muhammad Nagib ended early in 1954.) Many reforms in the
administration, in law, policy and society followed; political opposition, including that of the Muslim Brotherhood, was suppressed; and
in October 1954 an Anglo-Egyptian Agreement was at last concluded,
leading on agreed terms to evacuation of the Canal Zone. 'Positive
neutralism' was proclaimed as Egypt's chosen foreign policy, but a
large-scale purchase of arms from the Eastern bloc in 1956 was ill-
regarded by the West, and relations deteriorated further when an
anticipated loan, for High Dam construction, was unexpectedly with-
held by the Western Powers. 'Abdul Nasir thereupon announced
(July 1956) the nationalization of the Suez Canal, and vigorous international protest failed to shake him. Later in the year an invasion of
Egypt by Israeli forces, and a refusal by Egypt to withdraw, on
British demand, its own defending army, led to an Anglo-French
attack on the Canal and its terminal port; but strong and world-wide
protests, focused in United Nations, compelled the two powers to
accept a cease-fire and to withdraw from Egyptian soil. The clearing
of the blocked canal and restoration of relations with Britain and
France took time: the former six months, the latter three years.
Egyptian energies were thereafter devoted to its economic and
administrative affairs. The formation in 1958 of the United Arab
Republic, integrating Syria and Egypt, proved unhappy and short-
lived and was dissolved in 1961. Egypt in 1962 had the appearance,
with all its abiding problems and painful stresses, of a considerable
and strongly socialist progressive state, the most populous and
developed in the Arab world—and not without some pretensions,
shown in the speeches of Colonel Nasir and the extravagancies of
Cairo radio, to assume leadership of this. Meanwhile the governmental régime in Egypt (which continued to call itself the United
Arab Republic) was that of the military-dominated committee presided over by 'Abdul Nasir. Parliamentary institutions were in
abeyance, but support was forthcoming from the army, the mob, and
the single permitted 'party' which purported to represent the
electorate.

The Anglo-Egyptian SUDAN, as the upper Nile territory had become in 1890 (p. 73), passed, in the half-century ending in 1962, through a period of rehabilitation, internal stability and sound development. The administration, British and frankly paternalistic and (except latterly with a small Sudanese political class—and always with the Egyptian co-dominus) generally acceptable, made way after the Second War for the beginnings of self-governing institutions, and for long-drawn negotiations with Sudanese representatives, grouped in articulate but discordant political parties, with the government of Egypt, and with the constitutional experts invoked. A régime of subordination to Egypt being rejected by the Sudanese majority, an independent state of the Sudan, as a parliamentary democratic republic, was proclaimed in January 1956. It joined the Arab League and United Nations in the same year. But late in 1958 parliament and all political parties were suppressed by an army-led revolutionary movement, under General Ibrahim 'Abbud, since when a military 'provisional régime', frankly authoritarian but benevolent, has been in power.

The ARABIAN peninsula has changed in half a century less than any Middle Eastern area: socially and culturally little, economically much (by reason of oil development), and in politics more apparently than profoundly. The Najdi, central Arabian, Wahhabi state of the Sa'udis, after preserving its neutrality during 1914–1918, managed to suppress its rival in Jabal Shammar (p. 74) in 1921, to evict the Sharifian rulers of Mecca and the Hijaz four years later, and to add all western Arabia including 'Asir (p. 74) to their empire, which in 1932 was renamed by its outstanding ruler and creator, King 'Abdul 'Aziz ibn Sa'ud, as the Kingdom of SA'UDI ARABIA. A member of the Arab League and of United Nations, and without rival in its vast inhospitable peninsula, Sa'udi Arabia was constitutionally primitive —a theocratic, despotic monarchy too often ill-advised—and economically dependent solely on its oil royalties, yet by no means without weight in the Middle Eastern international arena. Mecca and Riyadh are the joint capitals. There is no constitution or National Assembly. The Cabinet, which could never imaginably oppose the King's wishes, is nominated by him; he is sometimes his own Prime Minister, sometimes (as, latterly, in November 1962) delegates that office to his brother. Wholesale reforms on modernist lines (but with a Koranic framework) were announced as imminent late in 1962.

The YEMEN, freed from Turkish overlordship by the 1914–1918 war, maintained an isolated uneasy, backward but internationally recognized independence under its archaic Imamate; this, and the territory's separate existence, were magnanimously spared by ibn Sa'ud in 1934, when he defeated the Yemeni forces. The Imam's internal affairs appeared disordered and unprogressive; in the international world the Yemen was, though a member of United Nations and the Arab League, unqualified to play any appreciable part. From 1955 onwards some signs of internal dissidence appeared; there were Yemenis who had had enough of the Middle Ages. On the death of the Imam Ahmad in September 1962, his son and successor was overthrown after a week, and a group of military officers announced themselves, with early support from the U.S.S.R. and Egypt, as inaugurating a Yemeni Arab Republic. The ex-Imam, Muhammad al-Sadr, was, at the end of the year, struggling to enlist tribal support for a restoration.

The ADEN PROTECTORATE, continuously claimed by the Imam of the Yemen as part of his dominions, had by 1962 changed since 1914 only thanks to a general pacification and stabilization under British guidance, with the inauguration of some progressive works and projects, the beginnings of public services, and the foundation of a Federation among a group of the shaikhly or princely rulers. ADEN COLONY, transferred from British Indian to Colonial Office control in 1937, developed fast to become an oil-refining and bunkering centre of much importance, and a British military and air base and staging post. The Sultanate of MUSCAT AND OMAN gave up little of its isolation; admittedly independent and sovereign, it was a member of no international body, had only rudimentary and non-representative governmental institutions, imperfect control of its own territory (especially in the mountainous and persistently insubordinate hinterland, which claimed to be autonomous) and minimal resources. The Sultan, intermittently threatened by Sa'udi aggression and internal insurgence, received some material as well as moral support from Her Majesty's Government.

The small Arab shaikhdoms of the TRUCIAL COAST had little history in the present century, except for *inter se* boundary quarrels, fears of Sa'udi acquisitiveness, and hopes of oil discovery. As minute but independent political units under despotic shaikhly rule, they were a seeming anachronism in the present age, and their disposal presented problems; they were since 1952 linked by a common discussion group, the Trucial Council, contributed to a joint military force (1958), and were together a concern of the British Government in a modest, shared Development Plan. BAHRAIN Island had a recent history of oil development, of good administration but political suppression, and of economic and social progress—but not of serious constitutional advance: the shaikhly family of Al Khalifa declined to share its power. An inadmissible Persian claim to own the island persisted. The QATAR peninsula, under its shaikh resident at Doha, was equally independent but in effect British-protected; it had no recent history other than strictly internal, with peaceful succession of its rulers, quarrels with the ruler of Bahrain, and, since 1950, sudden fantastic wealth due to oil discovery, production and export. KUWAIT, free of even nominal Turkish claims since 1914, passed thereafter through phases of bad and good relations with Sa'udi Arabia and 'Iraq, but maintained its sovereign status. The older Anglo-Kuwait treaty, whereby the territory was (externally) protected by the British, was annulled in 1961 when a new agreement was made whereby British help would be available only if called for. Kuwait joined the Arab League in 1961 but its candidature for United Nations was vetoed by Russia. The suddenly announced claim by the 'Iraqi dictator General Qasim in 1961 that Kuwait was an integral part of his country, which he prepared forthwith to occupy, was thwarted by British action, shortly replaced by that of the Arab League, in supplying the amir with a protective garrison; but the baseless and truculent claim was reiterated. The oil wealth of Kuwait, first realized in 1946, was on a fantastic scale. Constitutionally, all power still rested with the shaikh (or amir) and his family, though there were (1962) signs of a greater association of a limited circle of the public with the tasks of government.

CHAPTER FIVE

PEOPLES AND LANGUAGES

1. *Territories and Citizens*

SOME account has now been given of the past fortunes of the countries of our region, and their accession to the modern statehood which they enjoy today. We proceed next to deal in outline with the populations which constitute these Middle Eastern states. And, to begin with, it has appeared abundantly that no ethnically pure 'races' can be expected to people them—or indeed any other territories in the world. The extent to which one human accretion after another has, since the dawn of history, diluted or modified original stocks—whatever they were!—has been shown by many examples; and since this phenomenon has been region-wide and has in no way comformed to, or created, present-day political boundaries (which have instead been established by any and every blind chance of warfare, resistance, apathy or caprice), it follows not only that all the populations are deeply mixed and composite from a score of ingredients, but that significant differences in human physique between them are, in the end, not easily perceptible. Any attempt to differentiate, one from another, the average or prevailing human type found in Arab or Turkish or Persian city or countryside must usually fail; the criteria of physical distinction commonly employed give here hopelessly mixed and inconclusive results. Only in a small percentage of cases will there be found a visible survival of some feature held to be characteristic of identifiable 'race'; the small-boned fineness of a Najdi Arab, the flat head-back of an Anatolian Armenian, the (very rare) Mongoloid eyes of a Turk, the recognizable Arab-Berber-Negro mixture in some Egyptians. To these generalizations some keen and possibly over-subtle ethnologist will demur, claiming to find in this or that valley or tribe—or in whole countries —physical types, or single features, which recall a specific, determinable origin; but in four-fifths or more of cases no mere spectator, and probably no expert, could tell by his physique alone a Turk or a Kurd, taken at random, from a settled Arab or a Persian. Except where obvious negro strains are present—and these are found here to a considerable, there to a minimal extent—the dark-white pigmentation, the brown-to-black hair, the brown or grey eyes, the Caucasian features prevalent throughout the Middle East are scarcely to be differentiated by sub-regions. There are, however, perceptible differences in apparent pigmentation between those whose life is passed in the open air—cultivator, herdsman, transport worker—in the hotter countries, and the city-dwelling office workers; the dark hue of the former type, indeed, often leads uninstructed Europeans to exaggerate the duskiness of these populations. And skin-colour can in many cases be lighter in any of the northern countries of our region, among the upper class whose family is more likely to have received, by recent intermarriage, infusions of blood from western Turkey or Europe. But all the races of which we shall speak, except the Sudanis, are 'white races'.

The basis of a claim to belong to this or that national group in western Asia is as elsewhere *prima facie* the passport carried; but this basis is insufficient and can be misleading. It is obvious that Egyptian papers can be produced by a long-domiciled Greek or Italian in Egypt, without such resident becoming Egyptian in more than a formal sense. The same applies to Greeks in Turkey, as it does to Persians in 'Iraq, or Circassians in Jordan. There are, moreover, cases of more massive minorities of one race, or culture-group, domiciled permanently in the territory of another, and forming a considerable proportion of its population. Such is the extensive Turkoman population—'Turks' in a truer sense, probably, than most Anatolians—in north-western Persia, or the Persian and 'Iraqi Kurds, or the Arab tribes on the (Persian) Karun. If we aspire to identify race with nation, as would no doubt be ideally desirable— and as is demanded by one of the principal bases of the modern concept of nationality—we shall find these racially-linguistically heterogeneous enclaves within other people's frontiers an embarrassment and anomaly; but they exist.

For political and administrative purposes the passport should determine its bearer's obedience; but on the level of the deeper sense of belonging, the loyalty of the member of this or that group is established by other criteria. What makes an Arab, or a Turk? It is the sense of inherited, habitual attachment, even in exile, to the group so named, and this seems to rest on certain unchanging elements. The first is common language, which normally provides the strongest of all single bonds between individuals and peoples; the language of their childhood and maturity, of their shared press and cinema and broadcasts, of their business and society. And a common language opens up, with strong community of feeling, the past glories (real or mythical) of earlier speakers of that tongue, with all their heroic deeds, conquests, and cultural achievements. Add to common language habitual residence in (or at least near) the present-day national territory; in a claim to be accepted as a Persian or a Kurd, one's own or one's ancestors' residence in Persia or Kurdistan or on their fringes must be an appreciable factor. Add again to these a conscious participation in a characteristic way and tempo of life, shown in domestic or public manners, forms of speech, preferences and prejudices, and religion. All these amount to much; but the final criterion which makes a man a true adherent to this or that group—Arab, Greek-Cypriot, or Israeli—is his own essential desire and *claim* so to be. This claim—how difficult, if it is there, for the foreign observer to gainsay!—cannot by itself produce a passport, may be politically thwarted, and may lead to helpless irridentism. Moreover, all the elements basic to such a claim may be present, yet it may never be made; the Turkomans of Azarbaijan, or those of northern 'Iraq, are far from unanimous aspirants to Turkish citizenship, while many Jews scattered throughout the Middle East abhor the idea of Israeli citizenship. Nevertheless, the three bases for what in the Middle East passes for 'racial' grouping must be reckoned as language, present or past habitual residence, and a common emotional devotion to the mystique and heritage of the group.

In none of these nations is the country's population, except in the communities of the Arabian peninsula, limited to a single race or culture-group. Turkey, Persia, the non-peninsular Arab states, Israel: all contain important minorities. And in almost every case there are also groups resident beyond the frontiers which can yet profess more or less valid claims to 'belong'. These are phenomena not less familiar in Europe and elsewhere, and so is the circumstance of a specifically bi-national state such as Cyprus.

It emerges from all this that the racial or culture-group picture of the Middle East is, as we should expect, very much less simple than the political map; the hatching or colouring meant to designate cultural or linguistic groups, whether politically self-conscious or otherwise, splashes capriciously across frontiers in blocks or fragments. The chapters of this book later to be devoted to each territory in turn will try *inter alia* to answer the specific question 'Of what elements does the population of *this* country consist, and in what proportions?' At the present stage it is intended to say something of these elements themselves, wherever they occur; first, however, dealing with the great religion common to most of them, and a constant element in their lives.

2. *Islam today*

No one is ignorant that Islam, in one or another of its sects, is the religion of western Asia, all of which (except Cyprus and Israel) belongs, accordingly, to the House of Islam. It has been shown, moreover, in these pages, first, that the faith of the Prophet included in its original form no more than certain fundamental propositions and demands, and that for these it claimed universal application and validity; and next, that Islam had in the Middle Ages been vastly complicated and divided by rival doctrines, sects and communities many of which stood and stand far apart from the orthodoxy of early times. It is now to be asked, in what forms does Islam survive in our own day, and how far is it an element of continuing force in the private and public lives of its adherents?.

It could be a matter of surprise that, in spite of its comparative rigidity and lack of imaginative popular appeal, the Sunni, strictly traditionalist, element in the Faith (p. 65) not only survived, but has prevailed as a powerful majority up to and into our own age. This has been due to its fidelity to its principles, the high authority it can quote for these, the impressive formulation of the Shari'a Law so central to Islamic communities (and the greatest of bonds between them), the distinguished characters who have upheld the Tradition throughout the centuries, and the support given for half a millennium by the Sunni orthodox monarchy of Turkey, with its immense prestige, patronage and endowments. It has resulted that western Asian Islam is today predominantly of the Sunni branch, though there is, among Muslims, as all know, no centralized Church or priesthood. The outward observances of the Sunni faith—though not its degrees of governmental establishment—are uniform throughout the House of Islam, and its theological background, the result of centuries of controversy and cautious absorption in the Middle Ages, is stable and everywhere accepted. It offers the most moderate, reasoned, and (to a western mind) acceptable version of the faith and law of the Prophet, and undoubtedly the nearest to his own conceptions. The four schools of the Shari'a Law, which are admitted by all Sunnis as unexceptionable, differ between themselves in no very serious respect, and even so in specific provisions rather than basic doctrine. All four were founded, and their codes formulated, by eminent medieval jurists, from whom they are still named. The Hanafi school prevails among the Sunni Turks and, through Turkish influences of yesterday, has followers also in 'Iraq and Syria; the Shafi'i is dominant in lower Egypt, 'Iraq, Jordan, Syria, and part of the Yemen; the Maliki, in upper Egypt and the northern and central Sudan; and the less widely accepted Hanbali, in Wahhabi Arabia only. These adherences determine the school to which the *qadhis* appointed to the religious courts of the country shall belong; but they make to the general public no difference at all, and their variations can be ignored here. The earliest of Islamic seceding sects, the Khariji, retained the full Sunni doctrine, and left the main community solely on the point of practical application, about which they allowed no compromise. Their survivors, known as Ibadis, are found today only (within the Middle East) in the Oman Sultanate, where Ibadism is the official religion.

Of the numerous Sufi fraternities earlier mentioned (p. 65) as within, yet standing clearly apart from, the main Sunni community —groups or coteries and often institutions with widespread branches, of great vitality and emotional attractiveness, but ill regarded by the traditionalist Sunni *'ulama*—a number survive and still play their part; to many indeed (but fewer, perhaps, in western Asia than in other regions of Dar al-Islam) they represent the most living and attractive forms that Islam has to offer. The Sufi sects vary greatly in their material organization, as they do doctrinally between near-Orthodoxy (as in the famous and ancient Qadiriya order, with its venerated headquarters in Baghdad), through different degrees of Islamic (or scarcely Islamic) mysticism to others with more objectionable rituals. Such, for instance, characterized the followers of the great Bektashi order in Ottoman Turkey, long identified with the Janissaries but today no longer there since the revolutionary suppression of the religious orders by Atatürk in 1925; and such also the Mawlawi (or Mevleviya) sect known in Europe from its 'dancing dervishes' but now banished from modern Turkey to a few refuges in Syria. The Sufi or darwish (dervish) orders in Egypt—Badawiya, Bayyumi, Dasuqi—are still important and mean much to their faithful members. The same is true of an almost opposite form of the Faith, as remote as could be conceived from Sufism or any 'fancy religion'; that is, the rigid, unalterably established code of the dour Wahhabis of Najd, who permit no accretion to, or latter-day interpretation of, the Book—and despise the laxity of Sunni and Shi'i alike.

The Shi'i communities (p. 65), which form a large minority in the Middle East, derive politically from the original rejection by the partisans of 'Ali of the claims of all Caliphs subsequent to him, while doctrinally they draw from many elements imported from non-Arab, mainly Persian, sources in the first and second century of Islam; indeed, the fragmentation of the Faith's original ultra-simplicity was an inevitable result of the diversity of countries, communities and minds which Islamic conquests soon brought within its fold, including peoples far more mentally sophisticated than the Arabs of Arabia. To this factor may be added tribal, racial and personal rivalries which could not but arise, and which partly were the causes of combat on the spiritual and theological front as well as the political, and partly used the former as a ready weapon in the latter. Shi'ism, at any rate, had every occasion to grow apart from the Tradition, to gain ground (particularly in non-Arab territory), and to flourish in its various forms. The Shi'i communities, besides their rejection of the Caliphs from the fifth onwards, are united positively also in attributing to a true Caliph or Imam (as they term him) wide spiritual powers and a personal infallibility and authority quite foreign to Sunni conceptions, and in postulating a mystical interpretation of the Qur'an itself, a body of secret knowledge, and a unique relationship between the family of 'Ali and the Creator. The line of Shi'i Imams—valid successors, in their eyes, of 'Ali and the Prophet, as are the Umayyid and 'Abbasid Caliphs in Sunni—is, after the first six, itself in dispute between differing Shi'i sects. The majority (the Ja'fari) sect is dominant and official in Persia, is heavily represented in central and southern 'Iraq, and is fairly numerous in the southern Lebanon, western intermontane Syria, and Bahrain Island. These Shi'is hold that the line of the Imams, after the first eleven, ended with the mysterious disappearance of the twelfth and last incumbent (A.D. 873), who will one day reappear. The Ja'fari branch of the Shi'a has, with considerable background differences from the Sunna, much also in common with it, and may be held to keep the essentials of the Faith intact; but the variations are so far emotional, and have been given so much weight in controversy, that attempts to effect a reunion, and to recognize a fifth orthodoxy school of Law (the Imami), have always failed.

Of other varieties of Shi'ism, the Zaidi sect is free from metaphysical or emotional extravagances, attributes no divine qualities to the Imams, and differs from the Sunna upon relative unessentials; it is the official religion of the monarchy and the highland districts (though not of the coastal areas) in the Yemen. The Isma'ili sect is more widely diffused; its founders left the main body of the Shi'a in the eighth century on a question of the succession to the sixth Imam, and later on matters of mystic theology which carried them to the very fringes—or beyond them—of Islamic tolerance. Isma'ilis are found, in the Middle East, only in small compact communities in Syria and Persia and in the Najran district of south-west Arabia; nothing is left today of earlier sub-sects of the Isma'ilis, whose place in history is that of the Carmathian (Qarmati) rebels of the Middle Ages, of the Fatimid State and Caliphate of Cairo (p. 52), and of the infamous Assassins in their north Persian stronghold (p. 55). The head of the Isma'ili Shi'is in the modern world is the Agha Khan; their main present strength is in India and East Africa. The Druzes (Duruz) of the southern Lebanon, of the mountain named after them in the Syrian Republic, and of northern Israel can be regarded as, in religion, a yet more heretical offshoot of the Isma'ilis, formed in the eleventh century into a separate sect; it was based upon the deification of the Fatimid ruler Hakim—himself apparently a lunatic—and on various mystical and concealed non-Islamic beliefs. The Druzes form, socially and at times politically, a bloc clearly distinct from all their neighbours; their claim to be Muslims at all can, indeed, only with difficulty be accepted, though they seem, in their own secret and graded hierarchies, to accept the main elements of Isma'ili belief. The same may be true of the Nusairis (or 'Alawis) of the west Syrian mountains, an ancient indigenous community whose mixture of local pre-Islamic or non-Islamic beliefs with extreme forms of Shi'ism, and even with Christian observances, has produced a peculiar blend not easily qualifying for inclusion in the Muslim world.

The religion of a fair proportion, possibly 15 per cent, of the Turkish peasantry—notably the Yuruks or semi-nomadic tribes— of Anatolia, is widely regarded as a heterodox, impure form of Islam, and resembles that of the Nusairis in their incorporation of primitive elements from ancient times. Without these Turkey, in spite of Atatürk's destruction of institutionalized religion, would be a uniformly Sunni country. One more scattered, nowhere compact or formidable, minority, found in Persia and in Israel, is that of the Baha'is, founded by a Persian would-be reformer in the eighteen-forties. His syncretic religion, later distracted by schism and always detested by all good Muslims, is in some measure an offshoot of Isma'ili Shi'ism, mixed with ingredients from other faiths. The

Baha'is are of more account and better tolerated in America than in their native Middle East, where normal Islamic tolerance has failed to protect them from the rancour, at times the violence, of the public.

This sketch of the varieties of belief within Middle Eastern Islam, and the representation of these in often antagonistic communities, may lead too readily to the conclusion that the power of the Faith is thereby gravely weakened, or even has ceased to count. It is true that its old unity as the single social-religious body envisaged by the Prophet is no more, and that the initial conquering force of an aggressive creed has long disappeared. Moreover, the contrast between the successes and advances of the non-Muslim societies of the West —the Christian sovereign states of Europe—and the relative back-wardness of the House of Islam has discredited the latter in the eyes of some, in addition to the clearly rising or risen tide of world-wide secularism which has gone far in diminishing the power of all super-natural religions. In many *évolué* Muslim circles their religion is considered by the young and sceptical as something for the older generation, most respected among the least progressive; the out-standing practical reformers of our century—Kemal Atatürk, Riza Shah Pahlevi—were irreligious; and the legislatures of the most modernizing Muslim states, Turkey and Egypt, have replaced Islamic with secular codes even in the hitherto reserved field of family matters. The ideal of many, almost certainly most, young politicians and publicists in the Middle East is now not a specifically Islamic state but one of western-type secular efficiency. All these are facts; is it, then, true that Islam today can claim none but a humble place as a current social and political force, to animate or to restrain?

Such a conclusion would be over-hasty. It can be urged, on the contrary, that major movements in recent history have been pro-foundly Islam-inspired; such have been, among others, the Wahhabi movement itself, of which the force is not yet spent: that of Ahmad al-Idris (d. 1837) who, with the sanctity gained by founding a new Sunni 'way' which borrowed Sufi techniques, gained a principality in 'Asir on the Red Sea; that of the Sunusi (Senussi) family now on the throne of Libya by way of a similar religious and reforming movement in north Africa; that of the Amir Ghani (Mirghani) family in the Sudan, whose piety and religious-social movement left behind it, in the influential Khatmiya sect, a power in Sudan politics; and indeed the rising and usurpation, also in the Sudan, of the fanatical Mahdi himself, Muhammad Ahmad (p. 86). These examples prove that an effective relation between religion and politics can, or could recently, still exist. And other phenomena support this. One is the clear distinction in a Muslim's feeling towards a co-religionist as against a non-Muslim fellow-citizen (a Copt in Egypt, a Christian in Lebanon, an Armenian anywhere), in times of stress; a distinction no doubt deplorable, but significant of Islamic self-consciousness. Another sign is the force, in any mob street-demonstration, of an emotional appeal to Islamic fervour; and another, the continued basing of political parties—the Muslim Brotherhood in Egypt and Syria, the Fida'iyin i-Islam in Persia, and others in Indonesia and Malaya—on a programme of Islamic revival; and yet another, the visible success of Islam in making far more converts from paganism, in west Africa today, than Christian missionaries can achieve. And, within Islam's most responsible and devoted circles, the effort continues to find ways to restate the Faith in forms less rigid and dry-as-dust, more attractive to the young and western-ized, than the time-honoured, almost static expositions of the traditional Islamic apologists.

These are all signs that Islam is alive, has convinced, intelligent and numerous upholders, can be a force in public affairs. To millions throughout the Middle East it is still the Faith by which their daily lives would claim to be guided; though its future may be one of gradually lessening appeal in our rationalizing age, and though its force may be less than that of a century—far more, five centuries —ago, yet in any of its diverse forms it is still precious to millions, colours their lives, and, to some unascertainable extent, may direct their actions.

Meanwhile, the Muslim of any but the least polite, or the most emancipated, society still shows constantly the influence on social behaviour of his Islamic background and community tradition. It is revealed in his conversation as a familiar element in his thought, and the tempo of his actions is traditionally that of dignity—since haste is of the Devil. In spite of all the inroads of cynical modernism, the social observances of daily prayers, the mosque on Fridays, the fast in Ramadhan, and the great Muslim festivals, are still widely alive. The great annual pilgrimage to Mecca, pilgrimages also to Meshhed in Persia, to Karbala and Najf in 'Iraq, and to a dozen other shrines, tell the same story. In most countries a qadhi in every town adminis-ters the Shari'a Law within its now restricted sphere, and a mufti gives rulings on religious issues. Mosques are maintained, with their salaried staffs, the mu'adhdhin (muezzin) calls, sermons are delivered, mosque and saintly-tomb revenues (often very considerable) are allotted to charitable purposes, scandals are few, government supervision (a recent feature) is close. Except in Turkey, where its use is much restricted, the garb of religion is seen everywhere; the religious 'establishment' goes on, with dignity and, let us hope, true devotion. There is explicit respect for high Islamic lineage, that of the Prophet's own family, for instance, or of some famed divine such as 'Abdul Qadir al-Gilani. The Shi'i *mujtadhis*, doctors and interpreters of the Law, have still high authority, though no official countenance, in Persia and 'Iraq; dynastic claims, like those of the Sa'udis or the Sunusi, can be based upon it, or, like that of the Moroccan royal family, be enhanced by it. A reputation for Islamic saintliness, even in wild Kurdish hills, brings fame and reverence.

The tolerance traditionally extended to non-Muslim 'people of the Book' (that is, of a revealed religion: the Christians and Jews)—a tolerance which, viewed throughout history, far exceeds the best that Christian history can show—covers also, not without human lapses, the aberrant forms of Islam itself, provided that the essentials of the faith are intact. To pagans alone such forebearance is not owed.

3. *The Arabs*

The Arab-speaking people or peoples of western Asia and northeast Africa (Egypt and the Sudan) form, as all know, the great majority of the population of the Middle East as we have defined it. They number approximately 54,000,000 souls, and are divided into eight sovereign states which are members of the United Nations ('Iraq, Syria, Lebanon, Jordan, Sa'udi Arabia, Yemen, Egypt, the Sudan) and a score of minor but independent units which are not. The latter include Aden Colony and the many statelets of its Protectorate, the Oman Sultanate, the seven Trucial shaikhdoms, with Qatar, Bahrain and Kuwait. There are, moreover, expatriate Arab communities in south-west Persia (the province of Khuzistan, formerly known as Arabistan), the southern fringe of Turkey, and Israel—if indeed these last-named, living in their own immemorial homes, can be called expatriates! In passing, two points affecting Arab territory in western Asia are of interest. The first is that, except in the Yemen and (scantily) in Oman, and in a small area of Syria-Lebanon, Arabs are invariably people of the flat-lands; the process of Arabization by invaders failed to penetrate into the highlands of Persia or of Turkey. The second is that, in all the range of the (eastern) Arab countries (excluding, therefore, the southern Sudan) the sole considerable enclaves of non-Arab-speaking peoples are those of the north 'Iraqi Kurds and Turkomans, the recently-intruded Jews of Israel, and, at the extreme south-western fringe, the partly-Arab bilingual grazing tribes of the central Sudan, the African-type Nubas of Kordofan, and the Nubians of the middle-Nile banks. Elsewhere Arabic speech and consciousness is practically universal.

The vast majority of these Arabs are not so called by virtue of belonging to an ethnically distinct race; they are, as we have seen, except for the central Arabian folk, an amalgam, or rather a variety of different amalgams, of many original races including some, such as the black Africans, far removed from one's normal conception of Arabs. But these peoples have been Arabized, for centuries, to a point where their claim to this classification cannot be disputed if our already suggested criteria (language, residence, cultural devotion, personal claim) are applied. The acceptance, or indeed the proud declaration, of their Arabism by the vast majority of the group throughout the region, is not invalidated by the few cases, hereafter to be mentioned, where such acceptance is doubtful, or is rightly or wrongly rejected by outside observers. The dominating elements of unity throughout the group are many. The strength of these will be apparent when we pass, now, to examine them; and the same scrutiny will reveal considerations detracting, here and there, from their potency. We shall examine elsewhere (p. 197) a field, that of politics, in which Arab unity is notably far from realization.

The claim of the entire block of Arab populations to form a single Community, and to be heard with the greater respect by reason of this fraternal unity, is indeed, in the case of a people divided as they are into self-conscious independent states, a unique phenomenon in the modern world. The Anglo-Saxon nations, the Slav group, the Scandinavians, black Africa: none of these approximate to the educated Arab's conception of his overall singleness transcending national diversity. The uniformly Catholic, ex-Spanish, miscegenated, geographically contiguous states of Latin America offer the nearest approach, yet, for good reasons, do not come near to the Arab sense of unity and mutual belonging and are far from regarding themselves, as do Arabs, as in fact a single *gaum* (folk or people). The nearest parallel to modern Arabism, in this respect, is perhaps the shared and eagerly boasted common Hellenism of the politically detached, independent Greek cities scattered through the Mediterranean world in the seventh to fourth centuries B.C., with their superiority complex as against 'the barbarian', their immense pride in language and tradition, their unique right of entry to the Greek holy places and panhellenic ceremonies—and the Games. This is a far cry; yet the likeness is more than an accident of history, since there are similarities of character and attitude, between Arabs and Hellenes, which have helped to create the parallel.

The Arab countries can, at the outset, claim to form geographically a single block from the confines of Persia to the Atlantic and Indian Oceans. This would by itself imply but a slight and perhaps unreal contribution to unity unless it were accompanied, as among Arabs it is, by the constant intercourse of familiar age-long neighbours, between country and country. The Arabs have in fact for centuries travelled, traded and sojourned in each other's countries, established common enterprises, married each other's daughters, participated as privileged kinsmen in their neighbours' society, and shared in a rich common treasure of history and myth.

The community of language which, above all else, makes this possible is, as everywhere, the greatest of bonds. The Arabic language, almost without qualification that of all Arabs everywhere, is, far more than with most tongues and their speakers, a source of conscious pride and interest; and indeed the language of the Qur'an, of pre-Islamic poetry, and of a vast medieval and modern literature is in itself a rich, flexible instrument in which to indulge the age-long, especial pleasure of Arabs in speech and writing. But is it still a single language, everywhere mutually intelligible? The answer is Yes, to a surprising extent. Historically, the separate emergence of modern Arabic from among a dozen closely-allied Semitic languages seems to date from the fourth to sixth centuries A.D.; it appeared by the latter date in a single, elaborate, closely-developed form, in which its flexibility and curiously delicate mechanism of expression were already evolved (though the script, originally inadequate, was later improved) and which has changed extraordinarily little in the last thousand years—or indeed since the recording of the Qur'an itself. The latter, which made its form of speech a sacred though never a hierarchic language, has been of course a considerable element in establishing it. Since then a large number of words from Persian and Greek have been introduced, to meet administrative, artistic and scientific needs for which the Prophet's vocabulary was unequipped; grammar and accidence were codified by the labours of Arab grammarians, chiefly in 'Iraq in the seventh to ninth centuries; and the more severe and elaborate features of earlier written Arabic have, in the modern language, been allowed to lapse out of use in favour of simpler and handier usages. The Arabic of the present-day press, letter-writing and literature in all Arab countries is, therefore, a remarkably constant international language, not merely intelligible from 'Iraq to Morocco, but substantially identical throughout. In the spoken tongue there are greater differences, due to the absorption of local words from other languages—Persian, Turkish, Greek, Italian, African—and to other factors, and to regional preferences also in pronunciation (for instance, the hard G in Egypt, and the dropping of Q there and in Syria); but even these are not difficult for the traveller or newcomer rapidly to appreciate, and a 'higher colloquial' based on current press-writing is today a *lingua franca* among literate people, even though the speech of some outlying, usually tribal, communities (notably in the Sudan) has departed perceptibly, to say the least, from normal Arabic. It emerges, therefore, that the substantial unity of modern Arabic is even more an effectively unifying factor than could well be expected; and with it goes the press, of which the acceptability knows no inter-Arab frontiers, and the cinema, and, with great importance, broadcasting.

The Arabic language has been, obviously, the vehicle whereby has been preserved the remarkable singleness of the Arab inheritance: that of awareness and pride in Arab past achievement—hailed as such, in spite of sometimes dominant contributions thereto by Persian or Byzantine—in literature, art, architecture, public works; in military and political achievement, whether in fact truly Arab-led or not; in the shared sense of a consciously single social community, widespread over much of the known world, and enduring for centuries—the one Arab Nation, within an even wider House of Islam; in the common awareness of the peculiarly privileged place of Arabs and Arabism in Islam itself; in legend, myth, household story, early and later poetry, anecdote and proverb, and all the background of a people as acquired in childhood and maturity. To this sharing of and pride in the Arab inheritance is due, more than to anything else, the justified claim of its possessors to 'be Arab'. And if one must judge that such claim is less than entirely universal among Arab-speakers, the exceptions are worth mentioning, in passing. They consist of those who, while appreciative of the Arab legacy and unwilling to be excluded from it, yet give first place in their hearts to some other loyalty—that of a local, westward-looking, Phoenician

Lebanon, for instance, or that of an Egypt of the Pharaohs and the Nile, rather than of Arabs and western Asia; indeed, the self-realization of the Egyptians as Arabs, which is substantially complete today, was imperfect (or in some circles non-existent) a generation ago. Such non-Arab localisms are sometimes emphasized by European observers, as discrediting the full unity of Arab sentiment; and indeed they do so, but within narrow, mainly political, and broadly unrepresentative limits. The same is in general true of Arabic-speaking communities who, for reasons implicit in their own histories, have an intense and inward-looking loyalty of their own which doubtless transcends any which they can offer to the main stream of Arabism. This may be the case of the Druzes of Syria and Lebanon (p. 94), the Mandaeans of lower 'Iraq (p. 107), Arabic-speaking Jews everywhere, perhaps the heretical Nusairis of the Syrian coastal ranges (p. 94) and even some, at some periods, of the Christian minorities later to be described (pp. 103–109).

The contribution of religion to Arab or pan-Arab community feeling—the Islamic religion, that of nineteen-twentieths or more of Arabs—may be variously assessed, but cannot be ignored. Something has been said already of the cleavages and sects within Islam, which divide the Arab Nation rather than unify it; but they do not, at their deepest and bitterest, obliterate the boundary which, in the vast majority of Muslim minds and communities, divides Muslim from non-Muslim. There is in the unquestioned essentials of the Faith enough of spiritual and emotional content to make certain that shared adherences to any form of Islam must be a powerful bond between all Muslims—and, for our present purpose, all Arabs; even though non-Muslim Arabs have, in times and places, contributed notably to modern Arabism in the fields of literature, business, politics, society, for each of which it would be easy to quote examples in plenty from Egypt, Palestine, Syria, Lebanon, 'Iraq.

The religious bond in Arab international society may be less obvious to the interested traveller than another feature in their communities which not so much creates as reflects their essential unity: that of the shared way of life which dominates the Arab scene in every region. Here, like must be compared to like; nomad to nomad, tribe to tribe, village and city to their equivalents elsewhere. With this proviso, one can emphasize the close similarity between the form, manner, tempo and social observances of Arab society everywhere in homes, coffee-shops, offices and streets. These differ extraordinarily little, class by class and age-group by age-group, from

Basra to Aleppo or Upper Egypt; and even allowing for elements
that are universal in the modern world, and those common to the
whole of Dar al-Islam, there remains something appreciably Arab in
the forms of courtesy and conversation, the social approaches and
reactions, the domestic arrangements and communal institutions
which have persisted throughout centuries.

There exists, therefore, an Arab World, of which the states and
units in the Middle East which have been mentioned (p. 97) form
part. Within this world there are, it is clear, factors of disruption as
well as of unity. Is there also such a thing as Arab character? It would
be the line of safety, or of pedantry, to deny it; 'national characters'
are notoriously dangerous ground. Nevertheless, certain generalities
seem to be permissible, in the full knowledge that these are open to
countless individual exceptions. Arabs, members of the international
Arabic-speaking bloc, are beyond doubt less, or less efficiently,
warlike than Turks, less artistic or mystical than Persians. They are
courteous according to their code, curious of the unknown, proverb-
ially hospitable, instinctively generous. They are by any standards
highly intelligent, quick in apprehension, witty and humorous, eager
and accomplished formulators of their thoughts in speech; indeed,
facility and fluency can here be their dangers, since these can too
easily be unrelated to facts or to wisdom. Arabs learn quickly and
remember well, but are less disposed to patient inconspicuous research. They are rapid and habitually extreme in judgment and, in
this field, not free from caprice and prejudice. They are freedom-
loving, uncompromising, strongly individualistic, at their worst
egoistic, poor at team-work, reluctant to accept unwelcome decisions
or to subordinate their own wishes to those of a majority or of
superior authority.

4. *Some Arab-world minorities*

We have glanced at certain differences of doctrine, leading often
also to difference of social and political grouping, within Middle
Eastern Islam; and no more than a mention need be made here of
such other Muslim groups within the area, but essentially strangers
in it, as the considerable Somali element in the Aden population and
that of Oman; or the small settlements of Caucasians—Sunni
Cherkes or Circassians and Shi'i Chechens—planted by Sultan
'Abdul Hamid on the eastern borderlands of settled Syria, including
present-day Jordan, to form a stable element among wayward tribes-

men. One may add to these the Pakistanis who, mixed with Indians, are found trading in coastal districts of Oman, the Persian Gulf and Red Sea; or the West African Muslims who pass years, sometimes, in the Sudan or the Hijaz or both in the long course of their pilgrimage to Mecca. And here also we may refer to two other groups of Muslims who, while not Arabic-speaking, are yet, as far as their stage of evolution allows, within the sphere of Arab culture. These are the tiny tribal communities of south-eastern Arabia which speak (Semitic) languages of their own, remote from Arabic; and the part-Arab, part-African graziers of the central Sudan with their Islamic faith, cattle-breeding tribal way of life, but African physique and Hamitic or Nilotic languages. Nor would it be difficult to find other, but in the general picture unimportant, Muslim or indeed non-Muslim communities in the Middle East marked off from the surrounding majorities in their countries by language, type, or alien community consciousness. Such for example would be the long-enduring yet significant community of the Zoroastrians in the Persian provinces of Kirman, Yazd, and Teheran; they are some 12,000 strong, known as good traders and outstanding gardeners, and close kinsmen of the rich, progressive Parsees of western India.

Far more important numerically, politically, and in terms of area occupied, is an element not indeed of Islam nor truly of the Middle East, yet today politically included within it as forming part of the Sudan Republic: that is, the black-African inhabitants, two to three millions strong, of the three southernmost provinces, and a large enclave also, that of the Nuba Mountains, in the province of Kordofan. Here we enter an essentially African world, far removed in every respect save the topographical—that is, in physique, evolution, conceptions and beliefs, way of life, languages, social organization—from everything characteristic of the Middle East: the world of the Nilotic Dinka, the Shilluk and Nuer peoples, the Nilo-Hamites of Equatoria, the agricultural Zande and other peoples of the Ironstone Plateau. Of all these, fascinating to the anthropologist (and embarrassing to the present Sudani administration) the present work will say little more; they are no essential part of a Social Geography of the Middle East.

Returning, therefore, to the Arab world, we glance next at some minority elements of which the social importance far outweighs the smallness of their numbers; and indeed the continued existence of these Arab-Christian communities, in an area so long and deeply Islamized, calls attention once more to the geographical and historical forces which have produced or sheltered them. Such are the half-isolated topographical enclaves which have, in times of trouble, been their salvation; the successive waves of conquest and penetration which have introduced new and partly unassimilable minorities, seeking and finding new homes; the long and slow communications which have kept central government action away; and the resulting localism and pride in separateness. In the matter of religion, a separate faith is often the surviving outward sign of a distinct but unascertainable racial or tribal origin, or of an old political secession, and the number of these shows the readiness of Middle Eastern groups to cling to religious beliefs or to evolve new ones of their own: examples, the Yazidis or the Maronites. At the same time, the dispersal of some once compact communities shows the effect of former persecutions (as in the case of the Armenians, or Assyrians), or sometimes reflects their own wide-ranging commercial abilities and quest of opportunity. The recent history of the Christian minorities, at least since the sixteenth century, owes much to good sense and toleration on the part of an authority not often praised: the Ottoman Government. Onwards from the first occupation of Istanbul (1453) the Turks allowed the community cohesion of the Christians (and the Jews also), sect by sect, to form recognized and internally autonomous *millets*, under their own elected heads, with separate representation on local councils, and freedom in matters of religion, personal status, schools, properties and churches, and their community life. The *millets* thus, with exceptions only when the unwise and sometimes fatal patronage of European powers, or their own indiscreet nationalistic ambitions, aroused suspicion and ill will, retained their own individuality and enjoyed a treatment by the public and government which left them little cause for complaint, and which permitted them to advance in education and knowledge of the modern world notably faster than the Muslim majority; a feature tending, however, to diminish, through jealousy and suspicion, their popularity *vis-à-vis* their Muslim fellow-citizens, and perhaps to weaken, as time went on, their own sense of intimate old-fashioned Christian community ties.

Today it is normal for Middle Eastern governments, except those of peninsular Arabia, to declare their entire tolerance of religious differences, with full equality before the law and freedom of opportunity in public and private life; and some of the present-day constitutions are indeed explicit in this sense. Nevertheless, except in the Lebanon, where the Christians in their various communities form an actual majority of the population (though each is by itself a minority), and except (until our own day) among the impeccably Egyptian and usually nationalistic Copts of Egypt, the non-Muslim elements in the Middle Eastern states have been and are viewed not without suspicion as being less than true citizens, less than entirely loyal: a suspicion by no means always mistaken, and the more likely to be justified the more the local government employs Islamic slogans to rally mass loyalty, or shows itself crudely chauvinistic and hostile to the (Christian) West. It follows that the Christians are today in general less regarded and less comfortable than in most periods of the Turkish or Safawi empires; they remain, nevertheless, an integral part of these new nations, and a part full of ability, experience and progressiveness, which they ask only to be allowed to use on equal terms in the interest of the country—since they have no other. The host countries seem scarcely to realize the extent to which they, or their governments, may be judged abroad by the degree of reasonableness and humanity with which they treat their minorities, whom too often they regard, in troubled times, as a fair target for nationalistic rancour.

Of the Christian communities, the first we consider is the Greek Orthodox: that is, groups of Arabic or Turkish language in the Middle East subject to one of the Eastern Patriarchs of Antioch, Jerusalem, Alexandria, and Istanbul. The doctrinal differences of these from Rome or from Protestantism need not here concern us; there are variations also of ritual and of discipline (for instance, married priests), of organization and of personnel—the superior priesthood being in Turkey all Greek, in Syria and in Egypt only partly so. The Orthodox communities in each centre, other than in Turkey, tend to stand nearer to the Muslim and nationalistic majority than do the Uniate Churches (p. 107). They are strongest in Turkey (that is, in Istanbul and Smyrna), in Syria-Lebanon and in Egypt, and may number 350,000 in all the Middle East. The Greek Orthodox are usually townsmen, and contain many rich and prominent citizens in all walks of life.

The Nestorians (or, today, Assyrians) are a poor remnant of the powerful and widespread Church of that name in medieval times. They number perhaps 75,000 in all, whose rescue from the Turks in 1915–1918 and subsequent settlement in new homes have been tasks of extraordinary difficulty. Using a Syriac liturgy, and served by a rustic priesthood, their ecclesiastical organization is all their own. It is headed by a Patriarch, the Mar Shamun. The Assyrians are largely farmers, but some thousands have adopted town life. Many served in 'Iraq (1921–1952) with great credit in the armed forces. Those of the Urmia (Riza'iyeh) district of Persia were able in part to re-establish themselves after the cataclysm of 1915–1918; those of 'Iraq, now scattered in villages of the Mosul hill-country, have had many a sad adventure since that period, and owe their lives and livelihoods solely to British care. Those now in north-eastern Syria are an offshoot of the 'Iraqi settlements, made under violent stress in 1933 and onwards.

The Copts, with their Monophysite doctrine and their allegiance to the Patriarch of Alexandria (at Cairo), are almost confined to Egypt and the Sudan, to whose people they have always and integrally belonged while refusing conversion to Islam. Their total number may be of the order of 1,500,000. More is to be said of this interesting community in a later chapter (p. 143). The Syrian Orthodox (or Jacobite) Church has its Patriarch at Homs (formerly at Mardin) and, like the Copts, is Monophysite in doctrine, using a Syriac liturgy. They are found, as townsmen and villagers, in Syria and Lebanon, 'Iraq and Egypt, to the number of perhaps 70,000.

More significant than these, but equally Monophysite, are the Armenians, today scattered all over the Middle East—indeed, all over the world—far from their own historic, but now Kurdo-Turkish, Armenia. They preserve, physically, evident traits of the ancient Anatolian population; they retain their national culture, Aryan language and tradition, their schools, charities, national Church, and close sense of community and ancient nationhood; and they exercise in almost every Middle Eastern country their genius for commerce, finance and craftsmanship. Not infrequently suspected of tepid loyalty, or worse, to their countries of residence, and shamefully butchered by the Turks from 1895 to 1916, they have at times held high office in all these countries and are capable of being economically as well as socially an element of high value. Their main concentrations today are in Turkey (particularly Istanbul), in northern Syria and around Beirut, in Egypt and Persia (with important concentrations around Tabriz in Azarbaijan, and at Julfa, a suburb of Isfahan), with lesser numbers in 'Iraq and the Sudan. Only in Persia are the Armenians still, save exceptionally, rural cultivators. There are in all between 300,000 and 350,000 Armenians, of their own Orthodox Gregorian Church, in the Middle East. (The Armenian Soviet Republic, in Trans-Caucasian Russia, does not here concern us, except in so far as it provides a main centre of their Church and culture; it has, moreover, since 1945 drawn some thousands of Armenians, mostly from Turkey and Lebanon, to reside there.)

These then are the main non-Catholic Christian groups which concern us, to whom can be added the small Protestant congregations (Anglican, Presbyterian, etc.) created in most Middle Eastern countries by missionary work in recent years. One can add also, if dubiously, the small and harmless riverside Sabaean, or Mandaean, community of lower 'Iraq, perhaps 150,000 strong, with their famous skill as silver-smiths and their Christianity (if such indeed it is) mingled with a variety of other elements.

The Catholic Church itself is represented in our region in three ways, and on a major scale. First the Latin-rite Catholics, directly and solely subordinate to Rome, form a scattered community of not more than a few thousand souls, under a Patriarch of Jerusalem. Second, the Maronite Church in the Lebanon, with its compact community of some 400,000 faithful (30 per cent of the republic's total population), and with lesser groups in Egypt, Syria and elsewhere, is the most important of the 'Uniate' Churches—that is, Churches in communion with Rome and under Papal supremacy— but is also autonomous under its extremely influential Patriarch. It has its peculiar privileges, such as the marriage of the lower priesthood, and its own Syriac liturgy. The urban Maronites are progressive, virile, intelligent, French-educated folk, the peasants and villagers are hardworking, resolute types, mostly literate; they were from 1860 onwards the heart of the old Independent Sanjaq of Lebanon. They invariably supply the President as well as many ministers and officials to the Lebanese Republic, are prominent in every sphere, and form perhaps the most westward-looking element in all the Middle East.

Thirdly, the six other Uniate Churches represent Catholicized offshoots of the parent, non-Catholic Churches already mentioned. The Greek Catholics, converted from Greek Orthodox and still using a Greek liturgy, are found in all these countries to the extent of a few thousands, with their Patriarch at Cairo; they are a rich and progressive community. The Syrian Catholics, with their headquarters and Patriarch (today a Cardinal) at Beirut, and with important groups also in Syria, 'Iraq and Egypt, are a no less advanced and dynamic community, numbering in all perhaps 200,000. The Chaldaeans, chiefly found in northern and central 'Iraq, with a few in Syria, are converts from Nestorianism, and at present have far outdone the surviving 'Assyrians' in education, wealth, and social position; with a total of possibly 80,000, they are mainly townsmen, but also good cultivators in the Mosul plain; and they were, for a century, good crews on the Tigris river-steamers. Their Patriarch ('of Babylon') lives at Mosul. The Coptic Catholics are relatively few, and almost all in Egypt; their liturgy is in Arabic. The Armenian Catholics, widely spread but with their main centres around Beirut, follow a Patriarch of their own (named 'of Constantinople'). All of these Churches, like the parent bodies from which, largely through Catholic missionary effort, they seceded, have their substantial religious and community independence, their own pride and exclusiveness, their schools, orphanages and other charities. There is limited inter-marriage between them—and none with Muslims.

Of all these minority communities a feature strange at first sight to European newcomers is their complete, millennary habituation to life in the midst of a majority public and government of an entirely distinct and alien culture, and their normally cordial and familar terms with friends outside their community—yet the extent also to which the latter holds, by kinship, tradition, religion, shared tech-niques of living, and sometimes shared fears, their truest loyalty and sense of belonging. Nor are these communities immobile: thousands of Syrians and Lebanese have moved, since the early nineteenth century, to Egypt and the Sudan, there to excel in journalism, litera-ture and commerce. The interesting group of German (Württemberg) 'Templars', settled in Palestine in the mid-nineteenth century in and near Haifa, Jaffa and Jerusalem, is now no more, having failed to survive the Second War. Violence has repeatedly moved, and decimated, the Armenians and Assyrians, and in the Jazira province of Syria today groups of many Christian sects flourish who, trans-planted from Turkey, were not there a generation ago. And the emigration of Lebanese and some Syrian and Egyptian Christians to (and, though less, re-immigration from) the New World, West Africa, and indeed most parts of the world, is a constant feature of these minorities. Economically, the remittances of these exiles are an important source of livelihood for their stay-at-home friends. Few great cities of North and South America are without a valuable and nationally self-conscious community of Lebanese. Culturally, the bond thus created with richer and more developed lands has been interesting and valuable; Americanized Lebanese poets, essayists and scholars have written acceptably in English, as have, in French, Catholic ex-Lebanese or Syrians in France. The world-wide dis-persal of active, intelligent Armenians, varying from millionaires to cobblers, and holding every variety of passport, is a familiar phenomenon.

This often tragic mobility of the minorities is again exemplified by the recent history of the oriental Jewish communities found, for many centuries past, all over the Middle East, in which they had, under the Ottoman *millet* system and headed by their own Chief Rabbi in Istanbul, a recognized and protected place in society, and preserved their own privileges and characteristic occupations. Not as cultivators nor (save rarely) as landowners but, in almost every town in every country except Najd and the Hijaz, as bankers, traders, shopkeepers, promoters of enterprise, accountants or clerks, the Jews —politically unambitious, culturally remote, not often popular though but rarely maltreated—lived with self-respect and not unhappily, speaking the local language, represented on the local councils. But they have been ruined now by the militant Zionism of their American and European co-religionists, to whose success in founding their neo-Jewish state in Arab territory is due the new, hostile attitude of Middle Eastern governments and publics, and the catastrophe of a *millet* so long established and hitherto so safe. In Turkey the Jews have been reduced, by emigration to Israel since 1948, from perhaps 75,000 to 24,000, the remnant living almost entirely in Istanbul and Izmir. In 'Iraq the Jewish population has fallen from 100,000 to 10,000; in the Yemen, from 50,000 to a tenth of this; in Aden, from 9,000 to less than 1,000, and in the Protectorate, from 15,000 to scarcely any at all. In Syria, Lebanon, Egypt the record is much the same: the large Jewish colonies in these countries, at least 100,000 in all, have been since 1956 reduced by four-fifths. A lesser population of Jews, it seems, have left Persia, where perhaps 40,000 remain.

Of the Jewish citizens of Israel itself something will be said later, in the course of our account of that country (p. 188 ff).

The Europeans to be found in the Middle East at any one moment cannot be said to form a minority in our present sense, enormous as has been, is and will be the effect of their presence. They are subjects of Great Britain, France, the U.S.A., Italy, Greece, the two Germanies, Japan, and the U.S.S.R. and its satellites. We may exclude, as needing no comment, the armed garrisons, now extremely few, in Aden, Cyprus and (until 1958) 'Iraq, or the NATO establishments in Turkey; the foreign personnel of embassies and consulates; those employed by local governments in missions to their armed forces, or in specialized duties in their departments and institutions; those working on behalf of the government, or with its blessing, on industrial projects or enquiries, or busy on constructional contracts awarded by the state: in the ubiquitous oil industry, employed by the government-authorized concessionary companies; or in other state-approved industrial or research operations. None of the personnel thus far suggested, however important his contribution, is likely to settle permanently in the country; and the same is true of another category whose influence on Middle Eastern society over the last full century has been of the highest significance in all fields of culture and service—that is, the foreign teachers and missions, religious and secular; the staffs of institutions and establishments whether educational, charitable, medical; and archaeologists and students, and travellers and sportsmen. European permanent residents, less important than the above whether economically or culturally, are to be found nowadays in Turkey, confined almost entirely to Istanbul and, doubtfully, Izmir but still a substantial community; and to a lesser extent in Egypt, the Sudan and Persia. In Egypt and the Sudan thousands of Greeks, with lesser numbers of Italians, French and Maltese, have for many years been engaged (apart from the few dozen rich and socially established) in retail trade, clerical work, minor craftsmanship and other humble occupations; they are to be found, in numbers much reduced by the policies of the post-1952 Egyptian Government, not only in the cities but in scores of villages throughout the Nile Valley. These exiled Europeans, with often a lowly but never an abject standard of life, and with a brave blend of nostalgia and acceptance, have mixed little with the local population while forming a valuable element in it. But they have, probably, a doubtful future.

The Greeks of Cyprus will be further considered when we speak separately of Cypriot affairs (p. 185 ff).

5. *The Turkish-speakers*

Speakers of some dialect of the Turkish language-group are scattered widely throughout much of the Middle East, and form one of its three most important elements; the other two being the Iranian-speakers and, numerically the greatest, the Arabs. The Turks—to use a convenient abbreviation which must not mislead—are found as a fairly solid block in Anatolia and a small adjacent area in European Turkey; in communities of considerable but a far smaller scale, in Persia and 'Iraq; and in scattered households or tiny groups throughout the area.

The Turkish language-group, a member of the so-called Altaic family with its wide extension from central and northern Asia to south Russia and the Balkans, has a highly characteristic structure and a firm basis of similarity wherever found. It has at different places and periods been written in Syriac, Tibetan, Armenian, Greek and Hebrew characters, as well as in the Arabic script almost exclusively used for it in western Asia until 1928; and in Latin characters, in the Turkish Republic since that year. The language in its modern and western forms (which alone concern us here) has much attractiveness by virtue of its euphonious vowel-sounds, of which eight are distinguishable, its unusual regularity of structure, and its expressive and convenient system of prefixes and suffixes in both nouns and verbs, whereby the meaning is modified in a dozen ways from a single and simple root. The interminable and involved sentences of older-fashioned written Turkish—with the sole finite verb arriving, perhaps, after three pages!—are no longer in fashion; the Turkish of today is expressive, practicable and well equipped. Both in the Anatolian form (Osmanli Turkish, as perfected in Konya and Istanbul) and to a somewhat lesser extent in that of the Persian and 'Iraqi communities (whose dialects are often known, for contrast, as Turki) a wholesale adoption of Arabic and Persian words, carried out in medieval times, greatly altered the mass and expressiveness of the language. Most of this remains, but in Turkey itself officially sponsored efforts have been made since 1928, for reasons of national pride, to diminish the Arabic and Persian vocabulary and substitute true Turkish words. This process has been carried to great, sometimes inordinate, lengths, and it has been surprisingly accompanied by the needless adoption of French or English words to replace those available and familiar in Arabic or even in Turkish itself. A minor result of these processes is the widening difference between the current Turkish of the republic and that of Turkish-speaking communities elsewhere; these had been hitherto more closely united, linguistically, than is the case with other widespread language-groups. The gap increased farther by the adoption, under Atatürk's orders, of the Latin in place of the (fundamentally unsuited) Arabic script hitherto used in the Ottoman Empire; the details of the new transliteration were evolved by Italian scholars, on lines considered by them to be phonetic. A great gulf inevitably appeared between the old Turkish literature and the new—no unwelcome feature, perhaps, to a reforming dictator. The Turkish or Turki used in the Middle East outside the republic is still written in Arabic characters, and uses the old composite vocabulary. The Turkish language, however, whatever and wherever its evolution, must still be reckoned as relatively difficult for a European to acquire; its phonetics are subtle, its syntax unfamiliar to him, its vocabulary unaided by anything he will have known before.

The present subjects of the republic do not all speak Turkish, nor is their Turkish, notably as between educated city-dweller and uneducated countryman, dialectically uniform. Apart from resident Europeans and certain other small communities, there are appreciable groups of Arabs inside the southern border, of Kurds in the eastern provinces, of Lazes (a Muslim people of Transcaucasian, probably Georgian, origin) on the north-eastern coast towards the Russian frontier; and there are, as we have seen, Christian groups, Greeks and Armenians, whose Turkish is in most cases not their mother-tongue. To all these some Caucasians and the surviving Jews may be added. But the main community of Turks in European and Asiatic Turkey forms obviously not only by far the greatest group of Turkish-speakers in the Middle East, but 90 per cent of all subjects of the Turkish State.

This mass of population, fairly uniform in physique in spite of minor local varieties, is a mixture of aboriginal Anatolian with Phrygian, Hittite, Lydian, Kimmerian, Thracian, Persian and Greek, with medieval additions from Russia and central Asia, from Arabia and the Levant, and in later days from the Balkans. These Turks, welded first into a single group, then a nation, then a conquering Empire, yield to none in their conscious solidarity; and they now fill, with credit, all the occupations and careers usual in the modern world, including those previously reserved, until the revolutionary period 1922–1928, to members of the minority communities or to foreigners. Among the public as a whole stand, at the two extremes of social evolution, the fully educated, modern-minded, substantially Europeanized city-dweller, and on the other hand, the remote, backward cultivator or semi-nomad of the country districts. The former class has, in public and private life, most of the accomplishments, outlook and reactions of our own continent and age, with their full share of courtesy, social charm and humour; the latter has those of a tough peasantry everywhere, with its hard work, suspicion, ignorance, and naïvety. Typical Turkish qualities other than these are best shown in the middle and lower-middle orders of the towns and villages; they are those of endurance rather than speed, patience (which however must not be overstrained), discipline, personal honesty, shrewdness rather than brilliance, acceptance of self-criticism but not that of outsiders, loyalty to established and valued figures and institutions, hospitality and kindness, outstanding military qualities, as history proves, and a singular unawareness of class distinctions. Are there, it may be asked, survivals of the callous brutality of the old Turk of the Armenian massacres, or the treatment of British prisoners in 1917? Such lapses were due at the time, no doubt, to the low mental age of the Turkish masses, their egocentric sympathies and crude chauvinism, and malicious ill-guidance from above; but it is improbable that even today the strain of brutality has gone for ever. There is recent evidence that it has not.

As to religion, even though Islam has been disestablished in Turkey, the Turks are almost without exception at least nominal Muslims; indeed there has been in the period 1952–1960 something of a religious revival, fostered in part by politicians willing to use the more conservative popular elements for electoral support. Islam, therefore, whether in the form of the Sunni orthodoxy of the Sultanate and the old governing class, or that of the Sufi or heterodox sects which are widespread in Asia Minor, is still a force and a part of life in Turkey, city and countryside alike.

To the general Turcification of Asia Minor, substantially accomplished by the end of the Middle Ages, there have been latter-day additions, which indeed continue. In the nineteenth century there was a repatriation of Turks displaced by hostile occupations of Greece and Transcaucasia, and in the 'twenties of this century more Turks, probably three-quarters of a million, immigrated from Greece as part of the great population exchange following 1923. In the 'thirties and later between one and two hundred thousand Turkish immigrants arrived in Anatolia from the Balkan countries, especially Bulgaria; and the latter added to these in 1950–1951 by driving scores of thousands more, deprived of their possessions, across the border into European Turkey. A few hundred central Asian Turks have also made their way to Turkey in recent years from Soviet territory.

The Turks of Cyprus, numbering some 100,000 or about one-fifth of the island's population, are in part descendants of early, perhaps sixteenth-century, Turkish garrisons and colonists, and in smaller part later arrivals due to the disorders and population exchanges in Anatolia after the First World War. Their appearance, language, religion, manners and occupations and, it would seem, most of their features of character and attitude, equate them closely to their Anatolian cousins, with whom they were for so long (three centuries) fellow subjects of the Sultan. A fair proportion in the cities speak Greek, and fewer English. The Turkish villagers live in some cases distinct from, in others blended with, the Greek populations; in the towns the mixture is complete, with Turks usually a 10 to 50 per cent minority, but in places a majority. The resulting bi-nationality produced the grave political conditions (1948–1959), of sad and recent memory.

The Turkish-speakers of modern Persia, loosely known as Turkomans, are various and important. Those of the Azarbaijan province, with its capital at Tabriz, represent a Turkish immigration from the east subsequent, by many years, to the Seljuq or Ottoman. Many are today an industrious, reliable, progressive people, self-conscious as one of the main minorities of Persia, but differing from the main population of the country in language, orientation and cultural background. They extend, diluted, outside Azarbaijan into the provinces of Gurgan and eastern Mazandaran, the districts of Qasvin and Hamadan and other lesser localities. Many attempts have been made to seduce them from their adherence to the Persian State, and will doubtless be made again; but they have meanwhile a tradition of good recruitment into the Persian forces, and a high military reputation. Speaking the Azerbaijani dialect of Turki (easily intelligible to an Ottoman-Turkish-speaker, but written in Persian script), they are in political sentiment clearly distinguished from the main body of Persia, far also from the modern Turkish Republic, and nearer, it may be, to their cousins in the Soviet Socialist Republic of Azarbaijan, across the border. The proximity of the U.S.S.R. has inevitably affected both their social and political outlook, as well as the direction of their trade and travel. The Azarbaijanis are Sunni Muslims by religion, predominantly agricultural in habit, but good industrial workers also. There is, in all their region of settlement, a greater or less admixture of true Persians, of Kurds, of Georgians, Circassians, and Armenians. On the assumption that Persia as a nation will survive, it may be foreseen that this Turkish minority, and the others next to be mentioned, will tend more and more to be absorbed and assimilated, with the gradual disappearance of their dialects and separate identity.

These are not the only Turkish-speaking communities in Persia. In the north-eastern province of Khurasan there are Turkoman tribes both settled and (though now diminished in numbers) also migratory, whose territory is continuous with that of the Turkmen

Republic of the U.S.S.R. They claim descent from early Turkish colonists left by Chinghiz Khan; and certainly their community sentiment or attachment seems directed more towards the lands of their origin than to those of their Ottoman third cousins. Far to the south, two Turki-speaking tribe-groups, both seasonably nomadic within fixed routes and areas, have achieved fame, not least for their own internecine rivalries: the Qashqa'i of the Fars province, who show more than traces of Mongoloid physique, and a part though not all of the Five Tribes of the same province, the non-Turkish sections being Arab. In Kirman survives the Turkish-speaking tribe of the Afshars, which gave a dynasty to Persia. In central Persia not far south of Teheran, in the areas of Qum and Saveh, is the tribal area of the Turki-speaking Shahsevan, a group highly renowned in earlier days. Thus the Turkish- or Turki-speaking element in Persia is varied and conspicuous.

In 'Iraq, as throughout urban areas of (geographical) Syria, the long Turko-Arab connection, and in particular the Ottoman adminis-tration of Arab provinces for four centuries, has left a legacy of much Turkish, and later Ottoman-Turkish, blood and culture in hundreds, or thousands, of the town-dwelling educated class. In the old days Turkish fief-holders would settle and found families (some of which survive) in 'Iraq or Syria, and in later times—into the twentieth century itself—the same would be true of a few high officials of Turkish race. The age-long use of that language throughout the administration, from 1534 to 1918, by Arab, Kurd and Turk alike, and the Turkish education, civil and military, of hundreds of young 'Iraqis in that period (more notably in the nineteenth and twentieth centuries) gave a pronounced Ottoman colouring to much of the urban society of the three *vilayets*, not all of which has disappeared. But there were, and are, other 'Iraqi Turks than these; there are the Turkomans, strung out in townships along the old Baghdad–Mosul trunk road from Qara Tepe to Arbil. Turkish-speaking in a dialect intermediate between Turki and Ottoman, hardworking and generally law-abiding cultivators and townsmen, self-contained and politically unambitious, and providers (above all from Kirkuk) of far more than their proportion of government officials both in Ottoman and in present times, they have preserved their identity against Kurdish and Arab neighbours, disliking both. Feelings of attachment to Istan-bul or Ankara are not unknown, but have never been more than half-hearted; they revered the Caliph but were horrified at Atatürk's reforms. Their origin *in situ* may date back to Seljuq or post-Seljuq days; the leading families stood high with the Ottoman authorities, from whom many held fiefs which became nineteenth-century estates.

In the Levant States there are no grouped early-Turkish survivals, and the remnants of the Ottoman administration and its accompanying social influences are less obvious that in 'Iraq. Nevertheless, a number of the outstanding families of Syria are even today, among the older generation, Turkish-speaking in their domestic intimacy.

A Turkish cultural rather than physical heritage is still easily perceptible in Egypt, though remote enough from all modern features and tendencies of that country. Centuries of Turkish-Mamluk rule, followed by that of an Albanian-Turkish dynasty, and close social connections with the still suzerain Empire through the nineteenth century, left the legacy of a considerable remnant of Turkish speaking and Turkish manners in royal circles, and among the *deux cent familles*, under the now departed Egyptian monarchy. This will soon, no doubt, disappear.

6. *The Aryan-speakers*

The Aryan or Indo-European language-group—the correct use of the two terms is disputed by philologists—is extremely widespread in the world, and contains varieties within it far exceeding those of other groups, for example the Semitic. The languages of western Europe are but second cousins of the Slavonic group or of Armenian, and third or fourth cousins of the group (to which by some the word Aryan is limited) containing the Iranian tongues—Zend, old and new Iranian (Persian), and Sanskrit. The modern Aryan languages of western Asia all, except Armenian, belong to the more narrowly defined Aryan family. They consist of modern Persian, the sole official language of the Persian Kingdom; other modern-Persian varieties as spoken, often side by side with official Persian, in the provinces of Mazandaran (Mazandarani) and the Caspian area (Gilaki), and Luristan (Luri); countryside dialects spoken in Fars, Kirman and Khurasan differing less than those from standard Persian; and finally Kurdish, which differs more. Kurdish in its various and mutually unintelligible dialects is spread over a very wide area of Persia, 'Iraq and Turkey, and its era of separation from Persian dates from some centuries ago. The same may be true of the Baluchi language. All these languages, including Persian itself, use the Arabic script if and when they are written, with additional letters and a characteristically differing caligraphy. All have borrowed very widely from the Arabic vocabulary, are structurally unusually simple, and have no serious phonetic difficulties. Persian, with its very extensive literature, may be reckoned a language of much charm and resource; it greatly influenced the development of Ottoman Turkish, which borrowed copiously from it.

The Persian-speaking citizen of that ancient monarchy possesses qualities of which the origins are nowhere clearly traceable in his mixed ancestry of aboriginal Iranian, incoming Indo-European, central Asian, Mongol, Arab and the rest. His qualities are those of a quick, responsive rather than a profound intelligence, a leaning to mysticism and the unreal, with high accomplishment in words and the arts, easy acquisition of foreign cultures but always with a deep Persian superiority complex, and both broad and refined types of humour. Martial qualities, as those of patience and altruism, are generally regarded as poorly developed; tolerance is rare, unless in the form of cynicism. Manners are highly refined, impatience a sign of ill-breeding, the telling of bad news a *bêtise*. Personal honesty is assumed, integrity in public affairs notably less so. But a true appreciation of the Persian 'national character' would need to be based on a lifetime of close experience—and could then be widely erroneous; only a Persian, at his wittiest, should be entrusted with the task.

By great majority agriculturists (the pastoral tribes of the country being largely Kurds or Turks) the Persians occupy, otherwise than in a thin admixture, little of the north-west or the most westerly belt of their country, and only part of the south. The Persians, as distinct from the other Iranian and non-Iranian elements—Kurds, Lurs, Baluchis, Turks and Arabs—are concentrated in the north, west-centre, north-east and east of Persia, throughout which village life is as yet little changed from that of medieval times, while urban life has been advancing by strides.

Persians are found outside their own country principally in 'Iraq, where many households of such exiles are resident in Baghdad and Basra, and far more (though fewer than half a century ago) in the Shi'i holy places of Karbala, Najf, Kadhimiya and Samarra. No appreciable number, but at most some isolated Persian households, generally of religious complexion, are to be found elsewhere in the Middle East.

The reverse is true of other Iranian constituents in the country's population—the Baluchis, Kurds, and Lurs. The first-named, Sunni clansmen and peasants with typical tribal organization, part sedentary and part pastoral, live in the coastal area (that of the Makran province) of the extreme south, and are but a fragment of the main Baluchi group whose territory forms a major part of western Pakistan. Their interest, in the general picture of modern Persia, is strictly local; politically they are disunited and unformidable. The language is, like the Pushtu of Afganistan, derived from an Iranian group parallel to, rather than derived from, that of modern official Persian. There is a considerable Baluchi population across the sea on the north-east-facing Batina coast of Oman, and notably in the twin towns of Muskat-Matra.

In the Kurdish language, known as Kurdi or Kirmanji or both, it is not possible to trace the stages whereby, with the passage of centuries and the admixture of other local populations and their dialects, the present varieties of Kurdish were evolved, or the now clear difference between its main northern and southern branches established. The language has today, as compared to Persian, marked syntactical differences as well as many of vocabulary and phonetics, and speakers of the two languages cannot, or can barely and most imperfectly, understand each other. The Kurds as a people form an important group in western Asia; they have never at any time coalesced into a single united community, even though prolific, till the eighteen-sixties, in vigorous, short-lived local principalities. Kurdish nationalism is today a persistent, hopeless, largely expatriate growth, without a realistic programme or valid leaders. Their territory, shared on its fringes by other elements, stretches in a wide arc from Kirmanshah in western Persia across an extensive area of north-eastern 'Iraq to north-eastern Turkey nearby, as far as Erzurum and Kars, and westward almost to the great southward-flowing loop of the Euphrates. There are Kurds, perhaps some 150,000 in all, in Syria—in the Taurus foothills north of Aleppo, and in the city of Damascus, with settlements elsewhere; others, probably not exceeding 30,000 but with a full share of community conscious-ness, are found in Soviet Transcaucasia. The main body, however, lying athwart Persia, 'Iraq and eastern Turkey, has populations of perhaps 750,000, 1,000,000 and 1,500,000 respectively in those countries. Such figures would give an estimate of nearly 3,500,000 for the Kurds as a whole—conjectural as is this figure, and blurred as are the fringes of the community itself in terms of locality, purity and self-consciousness. The western Persian provinces occupied by a majority of Kurds are those dependent on the towns of Kirmanshah, Qasr-i-Shirin, Baneh, Sanandaj (Senna), Saqqiz, Mahabad (Sauj

Bulaq), Riza'iyeh (Urmia), Shahpur, Qutur and Maku, all in the wide strip of mountain country nearest to the 'Iraq frontier; to the eastward lie the Azarbaijani Turkomans. There are Kurdish villages, settled there by official action in the seventeenth century, far to the east in the Khurasan province.

The Persian Kurds, Sunni with rare exceptions, are in governmental eyes an unassimilated element of no great apparent loyalty to the Shah or to the Shi'i establishment. They have a background of age-long lawlessness, brigandage, local autonomy, and treasonable connections across the border with the Ottoman (Sunni) neighbours. Tribally organized, by habit agricultural with some pastoral tribes, feudally obedient to their Aghas, tough and warlike at need, the Kurds in their own countryside and deep valleys are peasants, in places nomadic herdsmen: a picturesque, attractive, far from uncivilized, virile type who have asked little, and received little, from the modern world. In the cities, which are nowhere entirely Kurdish-populated, the educated and outwardly westernized Kurd can well hold his own as writer, politician, doctor or mere conversationalist with any Persian or European, all provincial backwardness left behind.

The 'Iraqi Kurds, a 20 per cent minority in that republic are, with more Turkish and less Persian elements in their culture, similar in most respects to the Persian Kurds just described, with tribes of equal or greater fame, scenes at least equally majestic, and a broken history of valley autonomy sometimes rising to the scale of considerable principalities. For centuries the Ottoman Government, as nominal overlord, was disliked and distrusted; today that of Arab 'Iraq, for all the presence of a Kurd or two regularly in the Cabinet, is no better regarded. The many concessions made for years past in 'Iraqi Kurdistan to local feeling—Kurdish as an official language, Kurdish officials and regiments—have not availed to secure their loyalty, which indeed ceaseless Soviet efforts by broadcasts, agents and money are concerned to prevent. The 'Iraqi Kurds, with some few representatives in most towns of northern and central 'Iraq, live in the provinces of Mosul (that is, its northern and eastern districts), Arbil (but with Turkoman and Arab minorities), Kirkuk (the same), and Sulaimaniya (entire). The Yazidis, in two isolated communities in the non-Kurdish areas of Mosul province, are a puzzling fragment probably of mainly Kurdish stock though adhering notoriously to a separate religion. The latter is secret, but is known to contain non-Muslim elements including the propitiation (not the worship) of that

eminent though temporarily fallen angel, the Devil, and reverence
for Christian and Jewish, as well as Islamic, scriptures; indeed, their
religious services are in Arabic. No longer a danger to their neighbours and to travellers, the Yazidis are still dour, suspicious and
communally introvert. There are perhaps 30,000 Yazidis in 'Iraq,
and 3,000 more in eastern Syria.

In Turkey there have been, since the great Kurdish revolt of 1925
and lesser risings in 1930 and 1936, so many transplantations, restor-
ations and renamings (such as 'mountain Turks' for 'Kurds') that
the present strength or location and condition of the Turkish Kurds
is difficult to establish. It appears true that the Kurdish areas are
now (1962) reasonably peaceful, and administered with little difference from the rest. Their separate race and language are studiously
ignored, their traditional dress is forbidden near official headquarters,
their insubordinate airs, if any survive, are chastened by repeated
blows. The whole region traditionally Kurdish, or predominantly so,
includes the *ils* (*vilayets*) of Hakari, Van, Bitlis, Mush, Ağri, Siirt,
Diyarbakir, Mardin, Elâziğ, Tunceli, Bingöl, Urfa, Gaziantep,
Adiyaman, Malatya; that is, fifteen provinces out of sixty-seven.
And there are certain minor Kurdish communities—linguistically
varied, as with the Zaza-speakers south of Erzincan—outside these.
The essential character of the Turkish Kurds and their social organization were for centuries more or less identical with those of their
cousins in the Sultan's 'Iraqi provinces and in Persia; but processes
of assimilation have now been operating, with inspiration and assistance from government quarters at every level, for fifty years, and
this cannot be without effect both on the Kurds' separate national
consciousness and on their tribal organization. These processes and
this government attitude are in some degree, and will probably be
increasingly, those of the 'Iraqi and Persian Governments also; and
Kurdish resistance to them, for all their toughness, their topographical isolation, and their separatist tradition, cannot be expected to
last for ever. Meanwhile, the Kurds are a considerable element in
the three countries, and a major embarrassment to their alien rulers.

Speaking a dialect less remote from modern written Persian than
is Kurdish, but more deeply distinct than a mere bucolic variation,
the Lurish and Bakhtiari tribesmen of the middle stretch of western
and south-western Persia range from Dizful and Shushtar in the
south, the 'Iraqi frontier to the west, and a line north of Mandali-
Burujird to the north; in fact, a wide and beautiful mountain region,
its capital Khurramabad. The Lurs, with an interesting medieval

history of local statehood and dynasty, are today a major relic in Persia of the old days of regional separatism, aided in this case by a strong tradition and their own dialect. Along, and east of, the 'Iraq frontier region they are villagers and graziers, no longer formidable; they sometimes stray across into 'Iraq, form an element in the population of Badra, and supply, by long tradition, the famous corps of weight-lifting porters (mistakingly known as Kurds by the Baghdadis) in the streets and customs-wharfs of the 'Iraqi capital. Farther south and east the Bakhtiari, of the old-time Amirate of Greater Luristan, form a distinguishable part of the Lurish complex, speak a closely similar dialect, and are best so classified. Falling into two tribe-groups, they are among the most famous tribal folk in all Persia. With a number of fixed settlements—centres of a high culture among the sophisticated élite, which has on occasion played a decisive part in Persian politics—the majority are still seasonally nomadic, moving northward and eastward from the confines of the Khuzistan flatlands to the vicinity of Isfahan.

The important Armenian community, spread thinly but ubiquitously throughout the Middle East including Persia, is also Aryan-speaking (p. 106) in its own mother-tongue; but this has been already mentioned among the Christian minorities.

CHAPTER SIX

THE ARAB COUNTRIES

HAVING established something of the historical background, the present identity, and the constitutional forms of the Middle Eastern states of today, we pass next to a rather closer account of the facts of their geography as nature and man's delimitations have fashioned them. A few lines will be given for each separately on their topography, conditions, and climate, the composition of their populations, their natural resources and their communications. The reader who has glanced at the titles of subsequent chapters will realize that more information on the states from various aspects, but grouped by subjects rather than thus particularized country by country, is to be given later in the book. The countries' agriculture, their nascent industries, and their oil-resources will thus be described in Chapters Ten and Eleven.

In the present chapter and the next, the Arab territories and the non-Arab are for convenience grouped separately.

1. 'Iraq

The Republic of 'Iraq—a kingdom until July 1958, and effectively a military dictatorship since then—is the most easterly of the major Arab states, abutting, eastward and northward, on non-Arab territory. It has occupied nevertheless, as earlier pages of this book have shown, a leading (and for long the leading) place in Arab and Islamic history in past ages, and has claims today to be in the forefront of progressive Arab achievement—in spheres other than (at present) the political. The 'Iraqi *vilayets* were disliked by the Turks, who made them the theme of many pejorative jokes, and Syrians and Egyptians have habitually thought poorly of 'Iraqi culture and amenities. But times have changed, in 'Iraq's favour; such judgments, if ever true, are so no longer. And to the charm of 'Iraqi society, in tribe or city, such long-term residents as the present writer can testify.

'Iraqi territory amounts to about 175,000 square miles (though reputable authorities give strangely varying measurements); its extreme length is 620 miles, breadth 450. Its neighbours are, on the south, the principality of Kuwait, and Sa'udi Arabia: on the west, Sa'udi Arabia, a relatively narrow corridor of Jordan, and Syria: on the north, Turkey: on the east, Persia. The frontiers on the south and west are located in desert country, on the north and north-east in rugged mountains, in the east and south-east in the plain-country west of the Zagros ranges.

The country's sole outlet to the sea is on the mud-flats of Fao, with a frontage of some twenty miles on the Gulf, squeezed in at the Shatt al-'Arab mouth between Kuwaiti and Persian territory. Inland, though much of 'Iraq is dull and desolate country, it contains none the less great variation of terrain, including areas of wild and romantic landscape. Central and southern 'Iraq, the true delta of the twin rivers Tigris and Euphrates (whence its earlier name of Mesopotamia), is flat, stoneless, alluvial country, highly fertile, irrigable and indeed floodable, and extensively cultivated with crops and date-gardens. Its areas of broad marsh, as well as its stretches of unrelieved aridity, show that a completed drainage and irrigation system has yet to be achieved. In this region, the heart of 'Iraq, the population (exclusively Arab) is by great majority tribal outside the towns. The villages take many aspects according to the local types of cultivation and terrain, and the building materials available. The country west of Euphrates varies, except on the watered river-banks, from light steppe to true desert, the home of the great camel-grazing tribes of 'Iraq and neighbouring Syria. In the north, but short of the mountain zone, are broad plains (the ancient Assyria) cultivable, save in the driest years, on the rainfall. North and north-east of these, beyond an intermediate foothill belt, lies the Kurd-inhabited wild mountain system shared with Turkey and Persia. This is, for the most part, drained ultimately into the Tigris by the upper reaches and the tributaries of the Greater and Lesser Zab, the 'Udhaim and the Diyala. These mountain districts, which belong essentially to the Zagros system, form a region of grazing at seasonally varying levels, terraced or deep-valley cultivation, a mountain vegetation, rapid streams, hard winters and a radiant spring. The higher mountains reach more than 8,000 (and one 10,000) feet in height, and are snow-covered for much of the year. No conditions and no scenes could less resemble the average foreigner's ideas of 'Iraqi flatness.

Climatically, the country is known for its severity. In the mountains, summer heat is relatively moderate, often agreeable, especially in the 'hill stations' now available; winter cold can be intense. The foothill and undulating plain districts of the north are tropically hot in summer, with maximum shade temperatures of 110° to 115°, but they enjoy cool nights. In central and southern 'Iraq the summer heat is by 10° (sometimes by 15°) greater than this, but health and spirits are preserved by the dryness of the air and the refreshing coolness of the nights, which fails only in the southernmost parts of the delta. Rainfall varies from 4 inches a year, or less, in the uncultivable desert west of Euphrates, to 7 or 10 inches in central 'Iraq where all crops depend on irrigation, and to 12 or 16 inches on the northern plains where, in all years but the worst, rain-cultivation is successful. In the mountains, 30 to 40 inches of rain can fall, with, or in the form of, snow in the winter months. It is a country of high winds; in Baghdad summers the south-east wind is dreaded for its dust-content, the north welcomed for its comparative freshness. Fog is a rarity. On the whole, 'Iraq as a country of residence is neither unhealthy nor unpleasant—and yearly less so, thanks to the modern amenities, communications, and health services now available through the wealth due to its fabulous oil-development.

The population of the republic is about 6,500,000, a figure which represents a more-than-doubling of the numbers since the census of 1930. Of these, perhaps 1,000,000 are Kurds and Kurdish-speaking (p. 119), all of strong Sunni faith except minor (and not numerous) heretical communities. The Kurds, except a handful of town-dwelling households, are all to be found in the mountain and foothill zones. The Yazidis of Jabal Sinjar and the Mosul plain (p. 119) may number 40,000. The Turkomans (p. 115) of the north-east (the districts of Kifri-Kirkuk-Arbil) may number between 100,000 and 150,000. Other minorities are those of the Persians, a few thousand in all with their main concentration in the Shi'i holy cities: the Lurs (p. 120), a few hundred in the villages near the east and south-east frontiers, and in Baghdad: and the tiny Mandaean or Sabaean community (p. 107) on the south-'Iraqi river-banks. The once wealthy and numerous Jewish community, with its massive concentration in Baghdad, is there no more (p. 109); perhaps 10,000 or less remain. The Christian sects (p. 105 ff) are still a considerable element in the larger 'Iraqi cities, notably Baghdad, Basra, Mosul and Kirkuk, and provide admirable men of business, cultivators and craftsmen. There is no reliable guide to the numbers of each separate Christian community; in aggregate they may number 200,000. They include the different varieties of Uniate Catholics, and, among non-Catholics, the Greek Orthodox, Armenian, Assyrian (Nestorian) and Jacobite communities. The main body of 'Iraqi Muslim Arabs, some 5,000,000 in number between town and tribe, upland and delta, desert and date-garden, are probably about 55 to 60 per cent of the Shiʻi faith, the remainder Sunni. The post-revolutionary Constitution of the republic proclaims Islam to be its official religion.

The country is for administrative purposes divided into fourteen provinces (*liwas*), each named from its headquarter town. The provinces, which are mainly but not strictly those of the Turkish régime, are subdivided on normal lines. The fourteen do not include three further units into which the western desert area is divided, for police and tribal control purposes. Baghdad, the capital, with a population of some 800,000, is by far the greatest city, followed by Mosul and Basrah, with some 180,000 and 325,000 respectively; in the next grade of size come Kirkuk, Hilla, Najf, Karbala, ʻAmara, Arbil and Sulaimaniya, ranging between 35,000 and 50,000, followed by a score of lesser but largely modernized and flourishing towns. The standard of life, high or moderate among the *élite* and the upper-middle class, and self-respecting, with fair comfort, in artisan and the lower clerical circles, is low to the point of bare existence among the shanty-town or slum city-dwellers, and the less favoured of the rural villagers.

Possessor of extensive and potentially fertile lands and the water of its two great rivers, ʻIraq has an obvious—and historically verified —agricultural potential, at present in the way of increasing realization. Apart from this, has it fair material assets? Of its oil-resources, by far the greatest economic blessing and revenue-giver, more will be said (p. 255). Other minerals are unusually scanty; apart from quartz and dolomite, of which there are indications, and minor deposits of salt, gypsum, bituminous coal, and sulphur, there is little or nothing to support the economy and provide work. It is difficult to be optimistic about the further mineral deposits which recent geological research is said to have revealed; chromite, iron ore, copper, lead and zinc are claimed, but no projects for working these appear to be in hand. Forests of a scrubby, little-productive type exist in the mountains of the north, to an alleged total area of some 8,000 square miles, and scientific planting, both for timber and for soil-preservation, is proceeding. The timber now produced, mainly from the Kurdish valleys, is of walnut, plane and poplar; the oaks are stunted and of low value. Certain natural products afford interesting items of export —gum tragacanth, liquorice-root, gallnuts, and reeds for mat-making. Fishing is practised in all the rivers, with a useful but moderate rate of catch, all locally consumed without satisfying the demand; sea fishing is almost negligible. Stock-raising, traditional in its different forms, whether in the delta, the steppe, or the Kurdish mountains, has a major place in 'Iraq's economy both domestic and governmental. The animals concerned are, as elsewhere in the Middle East, sheep, goats and donkeys everywhere, cattle by the rivers and wherever pasture is adequate, buffaloes if water is plentiful, camels in the desert, mules mainly in the mountains. The export of live animals and animal products (wool, hair, casings, hides and skins) is on a considerable scale, and could be increased by improvement of breeds, processing and marketing. Existing types are of relatively low value except for meat and for draught purposes; the standard of husbandry is primitive, and diseases are widespread. Measures are in hand, however, to remedy these defects. The Arab horse, for which Basra was for centuries the trading outlet, is now in little commercial demand.

Though much remains to be done, 'Iraq has already developed an adequate system of communications. The railways are all state-owned. The line from the port of Basra to Baghdad, now metre-gauge, is in process of conversion, with Russian aid, to standard-gauge. From Baghdad a standard-gauge line runs on the Tigris west bank to Mosul, and beyond to the Syrian frontier. (It incorporates the original German-built Baghdad-Samarra section, built in 1911–1912.) A metre-gauge line crosses the Tigris at Baghdad and runs north-east to Khanaqin, Kirkuk and its oil-fields, and a terminus at Arbil. Oil pipelines run in and between oil-fields and refineries both in northern and southern 'Iraq, and on an imposing scale to the Mediterranean from Kirkuk. The road system of the country has always been embarrassed by the lack of stone in the centre and south, a deficiency now in part redressed by abundant bitumen for surfacing. Reliable roads now link all main centres, and passable fair-weather tracks run everywhere. Jordan, Syria and Turkey are all connected by road, and the two latter by rail also. There is road communication with Teheran, and with Medina by way of the central Sa'udi oases. Important road works and many new bridges have been incorporated in the development plans elaborated since oil revenues became plentiful, as they now are; further main routes of high standard are under construction. The sole seaport, Basra, is subject to the limitations imposed by its single approach (the Shatt al-'Arab) on the possible density of vessels using it, and on the draught of these by the maximum river-depth; but, within its limits, it is a well-equipped modern port. Its facilities are used by regular cargo and passenger lines of many nations. Oil export is not from Basra but from Fao and from the new mid-sea loading-base in the Gulf, 20 miles off-shore. Aviation needs are served by the airports of Baghdad and Basra, which are in constant use by 'Iraqi and foreign lines of all nationalities. Lesser but reliable landing-grounds are maintained elsewhere.

The 'Iraqi currency is based on the Dinar, equivalent to £1, and is controlled by its own Central Bank. The use of local and ex-Turkish weights and measures is still predominant within the country, for weight, length and area; but these will gradually yield to the metric system.

2. *The Lebanon*

Lebanese territory consists of a block of land approximating to 4,000 square miles in extent, roughly quadrilateral in shape but tapering in breadth from north to south. It is bounded on the west by the Mediterranean Sea with some 145 miles of coastline, on the north and east by Syria, on the south and south-east by Israel. The country contains a narrow coastal strip, flat or sloping; the high mountain range of the Lebanon, decreasing southward in height and wildness: the inter-montane plain of the Beka'a (Biqa') in which the al-'Asi river (Orontes), flowing northwards into Syria, has its rise, and the Litani (Leontes) flowing southwards and finally westwards into the Mediterranean: and the foothills and westward face of the Anti-Lebanon range, continued southward as that of Hermon. The highest peaks in Lebanon exceed 9,000 feet; the average altitude for the whole country is above 3,000 feet.

The territory, small as it is, is of great and varied beauty, with its Mediterranean aspect and string of picturesque (and extremely ancient) seaports, the wild mountain and valley scenery in its parallel ranges, and the fertile farmlands and gardens of the Biqa'. There is a relatively high rainfall and, in consequence, plentiful though capriciously located springs, often at high altitudes. The climate varies according to elevation and distance from the sea, from hot or temperate, humid, frostless conditions near the sea, to snow-clad mountain scenes a few miles inland, and hot summers with cold winters in the elevated but enclosed Biqa'. Rainfall diminishes fast as one proceeds inland, from 40 to 50 inches a year by the sea to 15 inches immediately west of the Anti-Lebanon. All rain falls between October and April.

The Lebanese population is of the order of 1,500,000, of whom slightly over half are Christian, the rest Sunni (290,000) or Shi'i (255,000) Muslims, with 90,000 Druzes and 6,000 Jews. The Christian populations (pp. 104–5) consist of about 425,000 Maronite, 155,000 Greek Orthodox, 70,000 Armenian, 110,000 Uniate and Latin Catholics, 14,000 Protestants. In race they reveal an immensely complicated mixture of many original, immigrant and neighbouring peoples. (This applies equally to the 100,000 'Palestine refugees' still living, in their hopeless exile, in the Lebanon (p. 137 f).) Almost all are Arabic-speaking (the official language), though the Armenians often retain, *inter se*, their own language, some of the Christian liturgies are Syriac or Greek, and French and English are generally understood in the towns; these, especially French, are habitually spoken by educated Muslims and Christians.

The Lebanese, to whom in spite of their diversity a 'national character' can with caution be attributed, seem paradoxically to combine toughness with gentleness, astuteness with naïvety, hard work with a Mediterranean reposefulness. They are able, progressive, emotional, articulate. With little surviving tribalism, of which confessional groupings here take the place, they exhibit strong local and community loyalties, which lead to anything between sporting competition and civil war. Outside the towns the Lebanese are village-dwellers and agriculturists, and attain a standard of life superior to that of much of southern Europe, aided not a little by remittances from tens of thousands of *émigrés* in the U.S.A. and elsewhere, who contribute a characteristic and materially advantageous feature to their society. The same phenomenon, combined with relatively advanced educational standards, many tourists, much foreign business, and the status of the Middle East's leading entrepôt and transit-station, gives the Lebanese cities their unusually cosmopolitan air.

The natural resources of the territory are scanty, yet the mixed ingredients upon which it lives produce, in effect, a greater economic stability than could be expected. Of its agriculture and industry, something will be said elsewhere (p. 241 f). Stock-raising, a feature of which is the seasonal migration between higher and lower pastures, is necessarily on an exiguous scale, though it produces dairy produce of high quality. Fishing makes a modest contribution to commerce and food supply. The area of forested land is small, but now carefully administered—in contrast to centuries of neglect; a sadly humble remnant of the famous cedars of Lebanon is to be seen. Minerals are of little importance; some lignite exists, traces of iron, a negligible

deposit of bitumen, salt derived from sea-water—and no oil. Important crude-oil pipelines, from 'Iraq and Sa'udi Arabia, enter and cross
Lebanese territory to the oil-loading ports of Tripoli and Sidon
respectively. More important than these is the country's tourist
traffic, persuasively induced and aided by the charm and interest of
the cities, mountains and ancient sites; and, transcending this,
Lebanon relies above all on its profits from the many commercial,
financial and social services which its geographical position, as a main
gateway to Western Asia, enables it to render, and which it handles
with great efficiency.

The country is divided into six provinces. The principal cities, in
which more than one-third of the population lives, are the capital,
Beirut (population 500,000), Tarablus (Tripoli, population 100,000),
Zahla (Zahlé, 33,000), Saida (Sidon, 22,000), Sur (Tyre, 12,000).
Beirut, beautifully situated between sea and mountain, is a city of
striking contrasts, between ancient East and modern West, with all
the phenomena of both. Its cultural and political life is as flourishing
as its commercial, and its politics, rooted in confessionalism and the
urge towards, or away from, Arab nationalism, are perpetually
mouvementés.

The communications of the territory are adequate. The main roads
are well engineered and maintained; one follows the coast throughout
its length, two more run inland from Beirut and Tripoli across the
mountains and into Syria, another forms an inland or inter-montane
trunk-road. Secondary and local roads give access to all villages, with
a multitude of 'buses and long-range hired cars. The railways are
(since 1959) both state-owned: the narrow-gauge line, very slow and
used for goods only, runs from Beirut across the Biqa' to Damascus
to connect there with the Hijaz Railway, and nearly 100 miles of
narrow-gauge track is also in use around the capital. The broad-
gauge line runs by the coast from the Israel frontier to Tripoli and
thence inland to Homs in Syria and beyond to 'Iraq and Turkey;
another broad-gauge line also connects Rayak in the Biqa' with
Homs. All the railways lose money; most goods and passengers travel
by road. Air services are highly developed. Based on the new Beirut
arport are four Lebanese airlines, and calls are made by large
numbers of foreign aircraft; the city vies, therefore, with Cairo as a
main international and inter-continental air junction and staging-post.
As a seaport, it is well equipped, extremely busy, and visited by
steamers of a dozen countries, for whom a score of agencies, nearly
all Lebanese, maintain offices. Tripoli and Saida have a limited

traffic, though both are, as we have seen, important oil-export outlets; the other seaside towns—Tyre, Jubail, Batrun—do little business. There are, it is needless to insist, no communications of any
sort between the Lebanon and Israel.

The currency of the republic is the Lebanese pound, officially
£Leb. 6·13 to the £ sterling, but on the free market anything from
£Leb. 8·5 to 9·5. The metric system of weights and measures is in
use, not without survivals of Turkish or earlier traditional measures.

3. *Syria*

The Syrian Republic occupies a territory of 72,000 square miles,
with a population of close to 5,000,000 souls. Its extreme north–south
and west–east measurements each slightly exceed 300 miles; its
Mediterranean coastline is rather over 100 miles in length. Its north-
western and northern neighbour is Turkey, throughout a great length
of open frontier; on the east is 'Iraq, separated by a purely arbitrary,
but diplomatically agreed, line across the Syrian Desert. To the south
is Jordan, across the Yarmuk river: to the extreme south-east Israel,
across Jordan and its lakes, with a common frontier of some 35 miles:
and to the west the Lebanese Republic, beyond Anti-Lebanon.

By far the greatest part of Syrian territory consists of open, flat or
undulating steppe-country, with considerable stretches of true desert
on both sides of the Euphrates and its left-bank tributaries, the
Balikh and the Khabur; the triangle between the great river and the
Turkish and 'Iraqi frontiers is known as the Jazira. Westward of the
steppe, which is the home of one-fifth of the Syrian population, lie
the more populous and geographically broken parts of the country.
These, from west to east, include the narrow, fertile coastal strip,
varying from 20 miles to a few yards in width: the mountainous
areas, oriented north–south and consisting of the Ansariya range along
the coast, and south of this and farther inland the Anti-Lebanon or
Hermon ranges, with the Jabal Druze massif in the extreme south.
Between and flanking these mountains are valleys and inter-montane
plains, traversed by the al-'Asi (Orontes) river and its marshes. The
eastern area of the mountain and hilly zone is of high—or, towards the
north, lower—plateaux, dipping farther eastward into the steppe.
Here are situated the fertile and thickly inhabited regions of the
Hauran, the great Damascus oasis with its rivers 'Abana and Pharpar'
and its wonderful gardens, the ancient but less welcoming cities of
Homs and Hama, and the most populous, perhaps the most ancient,

city of them all, Aleppo with its citadel. Syrian territory is therefore extremely varied, much of it invigorating and scenically attractive, and, except for the truly desertic areas and the lava-strewn border-lands of the Kingdom of Jordan, it is for the most part capable of development by irrigation—and some of it currently in process thereof. The country is rich in archaeological remains of all periods.

The climate varies from region to region. The eastern and southern zones are almost rainless, the north has a deposit normally sufficient to support light vegetation and crops, the west enjoys up to 40 inches of rain in the mountains, with less but adequate amounts in the plains, valleys and coast. The highest peaks, notably Hermon, are snow-covered for most of the year. Temperatures and humidity vary, as would be expected, as between the coast, the mountain zone and the plains. In the latter, summer and winter temperatures are both extreme, but humidity is slight.

The groups within the total population are those of Sunni Muslims (2,800,000), Isma'ili and other Shi'is (54,000), and the heretical sects of the Druzes (120,000) and the Nusairis or 'Alawis (410,000). Among nearly 500,000 Christians there are included Greek Orthodox (175,000), Armenian Gregorians (112,000), Syrian Orthodox (53,000), Nestorians or Assyrians (12,000), Protestants (15,000) and Latin and Uniate Catholics, including Maronites (130,000). About 20,000 Jews, it is estimated, remain in Syria. There are some 3,000 Yazidis. The language of Syria is officially, and for 90 per cent of the population actually, Arabic; Kurdish communities (included in Sunni Muslims above) speak Kurdish or are bilingual, the Assyrians speak their own Syriac, the Armenians mostly, among themselves, Armenian (and some Turkish), the Circassians and Yazidis their own dialects. French is familiar to the urban upper and middle classes, English less but increasingly. About 90,000 refugees from Arab Palestine have lived in camps on Syrian territory since 1948.

The territory is divided for administrative purposes into eleven provinces. The largest towns are Damascus (the capital) and Aleppo, both with a little less than 500,000 inhabitants, Homs and Hama both with between 150,000 and 200,000, Dair al-Zaur (75,000) and Lataqiya (62,000). Other considerable towns are Suwaida, Tartus, Banyas, Qamishliya, Hasaja, abu Kamal, Maskana, Raqqa and Idlib. Among the population outside the towns the characteristic forms of present-day Arab society are all represented: by the true nomads (badu) of the mid-desert camel-breeding tribes, who include some of the most famous; by the sheep-owning, partly cultivating tribes

of central-western Syria; by the wholly agricultural communities of
the open country and the river-banks, living in widely-spaced villages,
exposed to all the hazards and burdens of local tenant agriculture,
and tribal only in a diminished sense; and by the non-tribal villagers,
some in the mountain zone, some in newly-settled lands in the north-
eastern steppe-country of the Jazira. The rural standard of life is
generally low or very low, but here too there are hopeful signs. The
agricultural peasantry, who form by far the largest element in the
population, and contribute fully half of the national income, are, for
all their intelligence, so deeply conservative that the improvement of
their lot is likely to be a slow process. In the cities, the professional,
land-owning and mercantile classes are highly educated and sophisticated, and are playing a great part in developing the country in spite
of its poverty in national resources. Syrian politics, on the other hand,
appear to show many of the less favourable features of the Middle
Eastern political scene—disunity, excessive individualism, impatience, disorder. These tendencies, and their corollary that the
Syrians by their public character and attitudes must offer one of the
world's most difficult problems of civil government, are likely to
postpone the time when the country's economics, at present insecure
and needing fruitful infusions of capital and of confidence, can be
uplifted and stabilized.

The natural resources of Syria, other than the land and water which
make extensive agriculture possible, are in fact jejune. The wide
steppe-country lends itself to camel-breeding, and the less arid
inlying areas to the animal husbandry of sheep, goats and cattle.
These, in the aggregate, produce a number of the necessities of life
and of the economy; wool and hair, and live animals, are regular
exports. The improvement of breeds and products is a constant
care of the government. Forests in Syria are limited in modern times
to the Lataqiya hinterland and the Jabal Druze, and are here rather
picturesque than productive; proper maintenance and protection present problems not yet solved. Fishing, in fresh- or sea-water, is
practised on a minimal scale. The mineral wealth of the country, as so
far discovered, is of the humblest. Oil (p. 253) has been discovered in
quantities of no outstanding interest by Middle Eastern standards. A
little lignite but no coal has been located, one interesting asphalt
deposit behind Lataqiya is being exploited, another in mid-desert is
in view. There have been indications, but no more, of iron ore,
chromite, and lead; otherwise, no territory could have less to show in
mineral resources. Parts of Syria are traversed by oil pipelines from

Sa'udi and 'Iraqi sources; these pass on into Lebanon, except for one from 'Iraq which leads to the terminal and loading-point at Banyas, constructed in 1952.

A fairly adequate road-system, only in part all-weather, links the inhabited areas of the country, and extends into all neighbouring territories except Israel. The (British) Nairn Transport Co. has since 1923 operated a trans-desert motor-coach service between Damascus and Baghdad. The railways, designed long ago for quite different conditions, do not satisfactorily serve the present economy. One section of the old Baghdad Railway emerges from, later to re-enter, Turkey in the extreme north: the other is a stretch of the same Baghdad Railway, as extended in the 1930's, running from Qamishliya to the 'Iraqi frontier at Tell Kochek. Neither this nor indeed the rest of the system is a commercial asset to Syria. The Damascus–Homs–Aleppo line (or D.H.P.), which in its course enters and later again leaves Lebanese territory, and affords a further connection from Homs to the Lebanese frontier at Tell Kalakh, carries a useful goods traffic but few passengers. These lines together form the Syrian State Railways. The narrow-gauge railway running south from Damascus—the old Hijaz Railway of 1908—links the capital with the Jabal Druze area, and beyond Dar'a with Jordan, but is of little economic value. A railway to link Lataqiya with Homs and thereby with the Euphrates and the trans-Euphrates area (Dair al-Zaur, Hasaja, Qamishliya) has been proposed but not so far undertaken. The hinterland communications of the newly constructed port of Lataqiya—the sole important general-purpose Syrian port, since the loss of Alexandretta to Turkey in 1939 (p. 77)—thus remain poor. In spite of this, it is intended for nationalistic reasons that Lataqiya shall in due course take most of the Syrian share of Beirut's transit traffic. Tartus is a small fishing port, Banyas an important oil-loading terminal. There are a number of reasonably equipped landing-grounds for aircraft in the territory, with Damascus offering the best facilities and enjoying by far the most traffic. It is used by at least one locally-constituted airline, by those of nine more originating in neighbouring countries, and by nearly as many European and American.

The metric system of weights and measure is officially in force in all areas, though in fact other and older standards are still in common use. The currency is that of the Syrian pound (£Syr) quoted officially at 6·19 to the £, unofficially at rates between 8·00 and 10·00.

4. *Jordan*

The Hashimite Jordanian Kingdom (or Kingdom of Jordan), as distinct from the (mandated) Amirate of Transjordan, came into existence, with its changed name and status, in 1947. Its initial area was about 34,500 square miles, but in 1950 a further 2,200 square miles was added by the incorporation of the central-eastern portion of the territory of ex-mandated Palestine; that is, all of Palestine (except the Gaza strip) not included in Israel. Its present dimension is therefore 36,700 square miles. The territory is bounded on the west by Israel (a capricious haphazard frontier 350 miles in length), on the south and south-west by Sa'udi Arabia (but with a dozen miles of sea frontage on the Gulf of 'Aqaba), on the east by 'Iraq, and on the north by Syria. It has no common frontier with Egypt.

The territory west of Jordan, which contains a fair proportion of the ancient Hebrew principalities of Israel and Judah, represents a part of Palestine in which the purely Arab character had not been threatened by Zionist colonization. Roughly quadrilateral in shape, but with a deep wedge driven into its western flank to secure Israeli access to Jerusalem, the territory runs, north to south, from the neighbourhood of Janin to (and beyond) that of Hebron. It contains the Arab towns of Nablus, Tulkaram, Ramallah, Jericho (Ariha), Bethlehem (Bait Laham), and Hebron (al-Khalil), as well as the walled city of Jerusalem and most of its northern and eastern suburbs, with nearly all the holy places of the three faiths. This is a pleasant, temperate region of hills, with olive groves, fruit gardens and terraced as well as open-field cultivation. The Jordan Valley, deeply sunk between its lines of hills rising on either side, lies within Jordan territory to the extent of some 50 miles as the crow flies, far more as the river winds. The riverain plain, extremely fertile, is in places 12 miles wide and is all irrigable; it ends, on the south, where the river pours its waters into the bitter saltness of the Dead Sea, 1,290 feet below sea level—the lowest place in the world. The east bank of the Dead Sea, and south of that the median line of the broad, barren Wadi 'Araba, become the frontier with Israel as far as the Gulf of 'Aqaba.

East of the valley lies a broad upland, rainfed belt of which the favourable, cultivable section lies to the west of the Hijaz Railway. The belt is some 30 miles wide on its northern face at the Syrian border, which is formed by the Yarmuk river, and is narrower and less fertile, to the point of almost total aridity, as it falls southward

to the latitude of Ma'an and beyond. South again of this, and everywhere east of the railway, Jordan is a desert country, too dry for
cultivation, largely lava-strewn, and humanly valueless except for the
scanty, almost invisible camel-pastures of the desert tribesmen. The
cultivable area contains the towns or major villages of Irbid, Mafraq,
Jarash (with the famous ruins), Zarqa, 'Amman the capital, and
al-Salt.

The ex-Palestinian minority west of Jordan is typical of the
Arabized amalgam of peoples familiar in every country of the
Levant—'Arabs' in every valid test as well as in their own opinion,
and the world's acceptance, for fourteen centuries. East of Jordan the
mixed relics of earlier peoples are probably scantier, the purer stocks
of Arabia a majority; but the difference may in fact be slight. Tribalism, widespread in the old Transjordan, is little represented west of
the river; there, and in the uplands from Irbid to 'Amman, the
population are village-dwelling cultivators, devoted to the soil and to
their homes. The total population of Jordan is, according to the 1961
census, 1,725,000. More than half live west of the valley, including
about 500,000 refugees from Israeli territory; about 850,000, including 130,000 refugees, are in Transjordan. The total of refugees in
Jordan is, therefore, some 630,000, a figure which has fluctuated year
by year between 465,000 and its present level according to the
number of births, deaths or departures, or the vagaries of the counting
officials. The Jordanians (excluding the refugees) are believed to
consist of 75,000 to 70,000 nomads or semi-nomads, nearly 500,000
townsmen (including 250,000 in 'Amman, and populations exceeding
65,000 in Bethlehem and Jericho), and 450,000 cultivating villagers.
Against a great majority of Sunni Muslims there is a far from
negligible minority of Christians, perhaps 30,000 among the refugees
and 70,000 among original Jordanians. The proportion of Greek
Orthodox is probably highest, followed by Catholic Uniates and
Armenians. The Cherkes and Chechen settlements are mentioned
elsewhere (p. 102); they are not numerically important.

Jordan has no mountains other than those, reaching a maximum
height of 5,000 feet, which form the eastern escarpment over-
looking the river. There are no considerable rivers other than
Jordan, and no lakes except its share of the Dead Sea. The climate
of the territory is one of great heat, whether in the Jordan Valley
or on the plateau to the east; in the latter, the winter can be severe,
with hard frosts and snowfalls. Rainfall is in most years adequate
to cultivation without irrigation on the high land both sides of

Jordan, ranging from 15 to 25 inches a year; but east of the Hijaz Railway it falls to 8 inches or less, and crop-growing cannot be attempted.

Jordan is a poor country, viable within its present boundaries only on the humblest standard of life, and quite unable (unless with generous funds from outside) to afford the military, diplomatic and social-service *train de vie* which Middle Eastern states consider essential to their self-respect. It lives, therefore, and has always lived, largely on subsidies from its foreign friends, Great Britain and the U.S.A. Its natural resources are scanty. The greatest part of the country, being arid steppe-desert, is devoted to a sparse and penurious animal husbandry maintained, as their sole means of existence, by the nomad tribes; this keeps them alive, supplies some local needs of the sedentary folk, but leads to the export of only humble quantities of wool, hides and skins, and animal fats. Of agriculture in Jordan, something will be said elsewhere (p. 241 f), and the same is true of its industries (p. 249 f). No oil has been discovered. There are limited areas of forest, of some potential importance, in the north ('Ajlun district) and in the south (near Ma'an). These are now officially maintained, but irreparable damage was done to them in the period 1908–1918 by the Turks, seeking fuel for their Hijaz Railway. For a fishing industry, the Gulf of 'Aqaba offers the only possible location, and fish abound. Mineral wealth so far discovered is small, in spite of some hopeful indications. The salts of the Dead Sea, potash and bromine, are by far the most important source, and are under limited exploitation; further potash deposits have been found at Rusaifa near 'Amman. The export of the resulting chemical products is a considerable item. In the Wadi Hasa, south of 'Amman, potash, gypsum and manganese ore have been found, and are in early stages of development.

Great improvements have been made in late years, through funds allotted by United Nations, the U.S.A., and Great Britain, to the road system of the country. Excellent metalled roads now connect the capital to all main centres, including the port of 'Aqaba, the towns of central and northern Jordan, and Jerusalem. Passable un-metalled roads serve outlying areas in the agricultural districts, on both banks of Jordan. Bus, lorry and car traffic is light but adequate to needs. The Hijaz Railway runs from the Syrian frontier near Dar'a in the north to a point south of Ma'an, but not yet to 'Aqaba; it cannot compete successfully with lorry transport. The port of 'Aqaba itself has been improved beyond recognition, mainly by

British help, and its throughput has increased twelvefold between 1952 and 1959. The new 'Aqaba–'Amman highway, equally a British gift, was opened late in 1961. These two improvements jointly ended Jordanian dependence on a trans-Syrian route of entry. Air traffic, including that of Jordan Airways, uses the airports of 'Amman and Jerusalem, where a number of European, American and Middle Eastern lines call regularly. The territory is crossed by two oil pipeline systems: that of the 'Iraq Petroleum Company which up to 1948 carried oil from northern 'Iraq to Haifa (and has been unused and derelict since that date), and that, still operating, of the Trans-Arabian Pipeline Co. (Tapline) taking Sa'udi crude to Sidon in the Lebanon.

The currency of Jordan is the Jordan dinar, equivalent to £1 sterling. Where local or Turkish weights and measures have been outgrown, and for all international purposes, the metric system is used.

Some readers of this book may expect a fuller account than has been given above of the ex-Palestinian 'Arab Refugees' whose greatest concentration is in Jordan territory, and who represent so notorious a tragedy and problem in Middle Eastern society. To the approximate 600,000 of these now living in Jordan must be added about 200,000 in the Egyptian-administered 'Gaza strip', 90,000 in Syria, and over 100,000 in the Lebanon. These tragically unfortunate people left their homes in Palestine during the turmoil of threats, invasion and violence which followed the declaration of the State of Israel. Their flight was due partly to simple and well-based terror of destruction of their homes and families: partly to orders from their leaders, who wanted them elsewhere during the foreseen period of fighting, and who assured them, with an excessive optimism, of an early return: and partly to panic inspired by acts of outrageous brutality by certain Jewish militant elements, of which the wholesale massacre of the Dair Yasin villagers is the best remembered example. Once out of their homes, they have not (with a small number of exceptions) been allowed to return, in spite of a specific resolution of the UN General Assembly in that sense. Their houses, gardens and lands have been Israeli-occupied from that day, separated from their owners by a *de facto* frontier-line which represents the limits of the land held, on a given day of 1948, by the Israeli forces—a line, therefore, not defensible on any reasonable or humane basis, and one which cuts villages in half or separates them from their own lands. Amendment of this line in Arab favour has always been, and is still, refused; and meanwhile the refugees have been to only a limited extent absorbed in adjacent Arab countries. Many of those who had money or a profession, or a craftsman's skill or civil service experience, have been able to establish themselves in one country or another (including the oil-fields of the Persian Gulf) and to make new lives. Thousands (perhaps up to 100,000) of these categories have made permanent-seeming homes in Jordan itself—whence, in large part, the rapid expansion of its urban life, and a valuable contribution to the kingdom on many levels. Since all refugees in Jordan became, by King 'Abdullah's decree, Jordanian citizens, thus in a day doubling and greatly diversifying the population of the kingdom, the scale of the resulting social revolution in the territory is evident, with political effects at least equal; the incomers included dozens of *ministrables* and their educated followers, and the acquired territory in West Jordan contained such important political centres of Arab nationalism as Nablus and Jerusalem.

A very few of the refugees have been helped by work on agricultural projects within Jordan, notably in the Valley. But the majority are, fourteen years after their uprooting and flight, still without permanent homes or prospects, still a burden to themselves and to local society—and to the world at large which, through United Nations (UNRWA) funds, has played the main part in keeping them alive. Of those in Jordan, up to two-thirds have found some sort of living-quarters in villages or towns, but remain UNRWA-supported. UNRWA itself, the 'United Nations Relief and Works Agency for Palestinian Refugees in the Near East' was established by UN General Assembly in December 1949, and is supported by governmental and private subscriptions; its local headquarters is in Beirut. The rest, with practically all of those in the Gaza strip, and many of those in Lebanon and Syria, live permanently in camps without serious occupation and without hope, in a state of frustration and bitterness which, with opportunity, could be gravely dangerous. A proportion of the younger and more capable men have found employment; a few work in the camps themselves, but the percentage today of the aged and economically useless, and (thanks to the abnormal birthrate) of the young or very young, is estimated as up to 80 per cent; most have ceased to seek work; and the authorities of the host countries, while far from indifferent to their plight, tend on the human plane to regard them with a certain weary distaste, and, on the political, to dismiss major projects for resettling them outside Palestine as a politically and emotionally inadmissible confession that Israel is there to stay and that their own homes are lost forever. The problem of the refugees is, therefore, part of the central politico-social problem created by the establishment of a completely alien and strongly nationalistic Israel in Arab territory. With a not unnatural intransigence on both sides, and with implacable hostility to Israel an essential (and sometimes a seemingly competitive) feature, in Arab eyes, of one's status as a true patriot, the problem appears as far as ever from solution. It could be settled, one must suppose, only by a radically altered outlook on both sides: a genuine willingness, at long last, to compromise: a partial redrawing of frontiers, a partial re-admission of refugees to their own homes: more intensive agricultural development in Jordan itself (especially by Jordan Valley irrigation), and massive compensation, assessed by an international commission, for the losses of the displaced. But of even the first bilateral *démarches*, by authorized spokesmen, towards such a settlement, or any other, there is in late 1962 no convincing sign.

5. *Egypt (United Arab Republic)*

Egypt, which even after September 1961 has continued at its own wish to be known as the United Arab Republic, occupies a territory in many ways remarkable. Its geography is admittedly unique; its recorded history, as we have already seen, is the most extended of any, with but one possible rival; its surviving ancient remains in tombs, pyramids and monuments are the wonder of the world. Its strategic situation as a junction and through-way for world traffic is of unequalled significance. Its political and social position today among the Middle Eastern countries is one, not indeed of admitted primacy, but at least of claimed and partly accepted predominance in size of population, scale of commercial and industrial operations, social and cultural evolution, progress in education and the professions. These considerations, together with the social charm of so many rural and urban Egyptians at every level from *fallah* to Minister, make all the more regrettable both the undoubtedly grave economic situation in which the country finds itself, and, in another field, Egypt's seemingly wilful—and surely unnecessary—alienation of its Arab and other friends by the extravagances of its press, broadcasting and oratorical polemics.

As a habitable area the country is (as Herodotus remembered) 'the gift of the river Nile', claimed as greatest of all rivers by those sensible to its spell, and richest in history and legend; without the

Nile the whole of Egypt would be a mere uninhabited Saharan waste. Lower Egypt consists of all the country from Cairo (inclusive) north-wards to and with the Delta; the latter, 8,500 square miles in area, contains the various branches of the Nile-Damietta (Damyat), Rosetta (Rashid) and the rest: the flattened mass of fertile silt brought down by the river over many thousands of years: a dozen populous cities, hundreds of villages, and a teeming rural population. Between them and the open Mediterranean lie four shallow, partly silt-filled lakes, and east and west of the whole river and delta system stretch broad uninhabitable deserts of utter aridity. Upper Egypt is the river-side plain, from 2 to 15 miles broad, reaching from the Sudan frontier at Wadi Halfa to near Cairo. This is all cultivated to the limits of its waterable acreage, and is flanked on either side by rainless desert from the Red Sea to the Libyan border. The area of the whole country is some 385,000 square miles, of which 96 per cent is total desert, leaving but 15,000 square miles at most of cultivable land. The extreme length of Egypt is 675 miles, its greatest breadth 770. Its frontiers, drawn across sheer desert, are on the west with Libya, on the south the Sudan, on the north-east Israel; northern and eastern boundaries are provided by the Mediterranean and the Red Sea. No geography could be less complicated. The Sinai peninsula, separated from the rest of Egypt by the Suez Canal, can be reckoned as either Asian or African.

Otherwise than on Nile-side and in the Delta, the country is every-where uninhabited except by the scanty population of five oases (Faiyum, the most important, and Kharga, Dakhla, Farafra and Siwa), all in desert west of the river: by the towns and settlements along the course of the Suez Canal, and on the Mediterranean coast. The whole of these together contain little more than 5 per cent of the Egyptian population.

The First Cataract (first as we proceed up-stream), due to a partial blockage of the river-bed by hard rock, occurs near 'Aswan (Assouan) in upper Egypt and is the site of the famous (and earliest) Dam. (The other four Nile cataracts lie in the Sudan.) Between the Nile and the Red Sea is a belt of hilly or mountainous country, running parallel to the coast and in places reaching 7,000 feet. Elsewhere the Egyptian deserts are undulating rather than flat, and are varied locally by deep depressions of which the best known is that of Qattara in the northern-most quarter of the Western Desert. Sinai has a few coastal villages and a famous monastery, as well as the tragically over-populated 'Gaza strip' (pp. 134, 137). The largest cities of Lower Egypt are Cairo

EGYPT AND THE SUDAN

(2,500,000 to 3,000,000 inhabitants), Alexandria (1,500,000), Port Said (Sa'id, 240,000), Giza (250,000) Tanta (185,000), Mahallat al-Kubra (175,000), Inbaba (136,000), Suez (Suwais, 200,000), Mansura (150,000), Damanhur (125,000), Ismailia (Isma'iliya, 110,000), Zagazig (124,000); and in Upper Egypt, Asyut (Assiout 122,000), Faiyum (102,000), Minya (94,000), Bani Suef (Suwaif, 79,000), Sohag (62,000), 'Aswan (Assouan, 48,000), Qana (58,000), and a number more of some 50,000 or less inhabitants.

The territory is divided for administrative purposes into sixteen provinces, eight each in Upper and Lower Egypt; in addition to these are five special governorates (of Cairo, Alexandria, and the three Canal cities), and the five 'frontier districts', relatively scanty in population, of Red Sea, Sinai, Southern and Western Desert, and the Bahariya Oases.

The climate of the territory varies between narrow limits. Rainfall, almost non-existent in Upper Egypt, can amount to a maximum of 6 to 8 inches a year in the Delta and on the Mediterranean coast. Summer heat is everywhere severe, but least so on the Mediterranean, where the Alexandrian summers are reckoned tolerable. Sandstorms brought up by the south wind (the Khamsin) of early summer are a severe trial. Winter is everywhere delightful in its cool brightness. The annual rise of the Nile, without which Egypt could not survive, takes place from August to October; by December it has subsided, and in April is at its lowest.

The population of the country is well above the Middle Eastern average in respect of homogeneity. Not less than nine-tenths of the people are of traditional modern-Egyptian type, whose blood-mixture, except for minor upper-class nineteenth century Turkish additions, has long settled down to produce a prevailing physique: a type representing a thickened, more muscular, slightly darker Mediterranean. As a character, the Egyptian has on the whole been a popular figure in the world; an upper class of charm, high culture and wealth (though often with too restricted a social conscience) has pleased its foreign acquaintances; the professional and middle class, far more extensive than elsewhere in the Middle East, commends itself by its intelligence, courtesy, and capacity for progress; and the mass of the *fallahin* in Delta and Nile-side are known as laborious and patient, yet responsive and humorous. Only the lowest stratum of the urban proletariat shows itself at times to contain its full proportion, or more, of violence or delinquency. Among such European long-term residents in the country as were also sensitive observers, life among Egyptians has had little that was unpleasant, much that was delightful, to offer.

Of a total population of some 27,000,000, probably 25,000,000 are Sunni Muslims of the Hanafi and Shafi'i sects, and these, in the towns, include many adherents of one or other of the still vigorous Sufi fraternities (p. 92). Islam is, under the post-revolutionary constitution, the official religion of Egypt. Foreign communities, from among whom many individuals—Greeks, Italians, and other Europeans, and also Syrians and Lebanese—have in the past obtained Egyptian passports, have played a part in the country's affairs more than proportionate to their size, and have contributed largely in culture, finance, and commerce. This, since the modern upsurge of xenophobic nationalism, is much less clearly the case today; indeed, the numbers of such communities have of late been notably reduced by emigration or expulsion. The same is true not only of British (including Maltese and Cypriot) and French subjects, whose numbers in the Egyptian cities have fallen rapidly since 1956, but also of the long-resident Egyptian-Jewish community, now greatly diminished by movement to Israel. The position of the Armenians (including both Gregorians and Uniate Catholics) is, in the current political atmosphere, fairly but not wholly secure; of the other Middle Eastern Christian communities (Greek Orthodox and Greek Catholic, Syrian Orthodox and Syrian Catholic and Maronite) who are mainly of Syrian and Lebanese origin, substantially the same may be said. These are cultured, progressive, valuable members of society—but are imperfectly at their ease in the Cairo of 1962. The Copts (p. 106) are an Egyptian minority on a different footing; numbering perhaps 1,500,000, mainly peasants but also landowners and town-dwellers, these are authentic Egyptians with no other home or allegiance, and are differentiated from the Muslim majority only by their refusal, a 1,000 years ago, to change their monophysite Christianity for Islam— and differentiated also, in some measure, by the special and valuable gifts in commerce, the professions and administration peculiar to their community. The majority of Copts have kept their ancient faith, minorities have accepted Protestantism, others Catholicism, while conversions to Islam were, and perhaps are, not infrequent. The Copts have, as loyal Egyptians, played an active part in politics, usually on the side of nationalism, never in any non-Egyptian interest. Yet in the atmosphere today prevailing their Christianity and distinctness seem to militate against their acceptance by Muslim feeling as completely reliable compatriots. Coptic, as a language, is no longer spoken or written, but survives in their mixed Arabic-Coptic liturgy.

To the outside world it may appear that the main Egyptian effort of the time is being made in the field of foreign affairs, with the pressing of campaigns of threat or seduction, invective or persuasion, directed intermittently to Arab neighbours and the western powers; and indeed a restless, sometimes intemperate, yet usually intelligible foreign policy has been and is in process of development. Its objects have been those of Egyptian aggrandisement and prestige (in part, at least, with the purpose of increasing Egypt's own popular self-respect and dignity), pre-eminence in the Arab world if this prove possible, and the acquisition meanwhile, by a proclaimed neutrality, of maximum material aid in every form from both western and eastern sources. But in fact the thoughts and efforts of Egypt's ruling military clique and her more intelligent citizens are, and ought to be, still more anxiously concerned with her internal problems. The greatest of these is the assurance of her food supply, standard of living and economic stability in the face of a seemingly uncontrollable population increase which has almost trebled the body of the nation since this numbered 9,000,000 souls in 1897. The true object of policy would be to achieve the uplift everywhere of currently (and traditionally) low, or deplorable, living-standards among both rural and urban poor; and with it should go a massive increase of education, enlightenment and health, and the diminution of social inequality and injustice. These objectives are in fact being sought with much sincerity, though not always with patience nor the wisest of planning. The means by which, in the restless uneasy atmosphere of Cairo and its officer-ministers, these ends are being pursued include a major or indeed ruthless revision of the land-tenure system with strict limitation of privately-owned acreage, and of rents chargeable; they include trade agreements with all and sundry, a drive towards industrialization (with provision for profit-sharing and a ban on exaggerated salaries); they include a widening and tightening of state control and ownership, and a complex of social, technical and administrative steps taken to increase rural prosperity. Part of this is the planned completion, at the earliest date, of the giant High Dam at Aswan (p. 84), a project already well begun: and the establishment, for all to see, and using the confiscated wealth of the exiled Royal family, of an exemplary 'Liberation Province' devoted to showing what can be done, in Egypt now, with sufficient energy, capital and modern methods, to create a new type of rural life. Together with these objectives and methods, the administration of the Revolutionary Committee has in hand a rapid overhaul of, and much innovation in, the public services of education, medical establishments and village improvement. These and many other measures taken governmentally in the Egypt of today, amounting as they do to the adoption of a thorough-going socialist régime, do not and will not commend themselves to all—least of all to democrats (since personal liberty is largely sacrificed), or to the formerly privileged classes; some of the steps taken may well be misconceived, others ill-financed, others already a partial failure. But all show a genuine, almost a frantic, effort by the best leadership now available to deal with the appalling, yet visible and assessable, problems of this deceptively simple-looking territory. (The simple and effective expedient of birth-control, advocated by government authorities, is repugnant to the Egyptian masses.) Meanwhile, in all that pertains to social and economic organization a spirit of revolution, dating from 1952, still prevails in Cairo, activity throbs (sometimes painfully) in every field, aspiration towards social and material advance is limitless, and the voice of those (no negligible fraction) who detest the present methods and objectives is faint or drowned. On the subjects of Egyptian agriculture (including its all-important irrigation, and its famous cotton) and her industry, more will be said elsewhere (p. 243, 248 f); but it must be emphasized here how predominantly Egypt is still today (as it has been from all antiquity) an agricultural country in respect of its needs, its traditions and the livelihood of 75 per cent or more of its people, even while it is resolved more and more rapidly and widely to adopt modern industry as the prayed-for, perhaps the sole, solution of its problems.

Egypt is endowed, far less than its broad surface might indicate, with natural resources. Forests are unknown, fisheries make only a minor contribution to wealth or food, stock-breeding—in spite of current researches and pilot-schemes—must be impracticable on any important scale, mineral wealth is limited to very modest deposits of phosphate rock, gypsum and talc, manganese, iron ore, and lesser items. These are already under some limited exploitation, and are likely to be developed to maximum economic limits. Oil resources (p. 253), located mainly in Sinai, are useful and bring Egypt near to self-sufficiency. Sources of national livelihood more important than these are the unique Suez Canal, the extensive tourist industry based on the remains of antiquity and on climatic advantage, and the large-scale export of Egyptian teachers and technicians to other Arab countries—a resource of even greater political and social importance than financial. But, with all that Egypt's agriculture, its industries, and its every resource and ability can do for it, and with even the best of management and good fortune, it is still not clear how, short of miracles, this country—a paradise, perhaps, for a small or moderate population—is to support, and still less to elevate to living-standards far higher (as is desired) than the present, a population growing even now by 500,000 souls a year.

Flatness and aridity render the achievement of a communications system in Egypt perhaps less arduous than elsewhere. Roads, passable if often inferior, run everywhere. The railways, mainly but not exclusively state-owned, serve adequately the Nile Valley (including Kharga oasis) northward from 'Aswan, and the Delta, the Mediterranean coast, and the Canal Zone; some 2,700 miles of line, and a further 830 miles of light (agricultural) track are in use. Aviation is highly developed, Cairo competing with Beirut as the main Middle Eastern staging-post for inter-continental flight. All main (western) airlines regularly use Cairo; other airports in the country in daily use are those of Alexandria, Port Said, Matruh, 'Asyut, Luxor and 'Aswan. The state-owned United Arab Airlines covers the country as well as most of Europe and the Middle East. Many Egyptians are excellent pilots. A plan to multiply village landing-grounds is, late in 1962, in process of execution, in order to facilitate the spread of full social services to the villages. River-navigation (of which about 1,000 miles is on the Nile, the rest on its major branches and canals) is of great service. And the Canal stands alone as a highway of truly international status.

This unique waterway, which was authorized in 1854 by grant to de Lesseps from the Khedive Sa'id, begun in 1859 and opened in 1869, cost a mere £16,000,000; it would, *ceteris paribus*, cost ten times that sum today. It was for nearly a century administered by and for the Universal Suez Canal Company (an Egyptian-registered Corporation, with headquarters in Paris), until the abrupt nationalization of this by President Gamal 'Abdul Nasir in 1956, by an act whose legality some lawyers (and all Egyptians) have defended, others have attacked. Under Egyptian control, the administration (including pilotage) of the Canal appears to have been efficient; plans for its deepening, widening and improvement are progressively carried out, and this will continue. After all costs are paid, including the agreed instalments of compensation to the Canal Company, a modest income —but substantially greater than was received before 1956—accrues to the Egyptian Government: a dividend of which the true value is much increased by Egyptian gratification at her successful defiant take-over and subsequent administration of the Canal, and the status of owning and controlling so famous and remarkable a work of man. The Canal, 101 miles long (excluding approach channels each end) has a minimum width of 200 feet and a depth sufficient, since 1961, for the passage of vessels of 37-foot draught; these and other measurements are in due time to be increased. Improvements in traffic control are being introduced. A railway and a freshwater canal run beside the Canal throughout its length. The traffic, of which some 70 per cent is that of oil-tankers, continues to grow in terms of vessels and tonnage, and this must persist as long as world trade (and particularly the seaborne oil trade) increases, and as long as the immense saving of mileage by use of the Canal is a vital factor; a voyage, for example, from London to Bombay saves 4,500 miles by using the Canal (as against the Cape route), and one to the head of the Persian Gulf nearly 5,000. It seems that, with all allowance for the possibility of more and greater trans-desert pipelines, cheaper (because larger-tonnage) tanker-transport, and more and cheaper air-travel, the Canal can never lose its special and irreplaceable value; and nothing—not even the Nile itself, or the Pyramids—is more closely a part of the world's image of modern Egypt.

The Egyptian pound, £E, had the value of £1 0s. 6d. sterling until May 1962, and since then of £0 16s. 0d. It is divided into 100 piastres, or *qurush*. The metric system is in general, always in official, use; but as a measure of area the Egyptian *fiddan* (4,200 square metres, or 1·038 acres) still prevails. The *rotl* of 0·99 lb is widely met. Many other local weights and measures are found in agriculture and trade; the *ardab*, a measure of capacity (43½ gallons), is much used for the sale of grain and cotton seed.

6. *The Sudan*

The Anglo-Egyptian Sudan of 1899–1955 enjoyed always the interested goodwill of the outside world, and not least that of Great Britain who, with her purely formal Egyptian partner, bore the entire responsibility for the country's nurture and progress. Critics of colonialism, indeed, would do well to study the condition of this territory before the first date mentioned above, and at the second; a greater transformation for good, in terms of human happiness, can rarely have been witnessed in any country in so few years. Here, it seems, was the colonial system—never viewed by Britain in the Sudan otherwise than as a temporary expedient for rehabilitation—at its very best; and in fact the administration, in this the solitary case where Great Britain enjoyed continuous years of power in an Arab country with no 'local authorities' to collaborate with or conciliate, was the work of able and devoted men. The superior type of a great majority of Sudanis, the picturesque vastness of their country, the magic of the Nile, perhaps also the unforgotten drama of Gordon and Kitchener, have added to the attractive popular image of the country abroad.

The Sudan Republic, as it became in 1956, has an area of 970,000 square miles (more than sixteen times that of England and Wales), an extreme length of 1,400 miles, a breadth of 1,200. Its boundaries were indicated on an earlier page (p. 14). Its frontage on the Red Sea is of over 400 miles in length, a strikingly desolate coastline with but two ports, Port Sudan and the now largely derelict Suakin. The country can be viewed as consisting of five main natural provinces, linked by their overlapping contiguity and by the all-dominating Nile. The northern area extends from Wadi Halfa (on the Egyptian frontier) to Khartum; here the river is flanked by rocky plains varied by isolated groups of hills, among which occasional but very rare rainfall can produce a few thorn-bushes, with, towards the south, acacias in the *wadi* beds. The whole region is denuded, almost soilless, and irrigable only by raising water from wells or from the river; it is the home of camel-grazing nomads, and of the sedentary owners of the narrow strip of cultivation and date-gardens along the Nile.

The Red Sea Hills region (the western flank of the great Afro-Asian rift-valley) contains a belt of impressive mountains, some over 7,000 feet in height, amid which are valleys where rough thorn grows on the lowest ground and increases, towards the Eritrean border, to a more copious vegetation. The higher hills, with greater moisture, can support small trees which include the wild olive. The maritime plain east of this hill-system is featureless and desolate, largely fringed with coral reefs; it can however after rain afford some grazing, and the deltas of the Gash and Baraka rivers, near Kassala and Tokar, are annually flooded and grow valuable crops, including cotton.

From south of Khartum, and stretching far west through Kordofan to Darfur, lies a predominantly sandy region, with light rains which are all locally absorbed without visible drainage. Towards the south, the undulations in the sand-plain die out. The vegetation comprises short grass and trees which include the gum-arabic acacia; grazing is good, and the crops grown in favoured districts are considerable. This, the central Sudan, is the most populous and developed area of the country, with the greatest present activity and the most hopeful projects in cultivation and stock-breeding. It includes, in contrast to predominant flatness, the steep Nuba Mountains of Kordofan province, and, far to the west, the Jabal Marra ranges of Darfur, which rise to 10,000 feet and look westward over the Republic of Chad and its westward-flowing rivers.

South of this central area lies the wide belt where red sand gives way to the dark soil which covers all but the most southerly part of the lower half of the Sudan. With little drainage within its own limits, the area is crossed by stream-beds carrying impermanent water from catchment areas at a distance. The surface is for the most part covered by vast treeless plains of grass or, to the south, by savannah forest. Grazing is plentiful, wide areas are cultivated. Scattered hill-systems break the monotony, and amidst these sufficient water accumulates, in wells, to provide for sedentary village life. South of the twelfth parallel of latitude heavy rain falls, and over many thousands of square miles the Nile disappears in the featureless, trackless swampy wastes of the *sudd*, through the dense growths of which a passage for river-transport is barely maintained.

South of this wide zone lies the typically African forest area, which, with its equally non-Middle Eastern population, covers three provinces of the Sudan Republic (Upper Nile, Equatoria and Bahr al-Ghazal), but, for reasons given (pp. 11, 103), will not detain us here.

It emerges from this too-brief glance at the country that it is characterized by vast spaces and intractable deserts which occupy the greatest part of its surface: by a rainfall varying, from north to south, from almost nothing to tropical plenty: and by an extreme summer heat. It provides in fact, even if we ignore (as here we do) the all-African conditions of the deep south, most varied environments; and to these, as elsewhere, the response is that of camel-nomadism, sheep and cattle semi-nomadism, and cultivation by villagers in river-side settlements, in irrigated estates, and on favoured rain-fed slopes and depressions in open country. Cultivation follows diverse, and in cases unusual, methods (p. 245); and its serious increase, in extent and productivity, can only follow the development of irrigation, for which the single source is the river.

The Nile—its 4,160-mile overall length compares with the Mississippi's 4,520—is the dominant feature of the country, as it is of Egypt. The river is the supplier of drinking and irrigation water, and of fish; it is also the unique central highway. Its waters, contributed by Uganda, Kenya, Ethiopia and Eritrea, have been the subject of many diplomatic exchanges. The most important of all these rests (at present) with the Nile Waters Agreement made between the Sudan and Egypt in November 1959: an agreement which, superseding a British-sponsored arrangement of 1929, seems to secure the reasonable interests of both countries, makes possible the Egyptian High Dam (with payment of £15,000,000 compensation for 40,000 evicted Sudanese), and enables progress to be made currently in Sudanese irrigation plans—notably the dams on the Blue Nile at Roseires and on the 'Atbara at Khashm al-Girba, at both of which work has begun. Some arrangement with the government of Ethiopia regarding the control of the Blue Nile, which originates in Lake Tsana, must equally one day be made. In the Sudan, the extent to which irrigation from the Nile is practicable (otherwise than by hand or animal-lift, or by the now numerous mechanical pumps) is limited by the relative smallness of the area accessible to flow canals; none is thus accessible from the White Nile, and little from the Blue Nile other than the extremely important Gezira area, between the White and Blue Niles just above their confluence. The Gezira Scheme is described elsewhere (p. 245). The annual rise of the Nile, unique among rivers for its regularity, begins in June, and its high level continues till October. The flood-season water is derived mainly from the Blue Nile, with its enormous seasonal variation, and the 'Atbara, the seasonal discharge of the White Nile, below Khartum, varying comparatively little. When all is considered, it does not appear that the Sudan (especially with its vast but ill-manageable reservoir of the *sudd*) will foreseeably suffer from water shortage; but full and fruitful utilization is another matter.

The human occupants of the Sudan, about whom something was said on earlier pages (pp. 103ff.), are within limits diverse, even if we omit the pagan Africans in the three provinces of the south. Apart from a much greater variation between environments in this country than in Egypt, the basic Arabization of earlier population elements (themselves of differing stocks) has been less uniformly effected than in the northern neighbour, and no single prevailing Sudanese type can be matched to the relatively uniform Egyptian. For example the Nubians of the riverain area of northern Sudan, originally non-negroid, have in historical times been heavily mixed with negro blood, and later received a lesser addition of Arab; these are mostly bilingual between Arabic and their own dialect, and rarely intermarry with 'Arabs'. The Donagla, of Dongola (Dangala) province, are less negroid, more Arabized, but keep their own tongue. The Fung, on the other hand, though descendants of the old seventeenth-century Fung conquerors and imperialists, speak both Arabic and a Berberine (Nubian) language, but not their own. These varieties are matched by those found among the Beja tribes (who include Kipling's Fuzzy-wuzzies) of the Red Sea Hills; these are folk who speak their own Baidawi or Khasa tongues as well as Arabic, and had lived already for long centuries in their present countryside before the first Arab incursion—in spite of claims, among leading headmen, to descent from the Prophet's own Arabian tribe! Yet their social organization and way of life is strictly that of Arabia. The Baggara tribes, cattle-breeders (as their name implies) in central-western Sudan, use an Arabic of their own, but combine a large mixture of Negro blood with an outspoken pride of race and status; and even more do the camel-breeding nomads stress their pure Arab origins, which an unfriendly critic might dispute. The Nuba of south and east Kordofan must be pronounced non-Arab by most criteria, and so also the backward Fur people of the high mountains of Darfur.

The population, including 2,500,000 in the South, was estimated in 1961 as just over 12,000,000. Of the other 9,000,000 to 10,000,000, about 3,000,000 belong to the three provinces of the North (Northern, Kassala and Khartum), and between 6,000,000 and 7,000,000 to the centre and west (Blue Nile, Kordofan, Darfur). The vast majority of all these are Sunni Muslims, divided, however, to an extent politically important, between variant sects and fraternities with differences based more on personal loyalties (not least as between Mahdist and Mirghani leadership) than upon niceties of doctrine. Among the whole body of residents in the country, not more than perhaps 25,000 are Egyptians, Syrians, Lebanese or Europeans, another 25,000 varied African non-Sudani races, with 30,000 to 50,000 West Africans from ex-French or ex-British territories. The Christian elements are not numerically imposing; they include about 150,000 Catholics of the Latin or the various oriental rites, a few thousand each of Greek Orthodox, Armenians and Copts, fewer Protestants, and still fewer Jews. The resident Lebanese and European (notably Greek and Italian) element has made, over the last half century, an important contribution in retail trade, business and officialdom; but this is likely henceforward to diminish.

The country's natural resources, apart from its agriculture (p. 245), are not impressive. The search for exploitable minerals has been pursued for many years, and lately with intensity; the list of 'traces' or alleged prospects is formidable; but in fact nothing appreciable is under exploitation. No oil has been discovered, and the territory is of low promise. Hydro-electric sources, not having been provided by nature, can be secured only in connection with river-barrage works. Among wild products, gum-arabic is important and, after cotton, affords the most valuable item of export; the Sudan provides the world with about two-thirds of its requirements. Timber found in the south, and along the Blue Nile, is valuable, but insufficient for export; yet 'forest' areas are estimated at 400,000 square miles. Dum-nuts ('vegetable ivory'), mother of pearl, ivory and salt, are occasional exports. The inexhaustible papyrus of the *sudd* has little apparent value. Bee-keeping provides only for a local market. Stock-breeding is practised in nearly all inhabited areas of the country and, in whatever form, is a major source of livelihood; but exports from this source, amounting in value to less than 10 per cent of the country's total, are confined to limited quantities of live cattle and sheep, and of hides and skins. Fishing is a widespread occupation, and the Nile is bountifully stocked; some salted fish is exported. The relative paucity of the gifts of nature bestowed on this vast territory suggest, indeed, that its economic and in consequence probably its social progress must needs be laborious and slow; yet the Sudani scene appears at once more pleasant and hopeful, and less constricted or threatened, than that of its northern neighbour.

The nine provinces into which the Republic is divided have all been mentioned. That of Khartum is in population the smallest, but contains the 'metropolitan area' of the capital itself with Khartum North and Omdurman (Umm Durman), giving a joint urban population of some 320,000. The other provincial capitals are on a smaller scale; the Sudan is the least urbanized of all Middle Eastern countries. Wadi Madani, capital of the Blue Nile, has 55,000, al-Fashir (Darfur) 30,000, Kassala 45,000, El Obeid (al-'Ubaid, Kordofan) 60,000, Juba (Equatoria) 13,000, Malakal (Upper Nile) 12,000. Smaller capitals are Wau (Bahr al-Ghazal) and al-Damir (Northern). Major towns other than provincial capitals are Wadi Halfa, which is destined to be submerged by the reservoir behind the High Dam: Port Sudan (50,000): Mongalla in the far south: and 'Atbara (40,000), with its railway junction and workshops.

The roads of the country, except within towns, are mostly no more than formed earth or gravel tracks, passable except after rain; when the latter is heavy or persistent, road communication ceases. The radical improvement of this situation, by extending modern road-construction, is in hand. There are now in all some 30,000 miles of motorable track. Good bridges exist where necessary. A company-owned 'bus service works in the Khartum metropolitan area; a series of smaller-scale enterprises provide for access to most provincial towns, and the through route from Juba to Khartum is open from December to May. The railway system is extensive: a line runs northwards from Khartum to Wadi Halfa by way of al-Damir, 'Atbara, and abu-Hamad, with a branch from abu-Hamad to Kareima (Kuraima). From 'Atbara a line runs to Port Sudan and Suakin *via* Haiya, with another from Haiya southward to Kassala and on by way of Gadarif to Sannar (Sennar), site of the Blue Nile dam. A line from Sannar goes to Roseires. The former is joined also to Khartum by a river-side line *via* Wadi Madani, and westward from it a line crosses the White Nile at Kosti, and proceeds to al-Rahad and el-Obeid. Al Rahad has lately been connected with Nyala in Darfur province, *via* abu-Zabad. The most recent construction is that of a line which takes off from the last mentioned at Mujlad in Kordofan province, crosses the Bahr al-Ghazal, and reaches Wau in the province of the same name. This line was built entirely by Sudani engineers and labour. The total of lines in the country in 1962, all of 3 foot 6 inches gauge, is about 3,250 miles. They are all state-owned. A line joining the Sudani and Egyptian railway systems will no doubt follow the completion of the High Dam; the construction, as a joint project, has already been provisionally agreed. River steamers, owned by Sudan Railways, provide communication where there is no other, or to supplement land-transport; services, with a total mileage of 2,300 miles, run to and from Juba, and up the Bahr al-Ghazal to Wau, and on the Dongola loop of the middle Nile to connect with the Egyptian services.

Sea-transport facilities are necessarily confined to Port Sudan, distant 490 miles from Khartum. This is a fully equipped modern port, used by many inter-continental shipping lines. Air travel is locally in the hands of Sudan Airways, which operates both internal and international routes, the latter notably to Aden, Asmara, Entebbe, Jidda, Cairo, Beirut and London. Foreign airlines call regularly at Khartum.

The Sudani pound (£S), which has lately superseded the Egyptian, has a parity with sterling of £S1·03 to £1 sterling, and £S0·36 to the U.S. dollar.

7. *Sa'udi Arabia*

This enormously spacious, desertic kingdom, homeland of the Wahhabi sect of Sunni Islam (pp. 85, 95), covers some four-fifths of the Arabian peninsula. The north-Arabian extension into Jordan, Syria and 'Iraq is non-Sa'udi, as are the south-western (Yemeni) highlands, the south coast and its hinterland, the south-eastern mountains, and more than half of the Persian Gulf littoral. The rest, belonging all to 'the Kingdom' (as its neighbours call it), leaves it an area of 950,000 square miles, exceeded among our range of countries only by the Sudan, and more than ten times the size of England, Wales and Scotland. Its neighbours on the north are Jordan and 'Iraq: on the west it is bounded by the Gulf of 'Aqaba and the Red Sea, on the south by the Yemen, the Aden Protectorate and the Sultanate of Oman, on the east by the Trucial shaikhdoms, and the territories of Qatar and Kuwait. It enjoys, therefore, more than 1,000 miles of sea frontage on the Red Sea, and 300 on the Gulf. Its land frontiers are without exception drawn across desert country, officially defined only in the case of Kuwait and, in part, the Yemen, and disputed in the cases of Oman, the Trucial Coast, and Jordan.

Viewed from west to east, the narrow plain along the Red Sea coast is barren, without natural harbours, obstructed by reefs and coral, and carrying in its few miserable villages the scantiest of populations. The largest of these settlements, from north to south, are Wajh, Yanbu' (the port for Medina), Jidda (by far the most important, being one of the chief cities of the territory and the port for Mecca), Rabigh, Lith and Qunfidha. Behind and parallel to this desolate coast-strip, a line or belt of not less barren volcanic mountains stretches from the Jordanian to the Yemeni border, with its ridges and peaks higher in the north and south, lower in the latitude of Yanbu' and Jidda in the central sections. The terrain athwart, and east of, this mountain zone is of appalling desolation, relieved only by the scanty pastures used by a few fragmented camel-tribes, and by the oases created by the rare fortune of a water-source at Tabuk, Taima, al-'Ula, Khaibar, Medina (the famous refuge and burial place of the Prophet), Mecca itself, Ta'if (with 5,000 feet of elevation, and the summer resort of the Hijazis), Khurma, Turaba and Abha the capital of 'Asir. None of these, except the Holy Cities and Ta'if, would deserve mention except for their rarity as urban settlements. The population of Jidda and Mecca may now have reached some 200,000 each, Medina and Ta'if each perhaps one-third of that figure.

The whole Arabian peninsula is a plain of ancient rock severed from Africa (which is the same) by the deep fissure of the Red Sea, and disturbed locally by volcanic action, whence the Hijaz mountain ranges and the flat lava-strewn uplands which flank them. All Arabia is elevated on its west side and tilted gently downwards towards the east. The country east of the Hijaz mountains, therefore, is still high, covered by light layers, here and there, of younger rocks and varied by local ridges and depressions which have created the conditions for oases. The central area of the Kingdom is composed not of a single featureless plain, but a variety of desert surfaces (p. 16 f.), scattered ranges of low hills and broken ridges, hundreds of dry water-courses, and rare wells or water-holes which make life possible for the nomadic camel-breeding tribesmen. To the north of the central area lie the sheer deserts of the Nafud, to the east those of the Dahna, to the south that of the totally waterless, Sahara-like Ruba' al-Khali, or Empty Quarter, proverbial for its forbidding lifelessness. The oases of the centre, however—the true heart of the Sa'udi Kingdom—are considerable; and they permit, in changeless, inner-Arabian fashion, a not uncultured and not uncomfortable urban life, to which the recent and fantastic oil-wealth of the kingdom has contributed, for the fortunate few, a measure of modern luxury. The main oases are those of Jauf in the far north, Ha'il in the Jabal Shammar, Buraida and 'Anaiza in the Qasim district (with populations of perhaps 30,000 each), Shaqra and Riyadh (the capital, with a rapidly-swollen population of perhaps 200,000 and a galaxy of royal palaces) in that of 'Aridh, with Laila and Sulaiyil towards the south-west. These and a score of lesser oasis-centres, with their scanty but sufficient water, their gardens and exiguous crops and herds, their permanent mud-brick dwellings, mosques and mosque-schools, support the settled life of modern Arabia. In and around the palaces of the Sa'udi princes—and no royal house was ever more philoprogenitive—where the oil-revenues are spent or squandered, luxury and ostentation abound, and the old austerities are forgotten.

In Eastern Arabia, towards and along the Gulf coast, the flatness of the terrain is broken only by minor ridges and sand dunes, and these, in coastal areas, give place to flat gravelly plains and wide areas of salt-marsh. Inshore water is shallow and full of sandbanks, giving difficult approach to the land for shipping. The most populous oases—prior, that is, to the oil-age which has covered eastern Arabia with ultra-modern settlements of western industrial type—in the al-Hasa (al-Ahsa) province of the Kingdom, are those of Hofuf

(90,000), Qatif and 'Ujair. North of the province lie the two Neutral Zones—Sa'udi-Kuwaiti, and Sa'udi-'Iraqi—delimited in 1922 under British sponsorship because no boundary-lines between the disputing parties could otherwise be agreed.

The Kingdom is administered, under its King and a cabinet selected by him (largely from his own kinsmen), in five main divisions or provinces. These are the Hijaz on the west, a broad strip astride the coastal mountains: 'Asir in the south-west, which is permitted something of a privileged status: the Najran area, inland of 'Asir towards the Yemen border: the main subdivisions of Najd, the wide central area, which we have already named: and the al-Hasa province on the Gulf, with its capital at Dammam. Administrative methods are everywhere capricious and unformulated, but the current tendency is on the whole towards more semi-representative bodies in the towns and districts, powerless though these may be. There is no law save that of the Qur'an and the Shari'a.

The climate of the Kingdom is one of extreme severity. Rainfall over all of it, except the better-watered south-west area adjoining the Yemen, ranges from nothing to 8 inches a year; this can, exceptionally, be increased by sudden and violent falls which for a few hours turn the *wadi*-beds into torrents. Some of the rain, it appears, is carried below ground by aquiferous strata down the west-to-east slope to, or nearly to, the Gulf shores, where it furnishes wells and springs otherwise inexplicable. (Such water comes out in fresh springs in the sea off Bahrain.) The aridity of 99 per cent of Sa'udi Arabia is not improved by its high desert winds, its frequent dust storms, and its heavy coastal humidity; but days in winter can be sharply cold, in contrast to the extremely high summer temperatures of up to 120° in the shade.

The Sa'udi population is guessed by its outside observers to be about 4,000,000; some say more. Apart from a few hundreds of miscellaneous (but always Muslim) foreigners in the Red Sea and Persian Gulf coastal towns—Somalis, Baluchis, Negroes, Persians, Indians—the people are all Arabian Sunni Muslims, perhaps half of whom (including, of course, the royal family and court) profess Wahhabism, and half other doctrines. No Jews are permitted in the territory. The movements of the rare Christians who visit it, including diplomats, are strictly controlled; none are allowed in Mecca or Medina. Outside the towns, and in some measure within them, tribal ways prevail, in forms less modified or modernized than in any other country: a feature to be expected in view of the strength and antiquity of the Arabian tribal tradition, and the possession of a terrain in most of which no life other than the nomadic could be supported. Among these Arabia tribes still so organized, and still leading patriarchal lives in conditions literally unendurable to others, are found some of the most famous and historic of communities in the tribal world. Yet even here, in some material respects, modern ways are intruding, thanks to the ubiquity of motor transport in all regions passable for wheels, to recruitment of tribesmen in the King's armed forces, to wireless communication, and to service, even, in the mid-desert oil-seeking and oil-producing operations. Slavery still exists in Sa'udi Arabia at many levels of society including the highest; there may be 500,000 slaves in the territory; but there is little ill-treatment, public sales and the importation of slaves are now officially forbidden, and there seems to be little or no internal movement (certainly not among the slaves themselves, save for rare individuals) to press for liberation. Oil-wealth, it is said, has greatly increased the demand for, and prices of, slaves. The abolition of slavery in the Kingdom was announced in October 1962—with practical results which must be awaited.

Except for petroleum, whose superabundant presence and exploita-tion makes the whole country viable and the privileged class opulent, there are no minerals; a small gold mine in the Hijaz, worked for some years, has now been abandoned, and a recent country-wide American-aided geological survey and search has revealed little. Fish-ing and charcoal-burning are the occupation of a few hundred, at the lowest subsistence level. A little pearl-fishing is carried on from the al-Hasa coasts. Agriculture is possible on a small scale around the oases, where crops, dates and fruit are grown to the limits of the water supply, and the bedouin find it possible, in years of relatively good rains, to grow small patches of wheat in desert depressions. The rearing of sheep is similarly desired, but similarly limited, pastures capable of supplying herds being widely variable from year to year, and always inadequate to large numbers. Camel-breeding is the livelihood of the great tribes, and its produce enables them to buy their grain and other essentials from the oasis shopmen. An interest-ing experiment, begun fifty years ago by the great King 'Abdul 'Aziz ibn Sa'ud, was that of settling the *badu*, formed into fraternities and therefore called Ikhwan, or Brothers, in subsidized settlements intended to be static and agricultural, for which purpose they were sited where water could be made available. But the loss of their camels seemed to increase rather than lessen the Islamic zeal of the ex-nomads, and this turned often to open indiscipline; nevertheless many of the colonies persist, and may point a way to ultimate detribalization. The largest of them is Artawiya, in eastern Qasim.

In the days before the economic revolution produced by the oil industry, reliance of the State finances (then scarcely worthy of the name) was on the Mecca pilgrimage and the money which it was possible to extract in fees from the pilgrims, and by supplying necessaries to them. This, the greatest of all Islamic pilgrimages and a statutory duty for every Muslim, is now well organized; it is no longer used as a money-extracting occasion, though indeed the very large travel-organization to deal with the Hajjis' land, sea and air travel is not unprofitable, nor are Sa'udis excluded from its benefits. Careful precautions against epidemic disease are taken. Licensed guides escort the pilgrims who come in the sacred month in their tens of thousands (up to 200,000 in a year) from every Islamic land, to perform the ritual ceremonies at Mecca and to keep the Feast of the Sacrifice. Most, not quite all, visit Medina also. Religion apart, the Hajj has all the social importance of a universal meeting-place of the Faith, and politically that of providing opportunity, at the very heart of Dar al-Islam, for mutual information and debate, for reaffirming (one may hope) the part of Allah in wordly politics—and perhaps for admiring the wealth and achievements of the House of Sa'ud. All sects take part equally; it is a yearly return to Islamic essentials.

The two ports of Jidda on the Red Sea and Damman on the al-Hasa coast, in the heart of the oil-country, are adequate to all the country's needs for sea traffic; both have been constructed on modern lines, with foreign help. The deep-water Dammam port lies some eight miles from the coast, to which a causeway connects it. Surfaced roads run from Jidda to Mecca and Medina; otherwise, except for Company-built roads within the oil territory, the routes are mere tracks, usually passable, and these serve the central area, including Riyadh, and the east. All main oases, central, northern and southern are thus accessible. Telephone and wireless services, especially for official use, are relatively developed. The old Hijaz railway, from the northern frontier to Medina, has never been repaired since Lawrence's sabotage parties in 1917, though its rehabilitation is often proposed. A new 350 mile American-built, but government-owned, line connects the Gulf coast at Dammam, by way of the principal oil-fields, with the capital; a 975 mile line to join Riyadh to Mecca and Jidda is under consideration. Sa'udi Arabian Airways, owned by the State but American-operated, maintain air services with Beirut and Cairo as well as internally. The main landing grounds are at Jidda, Dhahran (the great ex-American base in al-Hasa), and Riyadh. A number of Sa'udis are efficient pilots.

The standard currency is the Sa'udi riyal, successor to that of Maria Theresa; it is equivalent in official eyes to one shilling and sixpence sterling, in those of the public to considerably less. The Sa'udi Arabian Monetary Agency acts as a Central Bank.

8. *The Yemen*

The Imamate—or, since September 1962, ex-Imamate—of the Yemen, scenically and climatically perhaps the most favoured region of all Arabia—it is the original Arabia Felix—has been also the most isolated inhabited area in the Middle East, and the least penetrated (if we except, perhaps, the highlands of Oman) by European influences. This has resulted, in part, from its geography, and its difficult routes of access which discourage all but the most persistent visitors: and in part from the policy of its rulers who, themselves medieval, remained for centuries highly suspicious of the outside world. Enjoying, at least in its upland districts, the best of climates and a generous rainfall, and threatened by none, the territory has yet contrived to be strikingly backward, insecure, and unhappy.

The area of the territory is some 75,000 square miles, with a sea frontage on the Red Sea (which forms its western boundary) of just under 300 miles. Its territorial neighbours are Sa'udi Arabia on the north and east, and the Aden Protectorate (persistently claimed by the authorities at San'a as Southern Yemen, unjustly occupied by imperialism) on the south. The land frontiers have in each case been the subject of joint diplomatic review on many occasions, but no accepted delimitation has been made. The Red Sea islands near the Yemen coasts (the Farsan group, Kamaran (Qumran), and Perim) do not form part of Yemen territory; the two latter are British possessions, under Aden Colony, while the Farsan archipelago is Sa'udi.

The country falls into easily distinguishable zones, of which the first is the flat, barren and almost uninhabited maritime plain. The main part of this is separated from the sea by swamps and lagoons, inland of which a sandy and rocky wilderness, traversed by arid river-beds, occupies the width of the plain, some 30 to 50 miles in depth. Next, inland of this, lies the western foothill area, trackless, deeply intersected by ravines, and rising to an elevation of some 3,000 to 4,000 feet; here more vegetation appears, and though largely of desertic type supports life for some villages and a scanty population of graziers. The highly elevated but deeply intersected region most characteristic of the Yemen, the high central upland, is heavily vegetated, fertile, and able to support a considerable population, reckoned as not less than 5,000,000 souls. The plateau maintains an height of from 6,000 to 9,000 feet, but many peaks and ridges are higher, and one, claimed as the highest mountain in Arabia, reaches nearly 14,000 feet. The highlands are, thanks to the rainfall, widely cultivable, whether in open areas or by an age-long system of terracing in which irrigation, from impounded rain, is practised with rare skill and profit. Inland from the plateau, where it slowly loses height and merges in the true deserts of southern Arabia, the population thins to vanishing point and Sa'udi Arabia is entered. The country contains no rivers; the westward- or eastward-flowing rain-torrents lose themselves in the sands of the Tihama (coastal plain) without reaching the sea, or in those of the central deserts. Rainfall is assessed as some 15 to 20 inches a year in the northern and central highlands, 30 inches or more in the south-west where the monsoon reaches in from the Indian Ocean, and an almost negligible deposit on the coastal plain. The winter season on the highlands can be cold, down to and below freezing point, with frequent snow-falls; but in summer the region is temperate, its near-equatorial heat tempered by altitude and cloud-cover.

The population of the lower, seaward slopes, that of the coastal towns and villages and of the terrain along the Aden Protectorate frontier, consists of Shafi'i Sunni Muslims, among whom on the coast is a small proportion of domiciled Africans—Somalis, Dankilis, and Ethiopians. The people of the highland area are Zaidi (p. 93) in religion, as is or was the family of the Imam; these may constitute in all rather less than half the Yemen population. In the deep hinterland a fair-sized community of Isma'ilis (p. 94) survives. There are no Christians, and the Yemeni Jews have, all except perhaps 5,000 to 10,000, left their homes for Israel, after the many centuries in which they formed an abiding element in the south-Arabian population.

San'a remains the capital of the country, with a population estimated at 100,000. It has not been latterly, however, the residence of the ruler, which has been fixed at Ta'iz (population 80,000). These cities are both at high altitudes, respectively 7,250 and 4,600 feet. Other major towns of the highlands are Ibb, Yarim, Dhamar, Manakha, 'Amra and Sa'da. The cities of the Tihama are Hudaida (population 30,000, the principal port), Mokha (a port once busy, now in decline), and Luhaiya, Bajil and Zabid. A static but largely operative tribal system, with all its means of control and its loyalties, has long pervaded much of the country, and can be a major element in its politics and district administration. The latter has been irregular and arbitary in the extreme: all real power, even over the smallest details, was in the hands of the Imam—as long as he could avoid assassination, or trust some of his sons! The assurance of his or the state's security by the holding of many tribal hostages at San'a was a usual method of Yemeni statecraft. In the cities, a refined Islamic civilization of ancient pattern, and some scholarly culture, persists and defies the modern world. A small beginning, however, has been made in recent years towards supplementing the old-type Koranic education of the country by a school or schools of modern syllabus, and by colleges for technical training. The rural standard of life is in general, at least on the highlands, less depressed in the Yemen than in most Middle Eastern territories.

Its natural resources are those already indicated—its soil and climate, agriculture and fruit growing, and, above all, its matchless coffee. There is opportunity and space for livestock breeding, that of sheep, goats, mules and camels; hides and skins are exported. Honey is produced on a scale unique in the Middle East. The narcotic drug qatt is widely grown, and universally used, with little regard paid to its debilitating effects on physique. There is little sea-fishing. Mineral wealth seems to be unknown. No oil has been discovered.

Facilities at the port of Hudaida (an open roadstead) have been under recent improvement by a U.S.S.R. mission, who are constructing another port, with deep water access, at Ras Kadhib near-by. The old port of Mokha has also been partly rehabilitated and improved. A small number of Yemeni-owned vessels ply in the Red Sea and outside it. A Chinese mission has completed a sorely-needed all-weather highway from Hudaida to San'a. Both Chinese and Italians have volunteered further help towards the beginnings of factory industry, and Soviet 'aid' is by agreement, to continue. The United States Government has made offers of help in communications or otherwise. There is every sign, at the time of writing, that comprehensive Egyptian help, in all departments, will be made available to to the new revolutionary régime in the territory, if it survives. Work has been done on the Hudaida-Ta'iz road, and others connect Ta'iz with San'a and (not without risk) with Aden also and with Mokha. Except these routes, newly constructed with foreign help, there are no surfaced or all-weather roads, and no railways. There is a roughly organized internal aviation service, under a local company with foreign pilots and operators. No western airline has used Yemeni landing-grounds.

The currency of the country is the Maria Theresa dollar, or riyal, equivalent (with many fluctuations) to about five shillings. There are no banks.

9. *Southern Arabia*

The composite territory next to be described consists of a belt of country, narrow at its south-western and deep at its north-eastern (Oman) end, in all some 1,500 miles in length and bordered, on the whole of its southern face, by the Arabian Sea. The western half forms the Aden Protectorate, the eastern half the Sultanate of Muscat and Oman. The inland frontier of the former is with the Yemen and Sa'udi Arabia, of the latter with Sa'udi Arabia and, at its northern end, the territories of the Trucial shaikhs. The inland frontiers pass everywhere through utter desert—that of the fearsome Empty Quarter—and are therefore undemarkated.

The main geographical feature of the Protectorate, which is divided administratively into a Western and Eastern half, are a dull, harbour-less, unfertile coastal plain of varying width, with Aden Colony and Makalla the only considerable settlements: a wide inland area of barren broken hills and valleys: a district of higher mountains, 5,000 to 8,000 feet in height, as Yemen territory is approached: and a high table-land region in the Eastern Protectorate, cut through by the great rift of the Wadi Hadhramaut and its associated depressions. Inland of it all, to north and east, lie impassable deserts. The two Protectorate areas include also the islands of Socotra (Saqatra) with the 'Abdul Kuri and the Brothers groups across the Gulf of Aden, and the Kuria Muria archipelago off the Oman Coast. The total area of the Protectorate amounts to some 112,000 square miles, that of Aden Colony to 75 square miles. The whole region with its coastal humidity, its extreme summer heat, its dust storms and aridity, has climatically little to recommend it, though a wild and desolate beauty awaits visitors to its remoter districts. Rainfall varies from some 3 to 5 inches a year at Aden to five times that amount, or more, in the mountains. The surface, when not wholly barren, is covered with a light thorny scrub and in places by incense-giving dwarf trees; cultivation exists along torrent-beds, in the Hadhramaut basin, in districts near Makalla, and elsewhere where well- or cistern-water can be spared. The population of the Western Protectorate may be some 500,000, of the Eastern perhaps 400,000. With rare immigrant exceptions, all are Shafi'i Sunnis. Aden Colony has a mixed population of some 150,000.

The Colony, which includes Little Aden and Shaikh 'Uthman, and also the Red Sea islands of Kamaran (Qumran) and Perim stands administratively apart from the Protectorate—unless and until the common Federation now contemplated (and already covering most of the Western portion), is to embrace both—and, unlike them, is a directly-administered British territory. Its population includes some 105,000 Arabs (including Adenis and Yemenis), 12,000 Somalis, 15,000 Indians and Pakistanis, and perhaps 5,000 Europeans; many of the last-named are to be found at the important oil refinery at Little Aden, completed in 1954 and economically the greatest of blessings. Other industries are on a small but growing, commerce and entrepôt activities are considerable, bunkering is on a scale scarcely equalled by any port in the world. The British garrison is economically and socially a major and vitalizing factor in Aden life; so are tourists and their hotels, and the traffic in luxury goods sold to them with 'free port' advantages. The port, immensely busy, is under constant improvement: but its dependence on the Suez Canal route was demonstrated when the latter was blocked in 1956–1957. The airfield at Khor Maksar is in use by the R.A.F., by Aden Airways, and by a dozen regularly visiting airlines. Aden society is, within its limits, cosmopolitan; it is also politically divided and uneasy (mainly thanks to non-Adeni influences), with its commerce and industry disturbed by chronic, politically-inspired industrial unrest. Attempts of subversion, both covert and overt, from the Yemen and from Cairo, are ceaseless.

The Western Protectorate contains a score of small sultanates, amirates and shaikhdoms, of which those of Lahaj, Baihan and Dhala are among the more important. (See Appendix A.) These and six more have been, since early in 1959, united in a Federation, which others (and perhaps Aden Colony itself) are likely to join. The Eastern Protectorate contains fewer but more considerable rulers, at whose hands a more developed type of administration is, or will be, possible. The main constituents are the (Qu'aiti) State of Shihr and Makalla, the (Kathiri) State of Sayyun, the (Mahri) Sultanate of Qishin and Socotra, and the (Wahidi) Sultanate of Balhaf. The ruler of the

Qu'aiti state has precedence over the other rulers, and he and his subjects for many years maintained close contacts with India. Throughout both Protectorates, covering territory which until the 1930s was largely lawless and unorganized, a very fair degree of security has now been achieved by the patient efforts of the handful of British representatives. An excellent start has been made in education by the foundation and inspection of primary, and even some secondary, schools; a beginning of other public services has been made, life and property are safeguarded, feuds and bloodshed ended, economic development encouraged by funds to aid practicable small-scale agricultural and other projects. The emigration of thousands of Hadhramis to the Netherlands East Indies (as they then were) was for a century a main source of wealth to the important cities of the Wadi—Tarim, Sayyun, Shibam—and, though this resource is now no more, Indonesian influences in the Hadhramaut are still visible, and have been a progressive agency; these imposing wilderness-surrounded cities remain, within the small circle of their social and religious élite, strikingly advanced and even luxurious. Elsewhere, penury is extreme, illiteracy until recently universal, and the world outside unimagined. The livelihood of the people derives from their scanty and precarious agriculture (which includes some tobacco and some cotton), fishing on the coasts, and limited sheep and cattle-raising. Camel-droving, once a main source of livelihood, has been superseded by motor transport. No oil has been discovered, and no exploitable minerals are known to exist. A local livelihood is often augmented (or replaced) by one gained by enlistment in British-sponsored (and British-paid) forces, or by flight to the towns or the sea. A number of Adeni and Hadhrami tribesmen have settled in Great Britain, others in Ethiopia, Sa'udi Arabia or East Africa.

The remote island of Socotra, where the Mahri Sultan lives, lies 150 miles from Cape Gardafui and has an area of 1,400 square miles and a population of 10,000. It is self-supporting in dates, cattle and sheep. The Kuria Muria islands, geographically belonging to Oman, were presented to the British Government by the Sultan of that country in 1854; the population is less than 100. Of the five islands the largest has an area of 20 square miles; their famous accumulations of guano have been removed, decades ago.

*   *   *

The Sultanate of Oman, with 1,000 miles of coastline, occupies the rest of southern and south-eastern Arabia, stretching eastward from the Aden boundary at Ras Dharbat 'Ali to the narrow entrance to the Persian Gulf. The total area of the Sultanate may be 90,000 square miles, its population 550,000. There are five main divisions of the territory. The first of these is the detached province of Dhufar in the extreme south-west, a district treated in all respects as the Sultan's private estate. It contains a pleasant and fertile coastal plain, flanked by the broad ring of the Qara hills, and is well watered by monsoon rains. There is some cultivation, and good cattle-breeding. Salala is its capital, Marbat its port. The second constituent district is the totally barren, uninhabited area of both coast and hinterland between Dhufar and the southern end of the main Oman mountain range. The third is the fertile and populated Batina coast running from north-west to south-east, to Ras al-Hadd, between the Gulf of Oman and the mountains. This is an area of famous date-groves, scores of villages, a passably motorable track, and the sea-side towns of Muscat (Masqat) with its twin Matra, Sib, Khabura and Suhar. The fourth district is that of the mountains—the impressive range of the Jabal Akhdhar (p. 16), wild and desolate but with its vivid green areas of vegetation, its rude urban or village centres, many *wadi*-bed camel tracks, and a few easier passes practicable for wheeled vehicles, improved to that standard during the last few years. This is a region of heavier though uncertain rainfall, less severe climate. It is made habitable by the cultivation of grain, dates and fruit in far from negligible quantities, by skilful irrigation, and by the breeding of the famous Omani camels. The fifth and last zone of the Sultanate is the sandy or gravelly plateau west of the mountains, sinking and merging westward into the Ruba' al-Khali, and containing rare oases, such as those of the Buraimi group, but otherwise only the scantiest of bedouin life.

The Omani population is, outside the towns, uniformly Arab, mostly Ibadi (p. 92), and devoted to its feud-ridden tribal organization. The latter is a complex of ancient devotions and antipathies, exacerbated by the theocratic claims of ambitious divines or their champions. The whole territory, therefore, in spite of the excellent intentions of its ruler, Sayid Sa'id, possesses little political or social tranquillity, while its prevailing poverty precludes any but a slow pace of development. It is further weakened, or distracted, by an active tribal or sectarian separatism in the mountain zone, and by the recent aggression of the Sa'udi authorities against its western flank—

insufficiently protected, it seems, by some hundreds of miles of utter desert! The capital, Muscat-Matra, is a city of mainly non-Arabs—Baluchis, Indians and Pakistanis, negroes. These elements are represented also in the Batina coast-towns.

The Omanis live on their dates, fruit, fish and grain, and the produce of their camels. There are no industries other than domestic. No important minerals have been revealed, though some coal exists; oil, for which the transmontane region seemed to offer high hopes, has been sought expensively, but so far in vain. The British government is currently contributing to a Development fund to assist progress and expansion, particularly in the fields of agriculture, roads, schools, public health and defence.

Airfields exist at Salala in Dhufar, on the barren Masira Island off the south-east coast, and at Bait al-Falaj near Muscat. A weekly air-service links Muscat with Bahrain. Steamers from and to India call at Muscat weekly, others occasionally. The small ports of Suhar, Khabura and Sur offer no protection from the weather.

The media of exchange are the Maria Theresa dollar and the Indian rupee.

10. *The Persian Gulf States*

The sole area now outstanding, from this cursory tour of the Arab countries, is the southern shore of the Persian Gulf, excepting that part thereof, the al-Hasa coast, already mentioned (p. 156) as a province of Sa'udi Arabia. This leaves us the Trucial Coast, the Qatar peninsula, the islands of the Bahrain group, and the amirate of Kuwait. The whole of this region is one of extreme desolation, almost totally without natural resources (save one!), devoid of natural harbours, without the possibility of any but the most exiguous agriculture, unendowed with adequate grazing, and lacking, indeed—except on a part of Bahrain Island—even a modicum of vegetation. The coastline is encumbered with shoals, deep water channels are hard to find, winds are sudden and unpredictable. Rainfall is scanty, though not quite unknown, and even minimum potable water-supplies can be a grave problem; they exist almost solely at Bahrain and in or close to the foothill area of the Oman mountains. The coast is humid and malarial.

The TRUCIAL COAST, the stretch of country extending some 400 miles from Ras Masandam (the northernmost tip of Oman) to the base of the Qatar peninsula, affords, with its featureless, sandy and salt-marshy hinterland, space for the domains of the seven independent Trucial shaikhdoms: an area amounting to some 50,000 to 100,000 square miles according as one may guess or claim an approximate, because never defined, inland boundary. The total population of the Coast may be of the order of 100,000 souls, of whom four-fifths would be found in the coastal villages, which are the shaikhs' capitals, and one-fifth in inland oases, especially those of the Buraimi group. All are Sunni Muslims, and all sedentary except a few camps of camel-herdsmen. The social organization is tribal. The occupations are date-tending, pearl-diving, camel breeding, fishing, rarely and scantily crop-raising, and, far more important, working in one or other of the great oil-fields of the Gulf. Of oil prospects in the Abu Dhabi shaikhdom, already in part realized, more will be said later (p. 254). An important source of livelihood since 1937 has been the 'interim payments' made to the rulers by the operating oil company on account of the oil concessions granted, and the employment given by field exploration parties; oil has in fact been located solely in Abu Dhabi territory—but here, very recently, on an important scale—and hope for the rest is fast diminishing. Apart from oil, the British government is currently helping with an embryonic local development plan, including agricultural experiments (which have given hopeful results) and technical training. The same government, which alone is represented diplomatically on the coast, pays also for a small inter-territory paramilitary force designed to maintain order.

The independent shaikhdoms are seven in number (see Appendix A); four are insignificant (though Ras al-Khaima is among the more populated), Sharja has some pretentions to stability and progressiveness, Dubai has the most accessible creek for shipping and the largest town (of perhaps 30,000 inhabitants), and Abu Dhabi has by far the most extensive territory, more than double all the rest together. Peace between the shaikhs is secured by the good offices of the British government, which also protects the territories from neighbourly (Sa'udi) aggression. There is no internal administration other than that, strictly patriarchal, of the rulers; in this the British play no part.

Steamers call monthly, or more frequently, at Dubai, which, with Sharja and Abu Dhabi, enjoys also a regular though not daily air service, whereby the rest of the Gulf, and Persian and Sa'udi cities, become accessible.

The QATAR shaikhdom, with an area of about 4,000 square miles and possibly 40,000 inhabitants (half in Doha (Dauha) town, the

THE PERSIAN GULF

capital) mainly of the Wahhabi faith, is in amenities for human residence no improvement on the Trucial Coast, with which it is geographically continuous. Its boundary with the Sa'udi Kingdom has never been agreed. Since the large-scale discovery of oil (p. 256) which since 1950 has totally transformed the economics of the peninsula, the old and miserable livelihood of the Qataris from fishing, pearling and camel-breeding is forgotten; the oil company is now the sole employer and benefactor, and the *per capita* income of the fortunate citizens is said to be the highest in the world—instead of, as but a half-generation ago, among the lowest. (Abu Dhabi, however, may soon wrest this unusual distinction from its Qatari rival.) As in Abu Dhabi, so in Qatar, the population is appreciably leavened by the presence, in oil-company employment, of hundreds of non-Qatari Arab technicians and office workers.

Besides Doha, now under transformation from a sprawling, squalid village to an opulent ultra-modern city and nucleus of a welfare state, there are three or four other villages, as well as the settlements, ports and multifarious activities of the oil company. Umm Sa'id is the deep-water port created by the latter, 20 miles south of Doha; Zakrit, equally a company creation, on the west side, has only shallow access. The shaikh of Qatar, himself no enemy of modernization, accepts the assistance of some British experts and advisers. The prevailing level of literacy and enlightenment among his own subjects could, until very recently, scarcely have been lower, but education for the young and for many adults (including that provided by the oil company) has made and is making rapid strides.

BAHRAIN is the largest island (30 miles by 10) of a group of eight, the others being Muharraq, Sitra, Umm al-Nisan, Hawar (close to the Qatar coast) and four more, all smaller except the last-named, they lie between the Sa'udi coast and the north-west tip of Qatar. The total area is some 215 square miles; the population may be 150,000, of whom the capital city, Manama, has rather less than half, and Muharraq about 30,000. Apart from resident or visiting foreigners (Indians, Pakistanis, non-Bahraini Arabs, Persians and British and American oil-men) the subjects of the Shaikh are about half (Shi'i) Baharina, who are alleged aboriginal islanders, and half Sunni Arabs, to whom the shaikhly house and most of *les gens bien* belong. The never-relinquished Persian claim to the island need not here concern us, though the large Shi'i element is not unconnected with it. The climate is of typical Persian Gulf type, but the many amenities of the island make it easily tolerable.

Plentiful water and cultivation exist in the northern half of Bahrain island, less or scarcely any in the southern part or on the other islands. Manama and its villages, deep in date-gardens and admirably tended horticulture, are the Gulf's most attractive centre. A causeway, with a central breaching-section for shipping, links Bahrain with Muharraq, where a busy, well equipped airport has been constructed. This in its improved form was completed in 1961. New port installations, additional to the simple moorings in use since antiquity, were completed in 1962 at Mina Salman. Both steamship lines and airlines make much use of Bahrain as a port of call. Much new building, notably housing, has been provided in recent years for Bahrainis and foreigners alike, and urban services—of public health, light and power, road transport, town-planning, education, broadcasting, and security—have now, after many years of enlightened if patriarchal rule and nearly a generation of oil-wealth, reached a high standard. Excellent artesian wells exist, and the main settlements enjoy piped supplies. The Anglo-American oil-field and refinery operatives, some hundreds strong, live in their own township, in the barren centre of the island; this does not include the Bahraini labour-force. Bahrain is host also to a British diplomatic mission, and a small naval base.

The occupations of the Bahrainis in oil-less days, pearling and ship building and maintaining the services of a main entrepôt for Arabia, are now of lesser importance; oil revenues, derived since 1934 from Bahrain's own production and from its major refining and exporting installations, cover most of the needs of the Shaikh, his administration, and the public. A number of British advisers and experts work in Bahrain government service, at the ruler's request.

The amirate of KUWAIT, north of the (Sa'udi) coastal province of al-Hasa and of the Kuwaiti-Sa'udi Neutral Zone, is unique among the sovereign states of the world for its combination of small and desolate territory, fewness of inhabitants, and enormous wealth. Its territory at the head of the Gulf, measuring some 6,000 square miles of almost totally waterless desert, contains, apart from a few camps of indigenous or visiting nomads, a single city, Kuwait. This, a mid-eighteenth-century tribal foundation, has grown from about 70,000 inhabitants in 1930 to 300,000 in 1962. A third of these may be native-born Kuwaitis, the rest are 'Iraqi, Egyptian, Syrian, Palestinian, Lebanese, Sudani, Omani and other Arabs, Indians and Pakistanis, most of these being employed either in the oil-fields or in the many enterprises, public and private, which oil-wealth has made possible. About 3,500 Europeans and Americans are temporarily resident in the amirate.

The state's accession to multi-millionaire status, amazing in its suddenness and scale even by Middle Eastern standards, has transformed Kuwait in half a generation from a small, isolated, impoverished community of medieval type, living hungrily on pearling, boat-building and smuggling, into an extreme form of welfare state equipped with every facility, benefit and adornment that money can buy, and confronted only by a problem unknown to its forebears—that of how best to dispose of its income. Nine-tenths of the old walled town has been destroyed, a modern city of planned boulevards, modern architecture and materials, fullest urban services, shops and banks, consulates, clubs and factories, hotels, offices and palaces have arisen. The new schools, colleges, technical institutes, clinics and hospitals, housing estates: the power stations, water distillation plants (since the principality is waterless), and sewage system: the airport and deep-water harbour: all these and much more are the pride and amazement of modern Kuwait, and the outcome of its successive Development Plans, initiated in 1949. All services are given free, all are immensely costly; and the contribution of it all to 'the Good and the Beautiful' and to human happiness in the person of the Kuwaiti townsman may perhaps remain, after all, a debatable quantity.

CHAPTER SEVEN

THE NON-ARAB COUNTRIES

1. *Persia (Iran)*

PERSIA, if a country of the Middle East, is not less one of Central Asia. Geographically it forms the western half of the Iranian plateau, of which the eastern half contains Afghanistan—an almost equally Iranian country, in population and language—and the Baluchistan province of West Pakistan; but its religious and cultural contacts have been predominantly, though by no means exclusively, with the Arab world, and its modern outlook and interests lie towards the West. The long continuity of the Persian record, the achievements of its early imperial conquerors, its artists, scholars and poets, its place in world-accepted romance and legend, and the high intelligence of its present *élite*, gives Persia a singular status among the nations of western Asia, or indeed of the world. This is little diminished by the evident weaknesses of Persian public life, and the seemingly insuperable difficulties encountered there in establishing a secure, liberal régime. Indeed, the talents of this gifted people seem to lie even less than might be expected in the direction of political wisdom, or sound administration.

The territory, of which Iran is the time-honoured and widely used designation—as it is of the 'Aryan' peoples and language group—was by official order so known during the reign of Riza Shah; since then the name Persia (taken from the province of Fars in the south) is again permitted.

It extends over some 630,000 square miles, having thus more than double the area of Turkey, two-thirds that of the Sudan, and almost half the extent of India. Its boundaries on the north-west run with those of the U.S.S.R., across the Aras (Araxes) river, and with those of Turkey across a wilderness of wild mountains. From deep in Kurdistan to the head of the Persian (now known, however, throughout the Arab world as the Arabian) Gulf runs the Perso-'Iraqi frontier. Persia's southern boundary is the Gulf itself, and, outside the Strait of Hormuz, the Gulf of Oman and Arabian Sea. The eastern frontier divides the country from Pakistan in the south, from Afghanistan in the centre, and from the Turkmen Republic of the U.S.S.R.

in the north, where the southern shores of the Caspian complete its delimitation.

Loosely described as a high plateau, Persia falls in fact into a number of diverse areas, each with a special character but close and overlapping intercommunication. The north-west, substantially the great province of Azarbaijan, contains a tangle of high mountains (up to 14,000 feet) continuous with those of eastern Turkey. They are in places stony or lava-covered, with deeply-cut intersecting valleys, the broad river-valley of the Aras, and a number of narrower raised or inter-montane plains. Lake Urmia, only less salty than the Dead Sea, and the marshes surrounding it lie in the heart of an extensive, flattish agricultural region. Tabriz, the second city of Persia (population 300,000) is the capital of Azarbaijan; other main towns of the area are Riza'iya (70,000, formerly Urmia) on the Lake, Ardabil (70,000), Maragha (37,000) and Khuy (35,000).

Western Persia, from south of Azarbaijan to the Strait of Hormuz, is dominated by a broad mountainous tract up to 150 miles in width, and containing peaks exceeding 12,000 feet in height. This is known, loosely and generally, as the Zagros range, the middle and southern sectors of which contain the famous Persian oil-fields. The mountain-ridges are of fairly regular north-west to south-east tendency, but with varying directions of river-drainage. The whole tract, in at least the northern part of which earthquakes are a looming terror, is diversified by hill-cultivation, in places terraced, by fairly abundant pasture-land which supports cattle-owning transhumant tribes, by some stretches of forest, by much barren rock and soil-less hillside, and, towards the east, by depressions enclosing sometimes salt-marshes, sometimes the low-lying, cultivated and garden-bearing plains which contain historic cities. Of the latter, the best known in western Persia (including the eastern fringes of its mountain-system) are Hamadan (100,000), Kirmanshah (125,000), Yazd (65,000), Kirman (60,000), Kashan (50,000), Burujird (50,000), Isfahan (500,000) and Shiraz (170,000). In, or on the hilly fringes of, the extensive flat alluvial plain (so untypical of Persia) formed by the delta of the Karun and Karkhan rivers, lying west of the southern Zagros and extending eastward to the 'Iraqi frontier, lie the cities of Dizful, Shushtar, Ahwaz, Khorramshahr (formerly Muhammara) and Abadan (250,000), the oil-city. On the barren and humid Gulf coast are Bandar Shahpur, Bushire (abu Shahr), Linga, Bandar 'Abbas, and Jask.

Eastern Persia, a broad belt of territory reaching some 800 miles

THE MIDDLE EAST: OILFIELDS AND PIPELINES

R. W. FORD

from north to south, contains the great and famous city and shrine of Meshhed (240,000) and the lesser towns of Quchan, Sabsawar, Sultanabad (Arak), Birjand, Zabul, and Zahidan (Duzdab). This region, intermediate between the central deserts and the Afghan and Pakistani frontiers, has no unified character or dominant features; the mountain ranges, in places high and imposing, follow no obvious system. Cultivation, except in the Meshhed area to the north, is limited to a few areas of higher ground, much of the land is sandy desert, and salt-depressions abound. The rivers, except for short streams running south into the Gulf, have no permanency or outlet. In the wide Sistan depression, athwart the Afghan frontier, salt-marshes and a lake are formed by the waters of the Helmand and other rivers which enter the country from Afghanistan; before ceasing to flow they afford water for considerable cultivation—and, in bad years, can produce dangerous floods. But most of the area is otherwise arid, windy, sandblown and desolate, though it would seem surprisingly to have supported a denser population in past ages. The south (Gulf) coast is separated from the central deserts by a stretch of desert barred, from west to east, by high barren ridges; these enclose the Jaz Murian basin, fed by enclosed rivers which produce an extensive salt-marsh area and lake; pasture is poor, cultivation scanty, and the date-gardens, where these can exist, are of low quality.

The heart of Persia consists, at an altitude varying from 1,000 to 5,000 feet, of a vast area of undrained, almost rainless desert, partly sandy and stony, partly of glutinous mud covered by crusts of salt, partly of marsh into which men, animals and vehicles can sink and disappear. The area is one of sheer desert, scarcely traversable unless at the fringes, and uninhabited; only on the higher edges that rise towards the enveloping ring of mountains is there human life and cultivation, the foothill areas themselves being fertile and favourable. Such are those of Teheran itself, and Qum, (90,000), Yazd and Kirman. The central deserts themselves cover more than a third of the whole area of Persia.

They are separated from the Caspian Sea by the last region of Persia to be here mentioned, the broad foothill belt and the massive range of the Elburz, with its westward and eastward extensions. These merge into the systemless massifs of Azarbaijan and of Khurasan respectively, with Elburz itself, surmounted by the superb Demavend (18,500 feet, the highest mountain in the Middle East) barring the central approaches to the sea. Elburz and its flanking ridges provide a rich variety of scenes, conditions and climates; they afford fertile soil for cultivation, good or poor grazing, forest, ravines and bare hillsides, precipitous as well as gentle slopes. Rainfall on the northern face of the mountains can amount to one hundred inches a year, the highest known in the Middle East except that of a small area of north-eastern Turkey. The coastal plain is fertile and thickly populated; a line of sand-dunes and salt-marshes lies between it and the sea. The Caspian itself lies 90 feet below sea level; it is sinking further annually, and thus renders life more and more difficult in the ports along its coasts. (It contains about a quarter of the proportion of salt found in normal sea-water.) Persian cities on this coast are Resht (120,000), Pahlevi (40,000), Babul (35,000), and Bandar Shah. South of the great ranges lie Teheran, the capital (1,550,000), Qazvin (100,000), Samnan and Shahrud; but this region is threatened with earthquakes, the most recent and disastrous of which occurred in August 1962, as this page was being written.

Though the modern capital has, thanks to its extraordinarily rapid growth since the Second War, more than three times the population of any other Persian city, in terms of prestige the situation is far otherwise; a dozen of the major Persian cities have an outstanding local and often imperial history, from which survive not only a world of history and romantic legend, but also buildings of great dignity and beauty or, elsewhere, of the highest claims—as at Meshhed or Qum—to religious appeal. Impressive Achaemenid and Sassanian, as well as early Muslim, ruins attract scholars and tourists.

The climate of the country contains, naturally, a score of varieties, from the extreme heat and high humidity of the Karun plain and the Gulf shores, with a rainfall of 4 to 10 inches a year, to the still greater heat and still scantier rainfall of the central deserts, and to lower but still severe temperatures on higher ground inland, alternating with harsh winters. Rainfall varies from the very high deposits of Elburz to almost none at all. In temperature and moisture, and therefore not less in vegetation and livability, the north and northwest of the country excel the south, centre, and east. The season of maximum rainfall varies; in the north, apart from the Caspian provinces, it is rainiest in early spring, in the south in midwinter. Deposits vary capriciously, between wide limits, from year to year. Humidity is high on the Gulf shore in summer, on the Caspian it is almost perpetual. The sun is everywhere powerful; the air, inland, is usually dry and clear except when dust storms occur.

Of the racial composition of the country—Persians, Kurds, Lurs and Turks—something was said on previous pages (pp. 116 ff.). The total population is assessed as of the order of 21,000,000; an accurate census is unimaginable. As against the overwhelming Shi'i majority, a Sunni minority of about 1,500,000 is estimated, including the Kurds. Lesser religious minorities are those of the Zoroastrians or Parsees, known locally as Gabrs (12,000), the Jews (40,000), the Armenians (160,000), and other small Christian communities, notably the Nestorians or Assyrians (20,000). The Armenians are divided between Orthodox (Gregorian) and Catholic. There is an Anglican Bishop of Isfahan. An uncertain number of Europeans, Americans and miscellaneous foreign Asiatics live in the highly cosmopolitan capital, Teheran. Persia is divided into twelve provinces, with the city of Teheran forming another. These are subdivided into districts and sub-districts. The provinces of Kurdistan and Baluchistan are classified as 'special', and lie inside two normal provinces.

The country's population, small in relation to its wide area, and influenced by its varied and largely desertic surface, lives rather in a multitude of smallish habitable areas than in a few major stretches of fertile country. The chief exceptions to this tendency are in the flat-lands of the Khuzistan province at the head of the Gulf, the regions of Lake Urmia and Tabriz, and the Caspian shore. In the rest of Azarbaijan, in an area of the central north-west (Hamadan-Kashan), and around Meshhed, population is relatively dense; but everywhere else it is sporadic and sparse and indeed, as we shall see elsewhere, in part nomadic. The great majority of Persians are, however, village-dwelling agriculturists, primitive and conservative in method, poor and lowly in living standards. Animals—sheep, goats and cattle—producing meat, hides, wool and hair, cheese and butter, and manure for gardens are the wealth of the transhumant grazing-tribes and of many villagers, and contribute something to exports. Cottage in-dustry is still extensive; it includes silk-weaving, embroidery, metal-working and wood-carving, as well as carpet-making. Factory in-dustry, greatly encouraged from 1925 to 1940, is still a relatively small contributor to national wealth or occupation (p. 247 ff.). Mineral output, other than that of oil, is slight but not unhopeful; there is a small production of coal and of iron; copper, lead, manganese and rock-salt are worked and other minerals have been located, but these are not developed or are worked only on a negligible scale, usually by state-owned enterprises. Certain of the latter are concerned with silica, zinc, antimony, fireclay, red oxide, marble, chromite and nickel. The vast petroleum deposits are mentioned elsewhere p. 255).

The forests of the territory—40,000,000 acres are so classified, though much of this is of low quality—have some importance, and produce useful quantities of walnut, maple, beech, box and oak. The usual pests of oriental (perhaps of any) forests have been operative for centuries in the form of goats, fire and wood-cutters; but with American aid good work has been done in recent years towards rehabilitation and a competent Forest Service. Fisheries in the Persian Gulf could, suitably organized, make an even more useful contribution than they do to food supplies, and to exports; the famous caviar-fishing of the Caspian, no longer under concession to the U.S.S.R., is now the care of a Persian state-sponsored body, and produces an export item of some value.

The construction and maintenance of an adequate communication system, in a territory on this scale and with all its land-surface problems, is a task far exceeding the capacity of the Persian treasury. Roads, of which limited stretches are admirable, are more generally indifferent or poor and, being used by very limited motor-traffic, are disproportionately costly to maintain. The high standard of road upkeep achieved on main routes by the Allied forces in 1941–1945 could not be sustained; indeed a first-class, country-wide system is scarcely imaginable, high as is the priority given to it by the authorities, and indispensable as it must be to the economic development of the country. Among the villages, animal pack-transport is still universal. Lines of railway, all dating from the '30s or later, now run from the head of the Gulf at Bandar Shahpur (and also from Khorramshahr, the lines joining at Ahwaz) to Teheran, *via* Dizful and Qum; from Teheran to Qazvin, Zanjan and Tabriz—with a branch line to Lake Urmia—and the U.S.S.R. frontier at Julfa; from Teheran to the Caspian at Bandar Shah and on to Gurgan, and also eastwards to Shahrud and Meshhed; and a line from Qum to Kashan, planned for extension later to Yazd. There are 'company lines' in the oil fields. The whole of this system of some 2,125 miles, achieved with great effort in a single generation, leaves, it is obvious, a great part of Persia with no railway communication, the construction of which would indeed be always uneconomic and, with better and more roads, perhaps unneeded. Increased strategic links with CENTO neighbours, Turkey and Pakistan, are under consideration.

The territory can boast no single reliable deep-water harbour, and its shipping is thereby greatly embarrassed. On the Caspian the small ports are in constant danger, or in actual process, of silting or sanding up, and only Bandar Shah has any considerable (nearly all Russian) traffic; of the Gulf ports, Abadan and Ganawa are solely, and the fresh-waterless Bandar Mashhur mainly, devoted to oil export; Bushire and Bandar 'Abbas, open roadsteads, have difficult interior communications; Khorramshahr, far up the Shatt al 'Arab (a water-way wholly 'Iraqi-controlled), is small and ill-equipped. Apart from the Shatt, the middle and lower reaches of the Karun offer the only river-navigation in Persian territory, and have been so used (under originally British initiative) for a century; transhipment at Ahwaz is necessary. Tug and barge traffic plies across Lake Urmia.

Persia is linked to Europe and the Middle and further East by a number of foreign airlines using Teheran airport, which was com-pleted in 1958. The other largest cities have each its own adequate landing-ground, for military and civil use. All internal civilian flights are the monopoly of the government-controlled Iran National Airlines.

The Persian unit of currency is the rial, with a parity of 75 rials to one dollar, or 210 to the £ sterling: or, as a 'selling rate', 76·5 and 214·2 respectively. The metric system is employed throughout the country, though older and indigenous measures are widely used in country districts. The Persian official year is solar, New Year's Day being 21st March.

2. *Turkey*

The Turkish Republic extends to an area of almost 300,000 square miles, of which some 9,000 are in Europe, across the Bosphorus, Sea of Marmara and Dardanelles, and 290,000 in Asia. Excluding its European remnant, the country forms a rough quadrilateral; its east-west length is 950 miles, and north-south varies between 300 and 400. In Europe, its neighbours are Bulgaria and Greece; in Asia its northern, western and (in part) southern boundary is formed by the Black, Marmara, Aegean and Mediterranean seas (excluding, however, almost all the Aegean islands, which are Greek), its south-eastern by the republics of Syria and 'Iraq, its eastern by the kingdom of Persia and the Armenian and Georgian republics of the U.S.S.R. None of these boundaries, except the sea, correspond with any geo-graphical realities; those on the east and south-east are drawn across wild mountainous country.

Eastern Turkey is a tangle of high ranges, barren and sometimes lava-covered uplands, towering volcanic cones which include Ararat (16,910 feet), a great lake (Van), and deep valleys with drainage which provides the sources of the Euphrates, Tigris and Aras. The population here is scanty, vegetation limited, communications difficult. To the south and south-west of this region lies another, entirely different in type; it is the northern extension of the north-Arabian Fertile Crescent, consisting of treeless, open, flattish or undulating lands, at far lower altitudes than the mountain zone but higher than the Syrian desert across the border. In this area of fair grazing and spacious rain-cultivation lie the cities of Gaziantep ('Aintab), Urfa, Diyarbakr, Mardin; in the high mountain zone are those of Malatya, Elâziǧ (Mamuret al-'Aziz), Erzurum, Erzincan, Kars, Van and Bitlis.

The central plateau of Turkey is largely barren, with a low population outside the cities and with cultivation confined to favoured, largely riverain areas. The region is ringed on the south, north and east by mountains, and has itself an average altitude of 3,000 to 5,000 feet; in some of its higher districts it is elevated to 6,000 to 8,000 feet with isolated peaks, or volcanic cones, ranging up to 12,000. The landscape is diversified by a number of salt lakes, mudflats and marshes, but elsewhere is drained by the considerable rivers which flow into the Black Sea—the Kizil Irmak, Yesil Irmak, and Sekariya. The main cities of this area are Eskişehir, Kutahya, Afyonkarahisar, Ankara, Çorum, Tokat, Sivas, Kayseri (Caesarea), Niğde, Konya, Karaman. On the north side of this region, and stretching west-east in a 20- to 40-mile strip inland of the whole Black Sea coast, is a broken mountain region barring the way to the central plateau to the south, and falling sharply to the sea on its northern face, leaving little room, except in limited areas, for a coastal plain. The mountains, which combine with the sea and the rich rain-fed vegetation to give delightful scenery, grow higher to the east, beyond Trabzon. Besides the major rivers which, having drained central Turkey, break through northward to the sea, there are a number of short, torrential streams falling in the same direction. Turkey has no navigable river. Coastal cities, on the Black Sea—containing, however, no good natural harbour—are Zonguldak, Inebolu, Sinop (Sinope), Samsun, Ordu, Giresun, Trabzon (Trebizond), Rize. Inland of the coastal ranges lie some comparatively lowland areas. The whole region is one of continuing, sometimes alarming, volcanic activity.

Turkey's southern, Mediterranean coastal region and its hinterland are divided from central Turkey by the wide, lofty and imposing mountain system of the Taurus, the irregular folding of which has determined the configuration of the coast. To the north of the ranges occur lakes and salt-marshes; in their midst, a broken desolate area of extreme isolation: and to the south, coastal districts even more isolated, but containing two considerable plains. The western of these is that of Antalya, which remains incompletely developed by reason of malaria and bad communications; the eastern is the Cilician plain, famed for its fertility and containing the major cities of Mersin, Tarsus and Adana. The plain represents the alluvial deposits brought through the Taurus by the rivers Çakit, Seyhan and Ceyhan. The last area of Turkey to be reviewed is that of the coastlands of the Aegean and Marmara. These provide the most favoured region of the republic, both in Europe and Asia; the area includes the Aegean hinterland along the course of the westward-running rivers—the Simav, Gediz, Menderes (Meander) and Daraman—as well as the broken, deeply indented coastline itself, and the broad flattish basin on both sides of the Sea of Marmara. This region contains a high proportion of the Turkish people, living in admirable climatic and other natural conditions in proximity to some of the most famous cities and beautiful and historic seascapes in the world. The role of this district in human history, from remote antiquity onwards, is well known, and not less its function as a direct gateway from the west into Asia Minor and beyond. Its famous cities are those of Istanbul, Edirne (Adrianople), Kirklareli (Kirk Kilisseh) and Tekirdağ (Rodosto) in Europe, and, in Asia, Adapazari, Ismit, Iznik (Nicaea), Bursa (Brusa), Balikesir, Akhisar, Izmir (Smyrna), Aydin, Denizli, Muğla.

The climate of Anatolia is as various as its land-surface, with extraordinary variations of heat and cold between districts as well as between seasons; in parts of the central plateau the summer temperature can be over 100 degrees Faht., the winter —15 degrees, and the rainfall can vary from 100 inches a year at the eastern end of the Black Sea coast, to 10 inches or less in some interior districts. The western and south-western coastal regions enjoy a perfect Mediterranean climate, with mild wet winters and hot summers. In the Marmara lowlands, conditions resemble those of Great Britain, especially in its rapidly changing weather. From all the above it will appear that almost any natural condition desired or dreaded by man can be found in Turkey, and almost every form of response thereto has been adopted by the varying ways in which life is lived, from Kurdish semi-nomadism to intensive fruit-growing, from extensive sheep-farming to the close area of tea or tobacco gardens.

Agriculture apart (p. 238)—and this in Turkey is extraordinarily varied—the natural resources of Asia Minor are considerable. Its mineral wealth, exploited in remote antiquity in the forms of gold, copper and iron, is the most considerable in the Middle East; if its development to some extent lags behind, this is by reason of the low grade or limited scale of most deposits, their scattered locations and difficulty of access, and the lack of available risk-capital to exploit them. Mining activity is largely state-controlled, under an Institute of Mining Research; most of the old mineral concessions have been annulled, or bought out, but private enterprise is still encouraged. The coal of the Zonguldak area of the Black Sea coast is important, and deeper search may find greater reserves; meanwhile, exploitation continues, a major asset to industry, and up to 8,000,000 tons a year is being produced. Lignite occurs at many locations and on a commercial scale, yielding up to 3,000,000 tons a year. Deposits of iron-ore are widely spread in Turkish territory; exploitation, however, today predominantly from the deposits of Divriği between Sivas and Erzurum, is no more than partial, owing to difficulties of transport and treatment. The other main source, the Camdağ mines, nearest to the Zonguldak coal, is government-owned. Chrome has long been an important Turkish resource, and exploitation of this mineral is reckoned the second greatest in the world. It occurs in western Anatolia and in the eastern highlands, west of Van, and elsewhere. Copper is mined at the Ergani and Murgul mines in Elâziğ and Çorum provinces and, besides local utilization, affords a useful export. Lead and zinc are both found at widely scattered locations, but are not more than marginally economic to produce. The same can apply even to the famous meerschaum clay deposits (near Eskişehir) in which Turkey enjoys a world monopoly; and even more to the wide range of minerals which diversify, without greatly enriching, production—alum, antimony, asbestos, manganese, mercury, sulphur, wolfram and emery. The last-named, found on the island of Naxos, gives an exportable surplus, as do antimony, boracite and manganese. The wolfram deposits have increasing importance. Production of minerals has, on the whole, increased encouragingly, and the search for more is being vigorously pressed. Petroleum (p. 253/4) is disappointingly scarce.

The forests of Turkey are the most extensive in the Middle East, and all, since 1937, government-controlled. They are found at different levels and in different conditions in many parts of the country, and cover an eighth of the surface of Turkey. Most are of low quality and meagre yield. A modern forestry administration has (at least on paper) been installed, and efforts, which should not be viewed with excessive optimism, are made to limit the progressive deterioration which has been continuous in the past through unauthorized cutting, charcoal-burning, fire, neglect—and goats. Some new planting is in hand. The annual value of forest output is low but not negligible.

Fishing is an activity of little economic importance, though practised in some degree in all seaside areas. Some recent development has taken place, with American aid. There is a limited export of fish.

The plateau of Anatolia affords a home and livelihood to the millions of livestock which are among Turkey's riches, and their immediate contribution in milk, butter and meat is a main support of hundreds of villages, even though modern forms of dairy-farming are little adopted; and is the whole-time concern of (a seeming anachronism in modern Turkey) the Yuruk (nomadic) herdsmen who move seasonally between higher and lower pastures. Draught-animals have still a high place in local agriculture and village transport. The export of hides and skins, wool and mohair, is valuable. The Anatolian wool is of coarse quality, though exported on a major scale; the silky hair of the famous 'Angora' goat, on the other hand, is highly prized and indeed unique. Water buffaloes are kept, for transport and ploughing and their milk, mostly on the Black Sea coast.

Turkish territory is divided for administration into sixty-seven Ils or provinces, subdivided into districts and cantons. The biggest city is Istanbul, formerly the capital; next come Ankara (660,000) the present capital, Izmir (370,000), Adana (230,000), Bursa (150,000), Eskişehir (150,000), Gaziantep (125,000), Konya (120,000), Kayseri (100,000), and a dozen more with populations exceeding 50,000; yet only one-fifth of the Turks are city-dwelling, four-fifths are countrymen. The population of the republic is: in Europe, 2,250,000; in Asia, 25,500,000, a total of 27,800,000. This figure represents a rapid growth during the last generation; the population was less than 14,000,000 in 1927, and has increased by an annual proportion varying between 2·3 and 3·0 per cent per year since that date, an increase due in large part, probably, to a lowered death-rate. Turkish resources, underdeveloped as they now are, could doubtless support a larger than the present population. Thanks to the long continuous Turkish occupation of Anatolia, their tradition of conquest and government, their religion, their policy of assimilation (aided at times by the expulsion or massacre of minorities) the present population is unusually homogeneous, not indeed in racial origins but in sentiment. A large proportion of the 1,500,000 Kurds, in the eastern provinces, is by now largely assimilated as Turks; the same may apply to the 30,000 recently immigrant Bulgarians, and to the 25,000 Lazes and 90,000 Circassians. It is probably less true of the 250,000 Arabs (all in the Mardin-Urfa area), and untrue of the surviving Jews, perhaps 25,000 in number, or the Greeks and Armenians in two or three main cities of the west. Not much more than 1 per cent of the population is non-Muslim, though a fair proportion, possibly one in six, are believed to be non-Sunni but to follow instead some semi-heretical Shi'i persuasion within Islam (p. 94). A proportion of the Arabs above-mentioned belong to the Christian sects of the Chaldaean, Syrian and Greek Uniates, and the Armenian Orthodox, but the numbers of each community are uncertain. Islam, no longer officially the State religion, is nevertheless widely revered and practised; the more old-fashioned Turk, in particular, is to all appearances a model Muslim. All races and creeds alike are treated, it is claimed, with impartiality by the government, though in practice certain discriminations (and, *vis-à-vis* the Greeks, a still powerful antipathy) continue to be observed.

The size of the country and the difficult terrain of tangled and passless mountain tracts, added to the prevailing (including governmental) poverty, render an efficient system of communications difficult to achieve, even though this is acknowledged as indispensable for social and economic reasons and to remedy the isolation in which live a high proportion of Turkish villagers, notably in the south-west, the extreme east, and the Black Sea littoral. The road system has, accordingly, been greatly extended and improved during the last generation, in part with American aid; there are now at least 15,000 miles (part macadam, part graded earth) of national highways, as much again of fair provincial roads, and an uncertain length of passable tracks. Work continues on all these, and all are used by a motor traffic which, still light by European standards, has trebled in the last fifteen years. Buses, fixed-route taxis and innumerable ox-carts are all constant road-users in addition to trucks and passenger cars. Railways, inadequate a generation ago, have been similarly developed with a view both to economics and to strategy, including internal security. They are since 1947 all state-owned, and give generally a reliable service. Much of the country is still, and will no doubt long remain, without railways by reason of the immense difficulty and cost of construction, and the unrewarding traffic; but most of the chief cities of the interior now enjoy railway communication, and this extends also to the east, up to and beyond Erzurum and to Lake

Van; eastward also from Diyarbakr to Si'irt; and northward to the Black Sea at Zonguldak and Samsun. New connections have been made also in central and western Anatolia. Single-track lines, the great majority, are now in some cases being double-tracked. With all this, it cannot be pretended that the combined road and railway system, improved as it has been at great cost, gives Turkey anything like an adequate communications system.

Partly for this reason, the country's merchant navy has, in recent years, been fostered and much increased. Total tonnage, all state-owned through the State Seaways Administration, now approaches 1,000,000 tons and nearly 3,000 vessels. These have a monopoly of the coastwise trade (in many areas the sole link with the outside), and a respectable share of Mediterranean and Aegean traffic. The chief ports besides Istanbul—by far the greatest, and now under further development on the Asiatic side—are Izmir, where new instal-lations have been added, Zonguldak, Samsun, Trabzon, Eregli, Mersin and Iskanderun. Each of these has its special function in view of inland resources, transit or strategy. Turkish State Airlines (the D.H.Y.), founded in 1933, now includes participants both domestic and foreign, and gives an excellent internal service. The main airports are those of Istanbul and Ankara, but twenty more are in use. Turkey is served, internationally, by the scheduled services of a dozen foreign (European, American and Middle Eastern) air-lines, with agencies and facilities at Istanbul and Ankara.

The Turkish pound, recently revalued, stands at £T 25·32 to the £ sterling. The money in circulation, apart from nickel and silver, consists of Central Bank notes. The metric system of weights and measures is in force, since 1934. The Gregorian Calendar, replacing both that of Islam and that of the half-westernized Ottoman com-promise, was adopted in 1925.

3. Cyprus

Cyprus is a territory markedly differing from any other in the Middle East by its racial content, its history and its current politico-social problems, and by being an island—the third largest in the Mediterranean. It lies some 250 miles from the Egyptian, 70 from the Syrian, 40 from the Turkish coasts. The area of the island is 3,570 square miles, its greatest length 140 miles, its greatest width 60, the average width (excluding the narrow eastern extension) about 40.

The dominant physical features of the country are at once obvious:

a sharply defined ridge of hills, rising to 3,000 feet and reaching from
west of Kyrenia to the north-eastern tip: a mountain massif, that of
Mount Troodos (6,400 feet), in the west-centre of the island; and a
flat plain, the Mesaoria, lying between these two and open to the
sea on its west and east flanks. Both the coast and the mountain
area, which is heavily forested, are of great beauty. The territory is
full of picturesque medieval and modern buildings, and of ancient
Greek and Roman remains. The climate is of normal Mediterranean
type, with a hot summer in the plain and a mild winter, and liability
to frost and snow above the 3,000-foot line. The rainfall can be as
much as 40 inches a year on the higher ground, but as low as 10
inches in the Mesaoria plain. The drainage of rain from the slopes,
and even that of melting snow, is so rapid that no rivers exist other
than short-lived torrents. Conditions on the island, despite its smallness, are remarkably varied, and nowhere disagreeable.

Apart from agriculture (p. 241), which is here obviously limited
by the chronic dryness of the agricultural lands and their restricted
acreage, and a few light industries on a humble scale, the resources
of Cyprus are not impressive. The tourist trade is valuable. Supply
to, and employment by, the British forces in their detached enclave
are assets; so also is the country's central position as an air-travel
halt and junction. The Cypriot forest, on and all around Mount
Troodos, covers nearly one-fifth of the island (or 670 square miles)
and, besides its uncommon beauty, can supply nearly half the local
needs in timber. The utmost care is taken to minimize the dangers
and evils of fire, goats and marauders. Neither fishing nor animal-
herding and breeding are of more than parochial importance.
Mineral exploitation, on the contrary, is a main source of the island's
activity and wealth. This concerns, to a limited extent, gypsum,
chrome, umber and asbestos; on a much greater scale, iron pyrites
(with export worth, in 1960, more than £2,000,000) and cupreous
pyrites, or copper, with an export value of £6,000,000. (These
figures are well exceeded in years of higher prices.) Mining is the
activity of American, Greek and British interests, and employs some
6,000 workers.

The population of Cyprus at present approximates to 575,000;
it is increasing by about 10,000 a year, and was less than 200,000
when the government of the island was assumed by the British in
1878. About one-third of the people are town-dwellers, the remainder
live in the Greek or Turkish or mixed villages, with a humble but by
no means miserable standard of life. There is a steady movement

from the countryside to the towns. Among the latter, each the head-quarters of one of the six provinces, are Nicosia, the capital, with a population of 90,000, Limassol (40,000), Famagusta (30,000), Larnaca (20,000), Paphos (8,000), Kyrenia (5,000). These populations include small minorities of Maronites, Armenians and other Christian sects, and a few score of European foreigners. They include also the considerable Turkish minority, one-fifth of the whole, of which we spoke on an earlier page (p. 113).

The bulk, approximately four-fifths of the people, claim, as is well known, to be Greek. It is true that no Greek territory lies nearer than 250 miles away, across the sea; that Cyprus has never, throughout history, been under Greek mainland rule; and that the Cypriot dialect differs appreciably from mainland Greek. Nevertheless, their own Greek culture, speech, sentiment and nostalgia combine to make unrealistic any claim that the islanders are 'not really Greeks,' and as such they must without question be considered. They are, of course, Greek Orthodox in religion, with their own auto-cephalous Church of Cyprus: their Archibishop having been, since August 1960, the first President of the Republic. Many members of both the major communities speak each other's language, and English is widely understood in the towns.

As to communications, the island's road system is greatly improved and now fairly, though not wholly, adequate to the demands made upon it by the growing motor-traffic. The number of road accidents, reported to be abnormal, is probably due to recklessness of drivers rather than to the roads, of which nearly 1,000 miles with hard surface exist, and 2,000 without; these are impassable on very few days in the year. Nicosia has an equipped airport, used by one locally-based company, and a dozen more belonging to Middle Eastern states or to countries of Europe. Air transport benefits by the poorness of Cypriot harbours, of which not one is adequate to modern needs. Limassol and Larnaca are open roadsteads with no protection from the weather, and the use of lighters is a necessity; Famagusta can offer berths only to vessels of shallow draught and moderate length. Greek, Italian and Israeli shipping lines provide regular passenger services, and others, including British, serve cargo requirements by at least weekly calls.

The Cyprus pound equals £1 sterling and subdivides into 1,000 mils. British weights and measures, those of the metric system, and miscellaneous Cypriot measures, which represent a survival from Turkish days, are all in use.

4. *Israel*

The State of Israel is situated in an area of the territory of Arab Palestine (as this had been before 1948) less extensive than the Palestine of the British Mandate, but larger by about one quarter than the area allotted to the Jews by United Nations decision in 1947. The resulting extent of the Israeli Republic is some 8,000 square miles. This represents mandated Palestine with the exceptions, first, of 150 square miles on the Mediterranean coast beyond Gaza—the 'Gaza strip', now occupied by Egypt—and, secondly, of some 2,500 miles of Samaritan and Judaean highland now forming part of Jordan, in central-eastern Palestine. Israeli territory consists in effect, of the fertile coastal plain of the mandated territory; of the foothills west of the central range, and part of that range itself; of the flat, rich vale between Mount Carmel and the Jordan, the vale of Esdraelon (or Emek Yezreel): the historic district of Galilee, which includes the plain of Acre ('Akka), an area of broken hill-country, the descent to the Jordan, and the lakes of Hula (now drained) and Tiberias. Besides these, Israel holds the extensive western suburbs (but not the walled city) of Jerusalem, and a wedge-shaped corridor leading up to it from the seaward lowlands: and disposes, finally, of almost the entirety of the southern desert of Palestine, bounded by the Sinai wilderness to the west and the Wadi 'Araba to the east; this, the Negev, gives Israel half of its total area. These two boundaries, converging on the Gulf of 'Aqaba, leave to Israel, as its priceless southern sea-outlet, a gap of some 8 miles on its shores. In terms of neighbours, the Republic is bounded on the north by Lebanon, along the old Palestine-Lebanon frontier: on the north-east by Syria, along the course of the Jordan and a winding line running Metulla-Dan-Hula: on the east, south of the Yarmuk, by Jordan, and again by Jordan from south of the Dead Sea to 'Aqaba along the bottom of the Wadi 'Araba: and on the south-west by Egypt. None of these boundaries have been stabilized by international agreement; all are those of the Armistice of 1948, which no peace has ever ratified.

Climatically, Israel is a typically Mediterranean country, with warm or hot summers and mild, rainy winters. The low-lying areas toward Jordan, and even more the Valley itself, can offer summer temperatures of over 100° F, and a high humidity. Snow is uncommon in the lowlands, not infrequent though rarely heavy in Jerusalem, and a regular feature of winter, to considerable depths.

in the hills of Galilee. This latter area has an annual rainfall of 40 inches or more, which decreases southward, by stages, until in the Negev and along the coast below Gaza it drops to 8 or 5 inches or less. Prevailing winds are south-westerly. On the whole, the temperate, sunny and delightful climate of Israel is among its uncontroversial assets.

The composition of the population, which was 90 per cent Arab in 1919, and between 60 and 70 per cent in 1940, underwent a total change in the year 1948 and thereafter; the great majority of the Arab population departed (for reasons elsewhere described, p. 137 f.) from the main part of Palestine which was thenceforward to be Israel, and the numbers of immigrant Jews rapidly and vastly increased: a process authorized and encouraged by the policy, or indeed the *raison d'être*, of the new state, which offered an unquestioning welcome to any Jew in the world who wished to enter. The population of the territory, in which about 200,000 Arabs and Druzes remained, rose rapidly; by 1962 it had reached nearly 2,250,000, of whom two million are Jews, 170,000 Arab Muslims, 50,000 Arab Christians (mainly Catholic and Uniate), and 25,000 Druzes. The surviving Arab element in Israel, while not excluded from the benefits of most of the social services, agricultural loans and co-operatives, and education opportunities (and the use of their own language), are subject to various restrictions, doubtless on suspicion of disloyalty, and enjoy generally a depressed and unequal status. They are exempt from conscription.

This formidable immigration of Jews, handled mainly by the pre-existing Jewish Agency for Palestine with its headquarters in Jerusalem and New York, has been the dominant feature not only of the demography but of the entire public scene in Israel from 1948 to the present date (1962). The immigrants, qualified or unqualified to start new lives, with every variety of capacity or helplessness, every age and background, came predominantly from Europe in the earliest years following mid-1948: from Hungary, Austria, Poland, Germany and the Balkan countires, with a few from southern, very few from western, Europe and fewer from America. From 1950 onwards began the flood of immigrants from eastern and African countries, whose situation there had deteriorated, to the point of unbearability, thanks to Muslim resentment. Scores of thousands came, accordingly, from the Yemen and Aden, from 'Iraq, Persia and Turkey, from Egypt and north-west Africa, from Ethiopia, Afghanistan, Turkistan and China. In the twelve years following 1948 the proportion between

European and eastern or African Jews entering Israel seems to have
been approximately 46·5 per cent of the former, 53·5 of the latter.
There is little need to emphasize the immense range of human types
involved, from blond Nordics and Slavs to Berbers, Mongolians,
Indians and black Africans; yet all were Jews, all became—and, with
allowance for emigration, nine-tenths remained—Israeli citizens. So
much, an observer might ruminate, for the ever-repeated assertion
that Jewry is a 'race'! The predominance of oriental immigrants
(one of numbers, not at all of wealth, skill, culture or standard of
life) will doubtless in future years be emphasized by their more
rapid rate of increase, and cannot but exercise a heavy influence on
the future of Israel.

No task of the young State has been more arduous, nor more
essential, than the assimilation and settlement of the immigrant
masses whom, in a high percentage of cases, fear and poverty and
misery, rather than suitability, had selected. They have been received,
fed, housed, set to work, instructed, directed and redirected until
somehow and in some occupation the point of 'settlement' has been
reached. The techniques for this series of co-ordinated processes,
always with emphasis (partly practical, partly doctrinaire) on the
land and on manual labour, have been constantly improved, and
have no doubt gone far to create, out of amazingly disparate
material, a feeling of single nationhood and of willingness to face
Israel's appalling problems.

The dominant language of the country is a revived and simplified
Hebrew, which is taught to all immigrants and has become the
lingua franca as well as the official language (jointly with Arabic) of
the state. This decision, involving the subordination of the languages
actually spoken by the multifarious incomers (Ladino, many forms
of Yiddish, and almost every major language of Europe and Asia),
has made assimilation and absorbtion more immediately difficult for
the novice, but has also, on a larger view, made possible a measure
of homogeneity and nation-wide communication as no other solution
could have done. Arabic is spoken by the Arabs and Druzes, and is
known to older Jewish residents. English is the most usually heard
of European languages, though English-speaking immigrants have
not in recent years exceeded 1 per cent.

Meanwhile, the face of the country has been changed. Not only
has a new, alien population, from the four corners of the earth,
replaced the former age-long dwellers in that familiar and delightful
countryside, but new settlements or villages, some temporary, some

permanent, have been sited and sprung up in many hundreds, existing cities have increased in size four or six or tenfold; examples of which are Tel Aviv with Jaffa (now 400,000 strong, and 98 per cent Jewish), Beersheba (increased from 2,000 to 45,000), Haifa (from 120,000 to 250,000), and, with similar increases, Ramla, Lydda (now Lod) the Jerusalem complex, Majdal (now Migdal Gad) and Naharia. Entirely new cities have been founded in Galilee, in the Negev, and on the Gulf of 'Aqaba. In spite of the ambition (and the economic necessity) to work the land and grow food, the Jewish population in 1962 was reckoned to be three-quarters city- or town-dwelling, one quarter engaged in agriculture. The latter has, nonetheless, a high priority among the employments to which the young of both sexes are canalized during their period of conscript service.

Israelis settled on the land have adopted, or have conformed to, forms of social organization peculiar to the country, and representative of its strongly socialist climate. Life in the famous Kibbutzim is entirely collective, with private property forbidden and all family life restricted; in the villages of more normal type private property and personal responsibility are allowed. In 1961, out of 830 rural settlements, 230 were Kibbutzim, with 80,000 settlers; a greater number lived under one of the less exacting régimes. Arab villages numbered about 100.

More will be said on later pages of Israeli efforts in the fields of agriculture and irrigation (p. 242 f.) and of industry (p. 247 ff.). In both, the scene in recent years has been one of phenomenal activity. This has been based in equal parts on scientific direction and planning, on the devoted labour of all concerned, and on the provision of capital. The latter has come from three sources: one, the now vanished Arab population (in the form of lands, citrus-groves, gardens, wells, houses, public buildings and installations); secondly, from international and foreign national agencies: and thirdly, and most notably, from the government of the United States and the immensely wealthy and influential Jewish public in that country, upon whose abundant contributions rests, in simple fact, the viability of the State of Israel.

The natural resources of the country are scanty. Its minerals, the search for which has been vigorously pressed, include some iron ore in Galilee and the Negev, and, mainly in the latter, copper (near Eilat), manganese, mica, gypsum, phosphates, salt, silica and china clay. These, although in initial stages of development, amount at present to very little; but the extraction of potash, bromine and

magnesium salts from the Dead Sea is a major enterprise—its installations have been resited since 1948—and it produces both valuable
raw materials for the chemical industry and useful exports. There
is no scope in Israel for extensive animal husbandry, but cattle are
raised intensively for meat and for dairy produce. Fishing on commercial lines is practised off the Mediterranean coast and in the
Gulf of 'Aqaba by a fleet of trawlers and other craft; the Sea of
Galilee is actively fished, and the breeding of carp in ponds in many
of the agricultural settlements is a developing industry. Forests, a
feature of the Palestinian landscape in antiquity, are today represented by some medium-scale but increasing modern plantations.

Israeli territory being small and unobstructed, an adequate system
of communications, mainly inherited from the mandatory government, presents serious difficulty only in the partly untrodden, sandblown Negev, and sometimes also in providing access to the remoter
new settlements. New main roads have been constructed, or old
tracks improved, in connection with the port of Eilat and the potash-
extraction installations, and to link Tel Aviv better with Jerusalem.
Road traffic is everywhere dense. The railways, maintained and improved, remain substantially as they were designed under the Mandate; that is, the coastal railway from the Egyptian to the Lebanese
frontier: the Tel Aviv–Jerusalem line: and the Esdraelon line from
Haifa through 'Afula to the Jordan Valley. A newly-constructed
line joins Lidda to Beersheba, another is planned to connect Eilat
with Beersheba across the Negev. The relations between Israel and
all her neighbours preclude any transfrontier communication, by rail
or otherwise. Of the country's seaports, Haifa is by far the best
constructed and equipped, and the most used. Inherited from the
Mandatory power as a well-found modern harbour, it has been
recently extended with new facilities and more space, and an auxiliary
harbour has been constructed at the Kishon mouth. Jaffa–Tel Aviv
has a joint lighter-harbour at the mouth of the Yarkon. A new deep-
water harbour at Ashdod Yam, north of Askalon, is currently under
construction. The new port of Eilat, invaluable by reason of its
access to the Red Sea and the East, is being equipped with all speed,
and handles an increasing traffic which includes cargoes of crude oil,
piped thence to Haifa for refining. The Israeli merchant marine is a
new and vigorous growth; it now includes tankers, dry cargo vessels
and passenger ships, to a total of some 50 (mostly new) vessels, with
300,000 tons displacement. This is regarded as an important asset
to a country whose land frontiers are all blockaded, and whose

needs of import and export are paramount. Considerable extension of the fleet is planned. In the field of aviation the country's main centre is at Lidda, with lesser airports at Haifa and Tel Aviv. Three local airline companies exist, the largest having major international scope.

The metric system is used in Israel; for land-measurement the Donum, of 1,000 square metres (a quarter of an acre), is the unit. The Jewish year 5723 begins on September 29, 1962. The unit of currency is the Israeli pound (I£), for which the (devalued) rate of exchange was fixed early in 1962 at I£ 8·40 to the £1 sterling, or I£3·00 to the U.S. dollar.

CHAPTER EIGHT

PUBLIC LIFE

1. *The Disunited States*

FOR the devotion of a chapter to governments and politics, in a work on 'social geography', there is more justification in the Middle East than could be pleaded in, for instance, a West-European or North-American area, since in these an interest in government and politics is for most people swamped by a score of others—business, social or sporting—and the visible effects of government action or inaction are less conspicuous. In the lands of the Middle East, on the other hand, 'the Government' is all-important, politics are the dominant concern for a large, and the most dynamic, part of the population. The State is the most pervasive of influences, the greastest and often the only repository of important capital, the initiator and controller in industry, communications and agriculture. It is the agency, far more than any form of private enterprise, responsible for creating the new conditions of life which have profoundly modified the ways of urban society. It is the sole provider of super-community and super-tribal authority, greatest direct employer of labour, possessor and bestower of the highest prestige. It is inevitably, therefore, from many angles a significant social factor. Moreover in every country, even Arabia, the servants of the government, the civil service in its every grade, form a highly important body, a numerous, characteristic, and privileged class. It is true that the transition from the low standard of nineteenth-century conditions in the Ottoman Empire, Persia and Egypt, to those of a more active, better trained, more honest official class, is as yet far from complete; there are still, almost everywhere, too many civil servants, too generally ill-paid, extremely diverse in type and merit—from over-meticulous to haphazard, from deeply entrenched veterans to the new and callow, from more than doubtfully to rigidly honest, from arrogant to democratic—and often infused with overdoses of political fervour or departmental narrowness. But the elements of scandal or comedy, or even farce, frequent enough in the Serais or police-barracks of Ottoman times, are by degrees disappearing; genuine service to the public is becoming a less unfamiliar concept, and a national is superseding a merely bureaucratic pride. Indeed, the *effendis* of today and tomorrow mark a vast advance on those of yesterday, and now form a generally creditable as well as an important social element; much goodwill and more competence are available in the civil services, and directors and ministers of excellent ability are far from uncommon. Indeed, the adverse factors which persist are generally those implicit in the backward, heterogeneous publics, in military interventions in civil government, and in the aberrations of dictators, rather than in the shortcomings of officialdom.

As to the shape of government itself, our survey of Middle Eastern populations may have suggested doubts about the applicability of the nation-state form of grouping to a region in which languages, races and minorities are spread so sporadically across the map; but could this be otherwise? To the sovereign-nation system there appears, in the modern world, no alternative; in the Near East the example of one self-conscious Balkan fragment after another breaking off from the Ottoman Empire long ago established precedents which the present Arab states—but, to their chagrin, never the Kurds, and never the Armenians—have been successful in following; and the similar record of imperial disintegration, or imperial policy, in favour of small independent states is, of course, plain to see in Africa, Asia and elsewhere in the mid-twentieth century. Moreover, in the possession of the recognized qualifications for nation-state rank, which are common territory, history, tradition, language, outlook, and sense of mutual belonging, or most of these, the modern Middle Eastern states, thanks in part to their long if often unedifying experience of politico-administrative forms and provincial delimitations under the Ottoman monarchy, do not fall short to anything like the same extent as do the new states of Africa; most of them can make a fair or strong case for national status, and all have successfully done so. That the secular nation-state conception is far removed from the original Islamic principle of a single religious-political community of all Muslims everywhere must, of course, be recognized; but this creates no practical difficulty, and is remembered only by the most conservative and pietistic elements in the states concerned.

Meanwhile among the Middle Eastern nations, as they now exist, national spirit is conspicuously developed. Those governments and publics which have enjoyed national status for centuries—Turkey, Persia and (practically, though not wholly in form) the central- and south-Arabian States—continue to be vigilant that no affront to, or implied diminution of, their independence be sustained; and this is even more the case among the nations 'liberated' to enjoyment of that privilege since the First War—the ex-Ottoman Arab States, with Egypt, the Sudan and Cyprus—in all of which their highly sensitive nationalism places insistence on 'complete independence' as its primary demand or pride. This, however, is not the only constituent of this ever-quoted (and in Europe largely decried) nationalism which is, and will for years remain, the strongest and most pervasive political force in the region. It contains, indeed, its element of genuine, perhaps idealistic, patriotism, its nostalgia for what was best in a glorious past, its resolve that the cherished State shall be not only free but benevolent, an inspiration towards uplighting living-standards and securing justice, and a visible negation of old inferiority complexes implanted by centuries of subordination. Nevertheless, and though few western nations are blameless in such regards, it must be said that nationalism in its Middle Eastern forms, with its visible elements of (often officially supported) xenophobia, chauvinism and boasting, too often takes forms inimical to liberty and enlightenment within these countries, and damaging to their prestige abroad: the former from its narrowness, insistence on uniformity, and competitive inflammatory influence on rival politicians, the latter from its malicious suspicion or rancour, and its easy adoption of bad international manners. It is, however, idle to expect the publics and leaders of Middle Eastern states to progress beyond nationalism, or even to purge it of its evident crudities, at a stage of their independent development in which manifestations of egocentric jingoism are, it seems, an inevitable phase of growth.

In view of this prevalent, deeply felt territory-nationalism can there be hopes of some form of multi-statal grouping—unity, federation, or association—between our territories? an association desirable, no doubt, on many grounds and perhaps made more conceivable by the peculiarly haphazard distribution of races and communities in the Middle East and, more positively, by the powerful factors of much common history, of propinquity and constant intercommunication, of largely similar conditions, as between the various states? Or can there truly be hopes, even, of the ever-proferred, everelusive Arab Unity? It must be answered that, for anything wider than the last-named possible grouping, there is no present hope whatsoever; Turkey, Israel, Cyprus, Persia—these are all far too distinct, too self-consciously isolated by their own exclusive national feeling, too suspicious of their neighbours, for any close link between them, or between them and the Arab states, to be presently conceivable. The Arab states themselves, as we have seen (pp. 101–2), possess solid and lively factors of unity; and a political extension of this, they repeatedly tell us, such as to create a new world-force and reflect the single voice of the Arab people, with more power and unanimity than their disappointingly ill-knit and ineffective League of Arab States has ever done, is one of their most cherished aims. Then, why not?

The reasons, sadly convincing, are various but interconnected. The first is the power and narrowness of the local patriotism (poles apart from the imagined Pan-Arabism) which the education and policy of the last forty years have exalted. Second is the very different orientation of the various Arab states, their diverse forms of government, their unequal stages of social and educational evolution. Thirdly, one must observe the strength of the vested interests—of royal houses, officialdom, the tribes, the minorities, the armies, the men of commerce and industry—which militate against any form of super-statal union which might (and in cases certainly would) adversely affect their personal or sectional interests. Fourthly, one must reckon with jealousy among the potential rulers or ruling cliques in any Pan-Arab formation, and even (as is so visible today) with a lurking or an explicit inter-statal lack of cordiality (to put it mildly!), together with doubts among many as to whether the task of managing the suggested super-national group (whether federal or federated or unitary) would not prove quite beyond the powers of any statesmanship at present sighted in the Arab world. In the fifth place come the existing specific animosities between the states—between 'Iraq and Kuwait, for instance, or Syria and Lebanon, or Egypt *vis-à-vis* most of her Arab sisters. And finally one recognizes the intensely individualistic strain in the Arab character, with its dislike of accepting outside (or any other) authority, and its poor record in unselfish co-operation. If at any time the Arab states, or some of them, can find a form of closer association, and make a success of it (as Egypt and Syria, in 1958–1961, did not), they would enjoy the good wishes of the world, certainly including Great Britain and the West; but the omens were, at the time of writing, unfavourable.

2. *The Field of Government*

In peninsular Arabia, rulers are still convinced that *l'état c'est moi*, and their families—habitually numerous, often idle and extravagant— are insistent that this formula (than which they can conceive no other) includes themselves. In these principalities, therefore, except in so far as world-opinion (or the urgings of European advisers, if permitted) may have faintly penetrated, very different conceptions of the legitimate sphere of government are held from those of the modern world, including their sister Middle Eastern states to the north and west. It is the latter, and the activities of their more developed administrations, that we pass now to consider.

It is needless, unless for completeness, to mention that in every such state is found a body of Law; a body far removed from its purely Islamic predecessor (the Shari'a), even though it may still permit the use of the latter (except in Egypt and Turkey) for cases of personal status—marriage, divorce, alimony, guardianship. The modern and repeatedly revised law-codes in current use, civil and criminal, are based on French or British or Swiss or Italian originals, and on local latter-day statutes. To administer these, all the governments maintain, properly separated from their legislative or executive branches, normally adequate Courts of Law, local and central, at all levels of First Instance, Superior, Appeal and Cassation, as well as the religious or community Courts limited in their jurisdiction to affairs of personal status. These systems, supervised by a Minister of Justice, are for the most part comprehensive and respectable. They are presided over nowadays by judges and magistrates of modern education, graduates of their law-schools, who have (except in the Shari'a courts) superseded the *qadhis* of old. It may be said that, not without their frequent short-comings, sometimes humours, occasionally scandals, the codes and courts of Middle Eastern countries now present on the whole a far from discreditable picture, are conducted with dignity and integrity, and are supported by a general public opinion in these qualities. There has been, beyond question, an important rise in standard during the last half-century. Both bench and bar provide careers for many of the professionally educated members of the middle class, for whom, too often, employment is difficult to find; and it is no longer anywhere (unless in the tribunals of Arabia) a near-certainty that the rich litigant will win his case, and the well-connected criminal be acquitted.

Trained and armed forces capable under normal conditions of securing law and order, and apprehending the wrong-doer, are no less a matter of course. A more or less adequate Police and/or Gendarmerie is maintained, reasonably drilled and equipped—as were indeed, in their time, those of the Ottoman (but far less the Persian) power. In these forces, and the Prisons administrations which accompany them, there is today more goodwill and honesty,

less oppression and corruption, than ever before. Behind these are
supported, upon a great or small scale (and often absorbing a lament-
ably large share of the revenues of the state) regular military, naval
and air forces, which range from the important formations of the
Turkish Republic to the relatively petty units of Lebanon or the
Sa'udis. Such forces have an appreciable social importance by reason
not only of the part they play in the maintenance of order, but also
from their contribution to visible national pomp, glory and ceremonial, and from the particular status of the officer-class—with, it
must be added, its notable readiness to stray into, and then to
dominate, the political field.

With the same difference in scale, and no less in effectiveness, the
Middle Eastern states follow all modern practice in assuming the
duties of a Public Health Service, and that of Education. Medicine
as a career attracts many of the best types of citizen; good medical
services are recognized as of inestimable value to the country, and
incidentally catch the eye of foreign observers; and the only limit to
governmental effort in this regard is that of material resources—
money, buildings, equipment and, in most of the territories, trained
men. Within such limits all the Governments, each in their degree,
aim at measures intended to decrease the danger of epidemic disease,
to stamp out those hitherto endemic (malaria, bilharzia, the eye
diseases), to minimize adverse local factors (bad housing, dirt,
polluted water, food infection, etc.), and to care for school children,
as well as to provide specialist and general hospitals, asylums, and
dispensaries in every district. There is, in this field, no lack of
intelligent goodwill, and progress is continuous, to an extent extremely
striking and heartening to those who have watched it for the last
four decades. The recruitment of a few foreign specialists is still
unavoidable, and the refusal of many local doctors to face village or
provincial life is unfortunate.

In Education the effort, in all but the least advanced of the states,
is equally sincere; all or almost all have would-be comprehensive
systems, from kindergarten to university, and in most of them
primary education is (at least in law and intention) nowadays com-
pulsory, even though in effect it reaches only a proportion of the
population, ranging from 5 per cent to 80, and may leave hundreds of
villages, still, with no school at all. But, aided very substantially in
some countries (Lebanon, or the Sudan, for example) both by
century-long missionary educational effort and by that of the local
minority communities, Christian and Jewish, the states have for

some years—indeed, ever since their attainment of independence—placed the advancement of education, and war on the still prevalent illiteracy, in the fore-front of their programmes: as part of which go also technical and professional training and the despatch of young men to foreign universities (British, American, French) for the higher levels of education not locally available. (Governments habitually show less interest in a question actually of acute relevance; it is, what careers, what outlets are available, or likely to be, for the new highly-educated class?) To direct scholastic programmes can be added the state Broadcasting services, the maintenance of cultural institutions (galleries, museums, libraries), and that of the ancient sites, monuments and objects in which most Middle Eastern countries are so exceptionally rich.

Nor are those of Health and Education the only public services which these governments today, in contrast to the conceptions of a century ago, feel bound to render to their publics. In most territories, legislation had been passed dealing with conditions of work in industry—hours, holidays, safety, amenities, minimum wages, compensation for injury; in some cases there is an inspectorate to enforce these, in others such regulations are largely ignored in practice, except by the foreign companies. Wages tribunals and Employment Exchanges have been set up by some of the states. Laws and regulations governing Social Security or Social Insurance have been published in most countries, and if in fact applied (which is no matter of course) do something, and will certainly do more in the future, to provide by pensions and care for the aged or distressed; the serious problems of financing and organizing such schemes have not in general, however, been fully solved. Both the law and the practice of Trade Unionism vary widely from one territory to another. In some, little has been done; in others, state-authorized Unions exist in some industries or in single factories, but are ill-organized and may or may not be permitted by law to withdraw their labour. In certain territories the Unions are predominantly, though not overtly, political, and strike incessantly, as at Aden; elsewhere, and often following European advice, Trade Unionism follows normal objectives by more or less normal methods. The grouping of individual unions into confederations is increasing, but is still limited by the specific and local nature of the demands and outlook of most, and by their untrained leadership. There is in some cases international affiliation to the W.F.T.U., in others to the W.C.F.T.U. The countrywide Histadruth in Israel combines Trade Union, Social Security, trading, contracting, co-operative and directly industrial functions on a very large scale and relieves the Israeli government of many of its functions in these respects. The Co-operative movement has taken root, with government initiative and fostering, in the industries or agriculture of a number of territories, and is capable of making an invaluable contribution. In this whole field of labour welfare and security, organization and self-help, the governments are increasingly aware of their opportunities, and progress may be expected as rapid as the evolution of the public itself permits.

The finances of the state call in the Middle East as everywhere for metriculous budgeting, accounting and auditing, processes which are lacking only in the patriarchal Governments, and are in course of introduction even there. The assessment and collection of revenue is still open, in certainly half of these countries, to well-based criticism for its low efficiency, its inequality, its favouring of some interests (such as landowning) over others, and its not infrequent scandals. Allied to financial administration goes the provision of central banking, the establishment of para-statal banks for special purposes connected with development and the provision of credit, and, through an *ad hoc* ministry or department, the control of a mass of state-owned, or endowment-owned (that is *waqf*), property in land and buildings. The government is bound to assume also the burden of overall development planning, often by Five-year or Seven-year Plans, for all types of progressive projects: projects which involve the allocation of a great part of the state revenues. Such planning (sometimes in touch, also, with outside agencies capable of providing funds) is usually entrusted, under the Cabinet, to specialized standing committees or Development Boards.

Government is equally concerned, centrally or locally, with planning of another kind—with *urbanisme*, street and park construction, slum clearance, water and electricity supply, and the provision of housing. In this field, so central to, and so revealing of, the current aspirations of the Middle Eastern states, the last forty years has important progress to show in every country, and indeed in almost every city except the poorest and most remote; many centres have been completely rebuilt, with wide streets, full public services and amenities, and an imposing range of buildings, public and domestic. The state interests itself no less in village improvement, with better road-access, modern water and electricity supply, and the telephone; it can, in 'Iraq or Syria, initiate schemes for summer hill-stations, and takes steps, almost everywhere, to provide for the important

tourist industry. All main communications—roads and bridges, railways, airports and their equipment, ports with dredged channels and
jetties, river navigation (in 'Iraq, Egypt, the Sudan), posts and
telegraphs—are within its activities. In the field of industry, most
Middle Eastern governments, as we shall see, have by now taken
steps, some upon an important scale, to build or finance factories,
develop mines, engage in (or, more commonly, delegate to foreign
concerns) the vast petroleum industry, and in general play the
dominant part in industrial development which in other regions
devolves more usually upon private or joint-stock capital. In the
domain of agriculture, still easily the prevailing source of national
livelihood, the state guarantees, or modifies, or today sometimes
essays to revolutionize, the land-tenure system and landlord-peasant
relationships, initiates research into plant-types and cropping
methods, teaches widely the results of such research, improves
marketing facilities, gives thought to stock-breeding, forestry and
fisheries, drains marshes, erects flood protection works, and
carries out irrigation projects on a scale vastly beyond private
capacity.

In these endeavours, fundamental to modern Middle Eastern self-
realization, countries of our region have had powerful and willing
friends. There have been first, the sympathetic, aid-giving governments of the United States, Britain, and the U.S.S.R., and, to a
much lesser extent, others. Such aid has taken the form of direct
help, in a crisis of famine or epidemic: or of a grant of funds, by
gift or loan, for a development project or series of projects, as of
Great Britain to Jordan, or Russia to Egypt, Syria and 'Iraq, or
China to the Yemen, or America to Israel, Turkey and Persia. Other
forms of aid have been missions of technical enquiry and appraisal,
or the compilation of economic reports, or the despatch of a military
mission, or gift of military munitions. In all these and other ways,
outside nations of both the western and the eastern blocs have made,
with whatever mixed motives of altruism or self-interest, the most
direct of recent and continuing contacts with the Middle East: have
trodden their streets, ranged their countryside, discussed business in
their offices, known at first hand their citizens and homes. The
greatest contributions in these fields have been those of the United
States who, through one or other of its specialized agencies, has
provided abundant funds, experts and goods in kind to most of our
territories, under the headings of Development Assistance, Technical
Co-operation, or Military Support, more particularly for development

in Israel and Persia, and (largest of all items) for military aid to Turkey. The U.S.S.R. has given less, and to a narrower range of countries; Great Britain has directly aided Jordan, has maintained in the Middle East staffs of experts in various fields, available for consultation by governments, and has organized regional locust control over all the Middle East and north-east Africa.

A second group of similar contacts has been multiplied by and through United Nations, of which almost all the Middle Eastern states are members. The part played by U.N. in the politics of our region in the last two decades has, indeed, been both various and continuous; here however it must suffice to mention the type of beneficent activity shown locally by certain of the many U.N. agencies. Such, obviously, are those of U.N.R.W.A. (p. 138), concerned with Palestine refugees and involving the maintenance of offices at five Arab capitals: of the U.N. Emergency Force (U.N.E.F.), concerned to keep the peace on the borders of Israel: and of the Truce Supervision Organization (U.N.T.S.O.), with its mixed Arab-Israeli Commissions based on the main near-frontier towns, devoted to the maintenance of the 1949 Armistice Agreements. The U.N. Children's Fund, U.N.I.C.E.F., is represented by an office in each of Beirut, Ankara, Baghdad, Cairo, (Israeli) Jerusalem, and Teheran. The Economic Commission for Africa, E.C.A., is concerned with Egypt and the Sudan; the similar Commission for Asia and the Far East covers Persia. The Economic and Social Council, E.C.O.S.O.C, itself has an office in Beirut: that of Food and Agriculture, F.A.O., in Cairo: that of World Health, W.H.O., at Alexandria: and the International Labour Office, I.L.O., in Ankara. There are U.N. Informational Centres at Cairo and Teheran. U.N.E.S.C.O., the U.N. Educational, Scientific and Cultural Organization, has held meetings on Middle Eastern soil, notably at Beirut. Finally, and of even more practical importance to Middle Eastern countries, the International Bank for Reconstruction and Development (the 'World Bank') has repeatedly conducted economic enquiries in the region, and has made loans for specific projects on a scale sufficient to give it locally a leading place as a development agency. The International Monetary Fund, I.M.F., has aided some of the states in their currency or exchange difficulties: the U.N. Special Fund has made many grants to governments to 'create the conditions' favourable to foreign or domestic investment: and the Expanded Programme of Technical Assistance, which works through all existing U.N. machinery and, jointly with the Special Fund, maintains resident representatives at virtually all Middle Eastern capitals, has spent and is spending millions in practical forms of aid.

3. *The Field of Politics*

The few pages to be devoted to this subject—pages which will show (if it were doubtful) how close is the connection in the Middle East between political activity and other main aspects of society—will deal in succession with the general character of local politics, the main issues upon which its debates concentrate, and the more characteristic political methods normally employed. Our account will necessarily be generalized for most, and the most typical, Middle Eastern countries, while not entirely true for any one of them, and will for this purpose ignore the entirely different conditions in Israel on the one hand and in the Arabian states on the other.

The days when government and its visible agencies were objects of fear and hatred to most of at least the non-urban public are over, except in the wilder tribes or remotest hill-communities; but the population elements are, on the contrary, still numerous among which the rule of law and the processes of orderly government have still an uncertain hold and little favour. Public opinion in support of lawful authority is far from unanimous; the admissibility of government 'interference' in fields unknown to earlier days—social, fiscal, administrative—is bitterly questioned; and, in brief, conceptions of the prerogative and obligations of the state and of its own optimum structure are, except in limited 'evolved' circles, very far from those generally accepted in the West. This wide difference is due, in general, to long ages of government based on unwestern, Islamic concepts, followed by centuries of arbitary maladministration or non-administration in substantial isolation from the main stream of world affairs. Our western axioms concerning popular representation, personal liberty, an independent judiciary, and human rights as applicable to political or governmental life, are not only not taken for granted as desiderata, they are commonly rejected, if not in words, then in action. Add to this that most of the nations of our region are essentially at quite different stages of their organic development from those of Europe or North America, differ widely in temperament, and are confronted with a dissimilar set of tasks and problems, and it will be apparent that hopes of merely transplanting to the Middle East western political or constitutional systems must be profoundly illusory—a fact too little realized in the last half century, both in the West and in our region itself.

The body politic in these territories is almost always plainly heterogeneous. It consists of elements differing much more than superficially in their strong, specific community loyalties, their economic
interests and way of life, and—most important—their level of
evolution and education. Society falls, if one may obviously over-
simplify, into two parts: the smaller, that of educated men with more
or less evolved ideas and desiderata in politics and society—that is,
the intelligentsia and the literate bourgeoisie: and secondly, the
numerically much greater part, that of the uneducated masses, rural
and urban. The educated class itself contains a small minority of well-
equipped potential statesmen, often of distinguished ability, and a
large majority from the literate, politically conscious, almost entirely
urban, middle and lower-middle class. The uneducated masses are
commonly dismissed by western observers as of little political interest
but as merely, at best, inarticulate folk misled by a 'handful of
agitators'. This is an error. The peasant or tribesman has admittedly
little information, backward (if any) conceptions in politics or
government, and an absorbing interest, above all, in his own circle
and in living: but politically he cannot be ignored. He is capable of
accepting and following a leader, or at least of supporting his own
local magnate or landowner; he can exhibit violent if uninstructed
political emotion, can demonstrate and riot, can destroy governments
or cause a reversal of their decisions; and many a political leader,
disliked by authority in office, can find formidable support among
the masses perfectly ill-equipped to judge the relevant issues.

This deep division in national society is doubtless diminishing, but
will not soon disappear; meanwhile, added to local, sectional and
community stresses and strains, it leads to that overall instability of
political life, or indeed of government itself, which is the region's
dominant and most disquieting feature. This instability is emphasized,
or increased, by the clash of personalities (sometimes of clans or
families) which is perhaps even more conspicuous in the Middle East
than elsewhere: by the crudely divergent interests which different
personalities or forces are publicly pursuing: by most political
leaders', writers' and speakers' immaturity in statecraft, and their
natural recourse to an extremism often competitive: by the constant
elements of restless movement, splintering and regrouping: by, in
fact, all the phenomena to which the excitable, intransigent, individualistic character of, at least, Arabs and Persians must inevitably
lead in public life.

Political leadership belongs today in all these territories, except

Arabia and in some measure Persia, no longer to the old ruling class of rich landowners, merchants, urban magnates, wealthy ex-officials or blue-blooded aristocrats. These, their lives and property often in danger from vigorous reformists—as in Egypt since 1952, or 'Iraq since 1958—are not today, as they were for centuries, the repositories of power, even though in wide rural or tribal areas they may, through their influence over the tribesmen or peasantry, and in opposition to the government's policies, still constitute a formidable force of self-preserving conservatism. But overt political power belong nowadays neither to these nor to the mob (powerful role as this can sometimes play) but, except when temporarily suppressed by a dictatorship, to the urban (including the military) intelligentsia, from which spring practically all leaders, politicians, organizers, military and civil executives—and the dictators themselves.

It is often asked, is there or can there be any true Middle Eastern democracy? There is little guidance here, paradoxically, in the authentic Arab social tradition of equalitarianism, the accessibility of old-type rulers to the petitioner, desert freedom and the like; all this belongs to history, and often to legend. And such phenomena as a vigorous, often an ultra-violent, political Press, and mammoth street · demonstrations, fail also to indicate the presence of true democratic instincts; most politicians and journalists exhibit these in no more than their speeches and leading articles, and demonstrators are available at little or no cost for any cause or occasion whatsoever, royalist, communist, hero-greeting, martyr-mourning, or any other. But if a true democratic régime demands a reasonably instructed, tolerably homogeneous electorate, this is absent. If it needs to express itself by political parties which stand for principles, or at least for coherent policies and programmes, these very rarely exist otherwise than in rootless and ephemeral forms, since few parties (except the communist) have a country-wide organization or continuity, or stand for much more than personal followings or tactical manoeuvres. Certain groups, it is true, in Lebanon, Syria, Egypt, Cyprus, Israel offer at least partial exceptions to this too-sweeping judgment; personal followings (as those of 'holy men' in the Sudan) can be permanent and fairly consistent: in Turkey the parties—or at least the Party, and the opposition to it—have both long continuity and a firm tradition, and in Persia both the (mainly Communist) Tudeh party and the conservative landlords' 'lobby' are seemingly permanent forces. But few profess a comprehensive, moderate programme to replace the current policies which they oppose, or can be conceived as an acceptable alternative government. If democracy, again, calls for a genuine system of popular representation, this is a most infrequent asset in the Middle East: if for a desire of political leaders to see power truly vested in the masses, this is rarer still, since nine-tenths of the statesmen who assert this as their ideal would reject with horror a veritable realization of it; indeed, the intelligentsia-politician has normally the lowest opinion of the brains or judgment of his illiterate fellow-countrymen. In spite of frequent advocacy by tyranny-hating orators of 'one man one vote', it cannot be pretended that democracy as a system (identified as it is, moreover, with the unpopular West) makes a seductive appeal to Middle Eastern ideologists; when not rejected as inefficient and sanctimonious, it appears with its debates, delays and squabbles as the enemy of national unity, and an impediment to dynamic progress. It will be long before Middle Eastern statesmen (unless, just possibly, in Turkey) can appreciate the value of a 'loyal opposition'; and even in Turkey the two-party system, installed in 1952, has had a tempestuous career.

We conclude at this point that, for the reasons given, the Middle Eastern political background is one widely dissimilar from that of most modern states in other regions: that the statal régimes, and their publics, are markedly heterogeneous, restless and unstable: that political power belongs today to the growing, literate middle class: and that the attainment of any democratic régime worth the name is far to seek. We pass next to deal with the question, what are the main political issues today disputed in these countries?

The first of these is evidently that of the struggle for immediate power in the state, for the individual, party or interest engaged. Such struggles take an infinity of forms and occasions, and, though always concealed under other names and pretexts, none are more bitter or recurrent. Their incidence occurs naturally in every sphere of government and public life—personal, procedural, financial and administrative, military and bureaucratic; and their frequency, normal in all politically-active societies, does not exhibit Middle Eastern politicians as lower or more self-seeking than others elsewhere, which they are not. On the constitutional side, habitual conflicts concern the general form of the government—monarchical or republican, 'popular' or oligarchic or dictatorial: the maintenance, or abolition, of a system of internal community balances as the basis of government (as in Lebanon): the limits or the achievement of popular representation: the wisdom, or alternatively the condemned weakness or folly, of allowing power or privilege to minority population-elements—Kurds, Druzes, Nusairis, or Sudani pagans—as against a policy of centralized uniformity. Behind this group of issues lie, more generally, the attitudes of those (found most commonly among semi-suppressed oppositions) who clamour for wide liberty of press and party action— in fact, for a free field for 'democratic rights'—and who resent all forms of authoritarian rule and all princely or shaikhly or ecclesiastical pretensions to extra-legal power. These or connected issues can take the form of autocracy versus so-called democracy, or of feudalism versus representative institutions; in extreme form they take shape as the forces of tradition or reaction against those of an extreme left-wing, or against Communism itself. The same issue merges, in the social-economic field, into the conflict between protagonists of a controlled or socialistic organization of society and economic life (such as President Gamal 'Abdul Nasir, or the étatists of Turkey and Persia), and the leaders who prefer freedom to run their own enterprises under minimum control. In the agricultural sphere the same issue appears as between old-type large-scale landlords, and state-organized redistribution into small-holdings.

A further type of divisive issue in Middle Eastern politics is that of foreign relations, embracing questions of antipathy to, or desire to amalgamate with, adjacent States: the relations of 'Iraq and Kuwait, of Yemen and the Aden Protectorate, of Sa'udi claims in Jordan, of Lebanese (and, on different lines, also Syrian and Jordanian) conceptions of a Greater Syria, of the unity of the Fertile Crescent, and indeed of Arab Unity itself. One or other of these or allied questions is a frequent hard-fought theme in local politics. Beyond them lies the whole field of foreign policy—western or eastern blocs, alliance or non-alignment, varying shades of neutralism: a field full of mutual recrimination but always united in wearisome denunciations of the sinister imperialism, colonialism, etc., attributed to whatever Great Power is for the moment most out of favour.

These, then, being the themes of political controversy, what are the methods characteristically in use? That of democratic elections must be placed first; yet, though popular elections are indeed frequently held and produce some sort of results, they are subject to various disabilities. Their processes can be blatantly falsified; they can be controlled under government orders by local officials; they can be limited to preselected candidates; they can be stultified by a boycott. Of all these phases of election-holding the Middle East can show abundant examples.

Of political parties, an indispensable element in any sound political system, we have spoken already. Apart from their habitual rootlessness and discontinuity they are readily suppressed by the dictator or dominant faction of the moment, or (as almost habitually with the Communist parties) are pronounced illegal and driven underground. But, inadequate as is the part they can play, they are prominent in the political field by their violence in speech and writing, their ready organization of mob and student demonstrations—the latter a constant and deplorable element—and often by their control of the (largely political) Trade Unions. The Communist parties are not unique in their possession of funds from abroad (to which their persistence is largely due), since subsidies to politicians or journalists (in 'Iraq, for instance, or in Syria) are known to have accrued at times from Sa'udi sources.

Other political methods in use are those of inspired intervention from inside the country but outside the normal political world, such as can be organized from or by the forces of religion in their more militant forms—from Sufis in Turkey, Shi'i *mujtahids* in 'Iraq and Persia, revivalists in Egypt and Syria. The same applies to provoked tribal uprisings (as in 'Iraq and Turkey), a manoeuvre dear to town-bred politicians who, in the event, can rarely control the resulting violence, and often suffer by it. In international politics, and scarcely less in internal, the use of violent broadcasting campaigns has become usual in the hands of dominant parties or dictators; and in this field, after all allowance has been made for the tradition of eastern hyperbole in political exposition, and the immaturity of many political publicists, it is difficult at times not to be pained by their repetitive and often foolishly mendacious outpourings. The active support of fugitives from other countries is a common way of expressing one's own Arab patriotism and creating difficulties for one's opponents— as, for example, by a welcome and support, in Cairo, for the leaders of Omani insurgence. Another technique is the discovery, at home, of a conspiracy by political enemies 'against the State', followed by arrest of the alleged culprits (often described as 'imperialist stooges') and an upsurge of loyal devotion to the threatened hero. The latter attitude is produced also by organized 'personality cult' of the ruler in power, aided by all the means of publicity and persuasion at his disposal.

Of interventions by the Army modern Middle Eastern history contains a score of examples; indeed, no major country is without one, and in most of them military dictatorship, short- or long-lived, is, as the world has witnessed since 1946, a recurrent phase. Indeed, the establishment of these dictatorships seems to confirm, by its witness against the practicability of successful democracy, the lesson of the scarcely less authoritarian forms adopted in Persia and Jordan, and temporarily in Turkey—and, of course, the totally undemocratic patriarchies or theocracies of Arabia. One might add here, regretfully, the often-used weapon of simple assassination, of which, again, no single Middle Eastern country fails to offer recent examples.

With all this, let no reader forget that, within the heated, confused, too often unedifying scene of Middle Eastern politics, there are actors not only of high ability, but of genuine devotion and patriotism. It is the more tragic that these qualities, so obvious and so valued in the quieter interludes or in private discussion, have but a limited force amid the stresses of a political arena dominated by slogans, obsessive antipathies, and competitive promises or boasts.

4. Going Communist?

No question is more often asked by observers of the Middle Eastern political scene than one at which we have already hinted: what is the likelihood of one or more of these territories 'going Communist'? Why and how could it happen? This deserves some consideration, partly because it is revealing of the present political— and, to an extent, the social—scene, partly because a move to the Communist structure and way of life, if it occurred, would have important social effects.

It is certain that the whole region has long enjoyed a high priority as a Communist, and before that a czarist Russian, expansion area: that the efforts of the U.S.S.R. since 1945 to expand its influence and penetration by swollen diplomatic staffs, abundant propaganda, acquired Press and personal allegiances, visits and missions, have been conspicuous: and that Communist Parties, whether subsidized or not, and whatever their precise relationship to Moscow, exist on some scale in most Middle Eastern countries, some with official recognition but most illegally. There have in consequence been evident signs of Communist intervention, in varying forms; the Party Line has at times been adopted by journalists, sometimes by broadcasting stations; high officials, of the fellow-travelling Left, have held their posts; mob demonstrations palpably Communist-organized have run their course, Soviet experts and trade missions have been welcomed, their loans and arms supplies received, their eminent representatives fêted. And in addition to occasions when, as in the 'Iraq of 1958–1959, the Communists formed an open and vital part of the political scene, there is little doubt that their less visible power, in their cells in the Trade Union movement and the armed forces, is very real. Admitting this, one may ask how far it will, given a favourable occasion, be able to manifest itself with success?

The Middle East, by virtue of the poverty and backwardness still prevailing among its masses, and the restless, unstable immaturity of its public in matters political, may seem a favourable area for Communist expansion. The political *dirigeants* proclaim neutralism, which means that they refuse Western allegiances; and they want maximum economic aid from outside, which in that field at least leaves the door to the East wide open. The Russians, because they have never invaded the Middle East nor shown their armies there, are regarded by the public (with however naïve an unreality) as non-imperialist. They have no past to live down in the region, as have the British, French, and Turks: no identification with the old, now dethroned, ruling class of landowners and the rich: no colour bar, no social taboos, no subjects, no local oil concessions or commercial interests. They refrain from singing the praises of that locally ill-regarded system, democracy: they have, currently, immense prestige through their exploits in space: they are gratifyingly anti-Israeli as well as anti-Western. They are seemingly generous granters of low-interest, stringless loans, signers of favourable trade-agreements, buyers of otherwise unsaleable crops. Above all, they are a people whom their own adoption of Communism seems to have raised, in a generation, from poverty, oppression, and near-serfdom to their present power and status.

All this would suggest an easy triumph for the Communists—that is, for the U.S.S.R., since the Chinese are not yet seriously in the picture—in the Middle Eastern region. Nevertheless, this outcome remains unlikely. The nature of Communist rule, and of life under it, are inevitably better appreciated as time goes on and public information improves, and the Russians themselves are less popular as they become better known through their representatives—experts, planners, missions, workmen—in the host countries, as a number of episodes have already shown; and as loan repayments become due, and the fulfilment of accepted obligations is expected, and occasions of friction have multiplied, cordiality is likely further to decrease. Moreover, the neutralism of the Middle Eastern states is sincere; no status tying them to the East, any more than to the West, would be tolerated. The idea of agreeing to close (which would mean exclusive) relations with a new, notoriously powerful and active Big Brother, after successfully getting rid of the Powers previously dominant in the Middle East, must be quite unacceptable; the convinced local Communists who would welcome such an alignment are very few, and unlikely to gain power. Finally, the powerful, emotional Nationalism of the states concerned, without exception, is bound ultimately to clash not only with the nationalism of Russia (which from some aspects has changed little since 1917) but also with the international element of Communism, a proclaimed world-creed; now that the 'struggles against imperialist powers' are safely over, in which the U.S.S.R. could support local aspiring nations, as such, against the West, it will be difficult to disguise the fundamental incompatibility between local nationalistic pride and entry into the Soviet system. For these and such-like reasons, here too briefly summarized, it is unlikely that, without war, any Middle Eastern state will allow itself to drift, or be forced, into Communist-satellite status.

A situation less improbable would be the acquistion of power in a Middle Eastern state by a party, almost certainly individual-dominated, of Marxist colouring in its economic and organizational predilections. In such cases a régime could be established in which a measure of internal Marxism (as today, for instance, in the Republic of Guinea) could be practised without adhesion to the Communist bloc internationally: in fact, a Titoist régime. The present social structure of almost all Middle Eastern countries, the power of the vested interests represented in them, the present weakness of local Communist adherents, the Islamic background (not by itself, however, a sufficient barrier against Communism), may render such a position improbable; but it is at least more easily conceivable than that of direct acceptance, by any one of these territories, of the status of satellite of the U.S.S.R.

CHAPTER NINE

PRIVATE LIFE AND SOCIETY

1. *Why backwardness?*

THE world at large, in both hemispheres, finds the Middle East a region of backwardness: picturesque perhaps but, as regards the mass of the inhabitants, socially retarded as well as poverty-stricken. The prevailing image (as the writer has found repeatedly in the United States) is that of the Arab as a scraggy, night-gown wearing, camel-riding nomad; that of the Turk as a truculent, water-pipe-smoking, harem-dwelling murderer of Armenians: of the Persian as a subtle, effeminate opium-taker. These pictures correspond very little to the facts of Middle Eastern life; but that there has been a lagging development in much of society as in public life, and wide-spread poverty, is all too true.

This backwardness, it is obvious, is not of uniform incidence throughout the region. It is at its most apparent in peninsular Arabia, in parts of the Sudan, in wide outlying areas elsewhere: and is at its least in urban and suburban areas of the more developed countries. Nevertheless, and although, thanks to the prevailingly high level of intelligence among the populations and their age-long contact with advanced civilizations, Middle Eastern backwardness is never at the abysmal level prevalent in most of Africa and great parts of South America, yet it is pronounced enough to justify the enquiry as to why a high proportion of the people of territories of such fame and outstanding cultural tradition should have allowed themselves, or been allowed, to fall, in the material and many of the cultural achievements of the modern world, so far behind those of other peoples not more gifted, and illumined by far less ancient glory.

The answer can be briefly summarized. The early and medieval greatness of the Middle Eastern region was obliterated by the conquests and catastrophes which it underwent in the later Middle Ages. The region, by nature poor and unfertile, and failing, after the Mongol visitations, to recover and provide the means of wealth and leisure, inevitably fell behind communities in the West, better endowed and less afflicted; and when the centre of gravity of the

civilized world, notably after the discovery of America, moved westward to the Mediterranean and Atlantic, the Middle East became no
longer central but peripheral to it. The discovery of a sea route to
India had a similar effect. The region had not escaped in earlier days,
though it had now long forgotten, the fertilizing influences of Greece;
but it missed entirely those of the Renaissance, which coincided
with its own darkest period, and it proceeded on its way as though
this immense upsurge of the human spirit had never occurred. The
reason for this apathy, or failure in communication, was the same as
that which was responsible, more than any other, more indeed than
all others together, for the present backwardness which we are dis-
cussing: the dominance of, and age-long uncritical devotion to, the
religion of Islam. Because of this faithfulness, a major part of the
thought, speculation and scholarship of the Islamic peoples was
canalized, after a period of unsuccessful attempts at freedom, into a
narrow, often sterile religio-legal field. Their activity, whether in
public or private life, was limited by a conservatism not far, at times,
from stagnation; and the range of this was the greater by reason of
the claim of Islam to cover, by prescribed rules which were invari-
able, every department of human life. With this immobility—
producing, as it did, a gracious but changeless manner of life—went
the marked 'superiority complex' of the Muslim, to whom the cultures and societies of the West, teeming in fact with progressive
dynamism, were unworthy, valueless aberrations and improprieties.
The Islamic world clung for centuries to its slow tempo, its restricted
horizons, its narrow education, its secluded women and lack of
western-type home life: to its ignorance of, or aversion from, mechanical and material progress: to its isolation from science, many of
the arts, and modern economic, strategic and political forms. It
was the victim of endemic, weakening diseases, among them malaria.
It accepted with fatalism the callous mis-government of Sultan and
Shah, and lived without security, justice or progress, until at last
compelled, in self-defence, to call in too late the special skills and
methods of Europe. These were accepted without discrimination or,
often enough, without any comprehension extending beyond the
most obvious and immediate. The process of catching-up, which
has been the outstanding feature of Middle Eastern life for the last
century and a half, is still far from complete; but it is well begun and
will continue without, it is to be hoped, the loss of the spiritual
values so abundantly represented in Islam.

2. Towns and town life

The traditional society of the Middle East was, as previous pages have suggested, conditioned by its peculiar and diverse geography, climate and resources, and notably by the great varieties in its land-surface. These created the environments in which life could be lived —by agriculture, gardening, nomadic or static pastoralism, fishing, and urban and village occupations—and determined the local density of population, from empty desert to packed city, from the menacing over-population of Egypt and Lebanon, to the man-power shortages of 'Iraq, Persia and Syria. The human history of the region bequeathed, with frequent changes of fortune and new ingredients, legacies of tradition and way of life; its religion imposed upon it a pattern only recently, but now progressively, in process of modification.

The factors by which this modification has proceeded have been suggested in an earlier chapter, where we mentioned the influences making for reform in nineteenth-century Turkey (p. 70 f.); they included all the channels and forces whereby western influences had by that time come to bear upon Middle Eastern society. Since then their action has been further intensified by other, and ever closer and more operative, links between the region and the western world, resulting in deeper penetration by the latter in almost every field of Middle Eastern society. This has occurred through the post-1919 Mandates, the constant flow of communication of every kind and level between east and west, the increase of international trade and industry, and widening education. Among such more recent factors one could emphasize the ubiquity of the motor-car, with its immense impulse to mobility and interchange: aviation, highly developed in the region, with its rapidity of travel and anni-hilation of frontiers and distance: the vast increase of newspapers, and of a literate public to read them: the never-ceasing broadcasts from western and eastern Europe: the cinema showing, in every city and town, scores of films of western society from which both the good and the bad—and too often the deplorable—features of Euro-pean society, morals and 'progress' are to be learned: and television, of which the same is true. These forces have operated unequally throughout society, which today in consequence presents the strange yet familiar spectacle of a region deeply divided in its manner of life, full of contradictions and anachronisms, and widely diverse as between its urban and its rural publics, between the old, traditional life and that of invading and prevailing modernity.

We pass, then, to review (with a degree of generalization too easily misleading, because allowing too little for great inter-regional varieties) the life of Middle Eastern towns, countryside and tribes, with the again-repeated proviso, however, that little of what follows is applicable to peninsular Arabia, where the ancient conditions, scenes and way of life are still (save in the small areas dominated by foreign industry) those of the Middle Ages: nor to Cyprus, culturally an outlying part of Greece and Europe: nor to Israel, a country totally remote (save in its Arab minority) from the region in which it has established itself. We speak here of the non-Arabian Arab countries, and of Turkey and Persia.

Middle Eastern towns of whatever magnitude owe their siting variously to the presence of an assured water-supply, to convenience as a caravan-staging-post in earlier days, to location at a point where some local resource could best be handled, to natural facilities for defence, or to some special sanctity (shrine or burial place) which attracted pilgrims and a resulting livelihood. To whichever of such origins, mostly now lost in remote antiquity, a given city was originally indebted, its present scale bears no visible relation to them, being due more probably to personal or administrative factors not always analysable. But in any event the region is one in which cities have played a dominant part in society, economics and government alike, and have maintained themselves as the providers of leadership, capital and social progress, if any, for thousands of years. And today, notably since 1945, the growth of urban populations, due to constant inward movement from the villages, is an outstanding feature of the times.

The urban life of the region is, evidently, the most changed, the least traditional, and furthest from the images of 'the East' dear to the uninstructed West. In its new setting, gone are the protective walls around the city, gone many (but not all) of the malodorous rubbish-heaps, the slums and the narrow alleys, the strings of load-carrying camels, the deep mud or swirling dust. Every Middle Eastern country today boasts its dozen or score of major and lesser cities in which can be studied, with many varieties, all that they have yet evolved in features of city life. Too often these cities are surrounded by an irregular ring of shabby, unfinished suburbs, by a mass or masses of shanty-towns where new arrivals from the countryside live in first hopeful, later despairing misery; but the inner areas of the city are very different. Apart from the still prominent monuments of the past—mosques, palaces, khans, barracks—there are everywhere signs of new town-planning, the pride of the local mayor and his council or of the central government itself. The new boulevards, parks, plantations, fountains are often of beauty and dignity, especially where helped by a favourable natural setting, and are the focus of a warm civic pride. Modern 'bus services run everywhere, taxis abound, private motor-cars and trucks throng the streets. Street lighting, upkeep and watering are a matter of course; so, though not everywhere, is a public sewage system. Well-planned, well-sited villas for the well-to-do, in whole streetfuls and quarters, replace their former town-houses, and modern-type housing estates have been developed in many cities to meet the needs of the public of the middle or lower-middle income ranges. Every government has provided itself and its cities with public buildings to its taste, which offer usually the greatest contrast to those even of half-a-century ago, and are the more diverse as state activities have increased. New mosques appear, though most of these conform to ancient pattern. New bank and office buildings, institutions, schools, clubs, hospitals, 'bus stations, garages, mark the contribution of private enterprise to the new scene, in which many cinemas and an occasional theatre or athletic stadium have their place. The hotels, mostly housed in new and grandiose buildings, give a high standard of modern service in the largest cities, and are nowadays usually reliable (not without occasional lapses) even in smaller provincial towns. Modern shops abound, with a range of European wares of every quality, as well as the familar merchandise of the bazaars. Restaurants admirably kept, and smart cafés, are among usual amenities attractive to 'the best people' and to foreigners. The latter, residents in or visitors to the city, and foreign diplomats if this is a capital, are a familiar element. Some state ceremonial may stir the citizen's pride, with a military band or a passing presidential cortège.

But this picture of the modern Middle Eastern city, varying in aspect with the scenes and taste of the country concerned, is part only of the truth; there remains always, on an important scale, remnants of the very different past. Such are the ancient, busy, noisy, arched or open bazaars, often miles in extent and scarcely changed in aspect for a millennium: old-type public baths and tea-shops, the craftsman in his workshop, the barber and the seller of cold drinks or vegetables: the archaic khan or caravanserai for the poorer wayfarer: the winding alleyways giving pedestrian access to windowless, airless dwellings: peddlars and street vendors, beggars, laden donkeys or mules, scores of ragged children and their black-clad mothers, and innumerable dignified, seemingly workless, sitters-in-the-sun. The easy co-existence in a single city of medieval and ultra-new, grandiose and sordid, eastern and western, progressive and static, with no boundary between them, and both wholly accepted, is to the new-comer a striking feature of life.

In the lesser towns, district or provincial capitals, the balance swings over to the ancient ways, as more of traditional building and planning—or no-planning—survive, threatened by less innovation. These centres are more compact because less magnetic to the drifting surplus rural population: more homogeneous, because unincreased by new-built quarters: more typical of the country in which they lie, because less cosmopolitan and more in unity with the surround-ing villages and tribes, for whom they form the natural centre and market-place. But all have, nonetheless, their share of new buildings, improved streets and gardens; the public services are well in evidence, with visible new-fashioned private ventures, and easy rapid com-munication to other centres. Thus, life is lived here half in the modern, half in the ancient fashion.

Within this general setting of part-modernized town-life, all the occupations normal in the modern world are practised. Religion keeps its own in mosque-staffs and seminaries, and in the officials charged with management of the extensive pious endowments. (Much the same is found, on smaller scales, within the Christian and Jewish communities.) Since every territory has its armed forces, these in all their ranks and branches occupy large numbers of the employable, as well as every type of supplier and camp-follower: and, with them, the gendarmerie, police and fire services. Reference was made elsewhere (p. 194 f.), to the importance of government service in all its departments and at every level, central, provincial or municipal; this, with the public services of every kind—teachers and medical staffs, engineers and transport workers—employs inevitably a large body of the citizenry who are, to their fellow-countrymen as to visiting foreigners, 'the Government'. Taking for granted the un-skilled or semi-skilled masses, pursuing their many livelihoods (but noting the recent appearance of an industrial proletariat created by new factory-type industry) and passing over equally the mere property-owner or 'idle rich', one may specify the diverse grades and varieties of skilled artisan in every industry, the technologists and managers who control them, and the capitalists who own and may direct such enterprises; and, with these, the executive as well as clerical grades in foreign-directed industry and commerce—banks,

insurance agencies, travel-bureaux, and the oil industry itself. Add
to these the practitioners of law or medicine, journalism or politics,
and the executives and staffs of all the multifarious businesses normal
in every city, from retail shops and humble *ateliers* to export houses,
shipbuilding or transport enterprises, and wholesalers or middlemen
in any and every commodity. The purpose of this list is not to be
exhaustive but to suggest that urban life in Middle Eastern cities—
conceived by some foreigners, it seems, as a simple affair of shaikhs or
pashas and a mass of ragged underlings—is in fact, as elsewhere,
a complicated and evolved microcosm. Closer examination of it
would reveal new social features of some interest, among which three
may be given as examples. One is the recent emergence of a new
upper-class founded on industrial or commercial wealth, side by
side with the old 'best families' who bear famous names. For some
of the new-made fortunes the war and its opportunities were
responsible, for others the immense influx of money through the
operations of the oil companies. Another feature is the modified
relationship between Muslim and minority-community society, a
relationship now easier by reason of less fanaticism and more modern
tolerance, but less easy through the upsurge of a Nationalism apt to
reject the non-Muslim as not fully a patriot. And a third is the change
of manners, among the younger middle-class, from their traditional
forms of courtesy to consciously anti-traditional western fashions not
always, one must admit, as pleasing: a change sometimes barely
appreciable, sometimes striking, and in any case inevitable.

How do they all live? There is here the familiar dichotomy between
old and new, running deeply through society. Among the proportion
(highest, obviously, in the less advanced territories) who even in
great cities keep the traditional ways of life, the clothes worn are the
flowing, picturesque garments of the country, in varying pattern
according to local usage, and in quality from rags to finery according
to personal wealth and taste. The houses of this old-fashioned, and
usually but not always poorer, city-element are of the ancient, enclosed pattern, with dark rooms, scanty furnishings, and few or no
services of light, water or drainage. Their occupants eat but poorly,
entertain at home rarely or not at all, isolate their women, observe
the Islamic taboos against drinking and card-playing, travel by the
crowded and noisy but not too inefficient public transport, conduct
their social lives in coffee-shop and bazaar, and fail to share, for the
most part, in such mixed blessings as modernity and the West have
brought. Illiteracy still prevails (though less than ever before) among

the lower orders, poverty is still oppressive, the death-rate among children needlessly high, malnutrition widespread, and disease commoner than it would be if the available medical services were fully used.

The line of demarcation between the exponents of the conservative way of life and those of the newer-fashioned, next to be described, is not merely one of wealth, since some rich families still prefer a little-modified version of the ancient way; it is one of education and calling. The followers of 'white collar' occupations are of the newer school, manual workers—but with many and increasing exceptions —are of the old, while in the middle, with a series of reasonable or awkward or sometimes half-comical compromises, comes the mass of the artisan and humbler clerical types. Ignoring these, one finds that the life of the modernizers—a substantial majority, in most cities, of those in easier circumstances or of modern upbringing—is characterized by the wearing by both sexes of dress of European type, often costly and well styled: the occupation of houses of western type equipped with all normal services, furnished à l'européenne, the scene of well-served meals (with local often preferred to European dishes) and pleasant social parties. These have, in fact, adopted living-styles either wholly European or of the agreeable Levantine pattern familiar among the socially élite (including Christian minority communities) in Turkey, the Lebanon and Egypt for centuries past. Their fashion of living is comfortable rather than luxurious, excess and ostentation are generally though not quite always avoided, the use of alcoholic drinks is far from universal, drunkenness rare though not unknown, gambling practised but by many disapproved. The two sexes, even in modernist circles, are still to some extent socially segregated by hard-dying custom. The more dashing members of such families meet in hôtels and cabarets, attend the cinema (as indeed does every class and age), frequent the racecourse if such exists, play cards (and play them extremely well), appear at athletic meetings, use freely their many and well-appointed clubs, delight in expensive motor-cars, and spend part of the hot weather abroad, or, where these exist, at the hill-stations of their own country. In their conversation, apart from gossip and personal matters, politics easily predominates; religion has little place, books and culture not much more. Literacy and a certain level of modern sophistication are assumed. The children, of both sexes, go as a matter of course to primary and probably to secondary schools, and often on to university or professional education, at home or abroad. The boys join the

Scouts and the local Youth Movement, play football and debate politics; the girls play tennis, follow the cinema, and accompany their mothers to their charitable societies and receptions or cocktail parties.

A recent feature of town life, which extends in large measure to the villages also, must be further specified; it is that of the changed position of women, so long a reproach, as many felt, to Islamic civilization. The movement towards emancipation, begun some decades ago, received great impetus from the legislation enforced by Kamal Atatürk in Turkey and Riza Shah in Persia, and from sympathetic but less conclusive movements in the same sense among the Arab countries. In the Middle East today the ancient restraints on veiled, uneducated, cloistered women, still prevail in the Arabian peninsula, in many country areas elsewhere, and, surprisingly, in some otherwise 'evolved' urban circles; and even in Persia and Turkey unveiling and emancipation, in spite of all laws and official sanctions, have far less than universal range, thanks mainly to the conservatism or shyness of the women themselves—the principal, if paradoxical, restraining factor in this field. Nevertheless, immense ground has been gained in the last forty years. The old polygamy of Islam is now relatively rare, and in 'evolved' circles is almost a curiosity. Full equality of opportunity for schooling or employment exists over a substantial, and increasing, area, and well-educated girls and women in open society, with thousands employed in clerical, technological and professional occupations, are now no longer an unfamiliar sight. (Significantly, the ancient theological university of al-Azhar, in Cairo, has now been opened to women students.) Less archaic conceptions of marriage, and a western type of home life, are fast extending. In her married state, in entering which she enjoys a freedom of choice unknown before, a woman benefits by much recently passed legislation which provides, in one country or another, for modification in her favour of the cruelly unequal rules for divorce, and those of polygamy itself. And the general, but still not universal, broadening of public opinion in favour of the new ways helps her, far more than laws—far more, even, than the vote which she can now, in most countries, cast in elections—towards a free place in society and the world.

3. *Cultural Aspect*

The Middle East has been, for centuries or millennia, a home of high culture and learning; but because much or most of its achievement belongs now solely to the historian (if not to the archaeologist), and because its immense and continuing contributions to Islamic law, religion and history stand clearly apart from the secular western world which here concerns us, the following pages will deal only with that part of Middle Eastern activity in the cultural field which links it to the present-day world: that, in effect, of the West.

The universities of the region which, mostly new but including some medieval foundations, exist in almost every country outside Arabia, are vigorous and thronged with students; and they contribute invaluably to enlarging the educated middle-class upon which these territories, administratively and economically, do and must depend. That they are making, also, valuable academic contributions to knowledge no one will wish to deny; but, not less undeniably, 90 per cent of students take a predominantly utilitarian view of their university work as the indispensable prelude to civil service or business appointments. Curricula are based upon European and American models. The language of instruction is that of the country, with English or French usually added—or, as in Lebanon, substituted. Premises and equipment vary from adequate to excellent. The status of the professorial staff is high. As in universities elsewhere, not all but most of the usual faculties and departments are represented, with less attention, obviously, to subjects little in demand, and less also to those requiring costly equipment or teachers of extraordinary qualification. Most universities, except the foreign, are state-financed and administered, though this does not prevent the seemingly endless addiction of the students to political demonstrations and strikes. The universities offer B.A., M.A., and Doctorate degrees. The standards of excellence for obtaining these can at some universities be respectably high, and a degree involves, generally, at least some study, some attendance at classes, and some intelligence. Nevertheless, the attainments of a high proportion of B.A. graduates are, it must be admitted, extremely moderate, and in at least some institutions the days when 'passing' was an unquestioned matter of course for every student are only now ending. There is, no doubt, as much variation between the merits and standards of Middle Eastern universities—Turkish, Persian, Arab, Israeli—as is familiar in North America. Among the best, by common consent, are such famous foreign foundations as the American University and the (French, Jesuit) University of St Joseph, both at Beirut; the (American) Robert College—not fully a university—at Istanbul: and the American University at Cairo. But these have no monopoly of excellence. There were in 1962 twenty-two institutions in the Middle East using the designation of university; these included new or embryonic foundations, but excluded the specialized colleges mentioned below. There was no university in Cyprus or Jordan, or the Arabian states, but six in Turkey, five in Egypt, three in each of Israel and the Lebanon, two in Persia, one in each of 'Iraq, Syria and the Sudan. The new (1962) 'international University under Turkish control' at Ankara, founded with strong western-world support, is full of promise.

Sometimes affiliated to, sometimes separate from, the universities are a wide range of colleges. These mostly offer, to approximately university standard, a variety of 'arts', scientific, technological, professional and commercial subjects, which include, in one college or another, law, fine arts, agriculture, economics, teacher-training and pedagogy, music, engineering, medicine and dentistry, veterinary science, oriental studies, and theology. The aggregate contribution of these is very important. They help to produce the membership of the numerous 'learned societies' and institutes to be found flourishing in all the major capitals and provincial cities. Some of these bodies are general in their cultural interest, some are specialized to certain fields, such as local folk-lore and linguistics, scientific (including medical) research, archaeology, education, orientalism, sociology and philosophy. There are societies for the practice and enjoyment of the fine arts and music, with exhibitions and teaching facilities. To these can be added the professional associations and societies which embrace the graduate practitioners of law, medicine, engineering, etc., and, finally, the official Academies of the local languages, literature and history.

One or more museums, general or specialized, are to be found in every major city. These are usually well maintained on modern lines. Some are of strictly local interest, others, like the museums of Cairo or Baghdad, have earned world fame. The more considerable are as a rule state-owned, but the non-Muslim communities, or specialized para-statal institutions, or private persons, are responsible for others. There is an interesting observatory, of French (Jesuit) foundation, in the Lebanon. The public or semi-public or collegiate libraries in the territories have grown in recent years to importance; most can be freely visited, some are of high value for serious students and contain works nowhere else available.

A cultural activity highly characteristic of our region, and one happily linking the interest of local and foreign scholars, is that of field (as well as study and museum) archaeology. The immense wealth of the region in ancient and medieval sites and objects has led to many projects of excavation by European and American bodies. These have been conducted with great propriety and the highest skill, and rewarded by 'finds' of unique interest in fully two-thirds of the territories. In this work local scholars, now trained thereto, have in recent years taken a creditable part, as also in administering the connected museums and libraries. The general public, to whom a generation ago the whole activity was one of 'foreigners digging for gold'—and smuggling it away when found!—are beginning to see it in truer colours; to the educated it is a source of interested pride.

To describe, and even more to appraise, the current output in the Middle East of modern-type literary and artistic work seems not to belong to the scope of this book. It must suffice to remark that a considerable public interested in these things, as distinct from traditional arts and writings, had by the mid twentieth century come into existence even in those countries where it was, until recently, insignificant; both the producers of such work and its readers or critics are multiplying. Not only in those countries which have long possessed a strain of western art and writing as well as the traditional types (Egypt, Lebanon, Turkey), but in every territory outside Arabia, there are now a number of writers of political and economic essays, of archaeology and history, of philosophy, poetry and fiction, whose best output has sometimes fair, sometimes admirable, merit. This applies to women as well as men, and to all the main Middle Eastern languages, including Kurdish and Armenian. If much of this output is based on western models, this need not deprive it of all originality; it can nonetheless reflect the personal attitudes and gifts of the writer, which often include realism, humanity, and a reforming spirit. The most copious single element, that of political analysis or diatribe, is perhaps the most difficult for the non-nationalist outsider to read with enjoyment. The techniques of printing and book-production, though still indifferent or worse, have immensely improved during the last generation, especially in Egypt and the Lebanon; but book publishing and distribution as an efficient and service-rendering business are still strangely backward, and give authors little encouragement.

In the visual arts, there is already a body of interesting work, but, it would seem, few products yet of such merit as to call for international recognition. Nevertheless, the fine arts are now a subject of higher study which attracts pupils, patrons are found to assist young artists, and the latter study in Europe and can arrange exhibitions of their work. Both here and in modern architecture and, in a very limited circle, western-type music, our region, which was until lately one of near emptiness, is filling to a surprising and encouraging extent with interest and inspiration; outstanding performance, in the near future, would be no surprise. The ancient arts of the region, in miniature-painting, delicate metal work, ceramics, carpet-making and carving, keep their place in public esteem (and as tourist attractions), but seem to have generally declined from their highest level.

The Middle Eastern publics are served by an abundant periodical and daily press. The dailies are, in a few well-known cases, of high or reasonable standard as news-carriers and commentators, with a solid organization behind them and some years of continuity; but the great majority are, for financial reasons, without any serious pretence of a news-service, are without sufficient subscribers or advertising income to maintain publication, and are too often, it must be confessed, without reliability or serious content. The inferior sheets, which by their numbers far over-supply the public demand, almost all represent the politics of a faction or an individual by which or whom they are briefly subsidized, and are devoid of other interest; they are often pointedly or wittily written, commonly by under-employed lawyers or journalist politicians, but ill-produced and likely to enjoy lives of no more than a few weeks or months—or sometimes days. Government censorship is severe, 'freedom of the press' a rarity. The periodical press, consisting of monthlies, weeklies, and some appearing at irregular intervals, is of higher standard. It contains material—political, literary, professional, scientific, scholarly, commercial—of often considerable merit and interest. Such publications are extremely numerous, with a score of weeklies in each of Beirut and Teheran, as many in Ankara-Istanbul, two-score in Cairo, and dozens elsewhere. They cater, in the appropriate languages, for all the main communities including the minorities, carry pictures and cartoons, and in spite of limited readership can be a valuable educative force.

In broadcasting, no Middle Eastern state has failed to equip itself with one or more stations and transmitters of varying power. In this field, for once, the Arabian principalities are no exception. Programmes, among which the Egyptian lead easily both in abundance and (on the whole) in the standard maintained, consist of the usual ingredients, professionally edited and produced, but with music (oriental and western) as the principal time-filling stand-by, and with heavy doses of strongly, sometimes rabidly, nationalistic politics or propaganda; indeed this powerful instrument seems often to be regarded by its possessor, the government, as more a political than a social or educational weapon. It is probable that broadcasting in most of our territories fails generally, as does the daily press, to satisfy the more educated strata of the public; but this, it seems, is scarcely less true in most countries of the world. Television, highly popular wherever installed, is technically efficient but is forced for its programmes to rely largely on the use of films—and, again, on opportunites for propaganda.

Film-making has made great strides in the more advanced Middle Eastern countries since the Second War, and in particular has produced 'documentaries' of excellent style and content. The social effect of these can be very appreciable. In this field Egypt is unquestionably in the lead.

4. *Villages and Tribes*

Since, in spite of the striking growth of the cities and the increase of industry, agriculture in one or another of its forms remains by far the greatest of Middle Eastern sources of livelihood in terms of labour, capital and extent, the life of the villagers devoted thereto ought to be among the most significant objects of our study. In fact, the infinite variety of village settings, in farmland and steppe, mountain and sea shore, wetness and aridity, in all of our dozen countries, would render this the task of a lifetime; and the significant content which would emerge, in terms of Middle Eastern current changes and tendencies, would be relatively small.

The tone and pattern of the life of these many thousands of agricultural villages has in fact changed little in recorded history. Many stand upon relatively new sites, others on ground immemorially occupied. The type, shape and material of the houses, the single room shops, the mosques, coffee-shops and caravanserais have scarcely altered. The furnishings, poor and scanty, are little improved. The food of the peasantry is that, probably, of the last half-millennium—and not more plentiful. Social inter-relations are not less permanent, the position of women scarcely less depressed; in spite of all laws and urban innovations the village way of life is substantially that of past ages, with few gaieties, amusements, amenities or hopes of a wider horizon. The labours of the bread-winner are not less arduous, his methods largely unmodified, his rewards, too often, those of bare subsistence. Drought, locust visitations and other agricultural misfortunes can still intensify poverty and increase indebtedness. These matters are viewed by the peasantry with a resigned fatalism, and they oppose an extreme conservatism to all proposals for change not immediately attractive. The local government still demands its due of land-revenue, landlords (often absentee) have their claims for rent, crop-share and debt-recovery, and tribal authorities, where these persist, must be served or placated.

Such, at least, would be the impressions of a visitor, and they are largely true. Yet there are both hopes and some signs of changes for the better. Landlords, where these survive the break-up of large, multi-village estates now widely in progress, are becoming more amenable, more enlightened both as estate-owners and as citizens. Government officials are for the most part more modern-minded, humane, accessible; many are themselves reformist and public-spirited, security is better than of old, bandits and prowlers less to be feared. The terrors of rain-failure are mitigated, in favoured areas, by irrigation works; specialist work has been done on seed-types and anti-pest measures, demonstrators from the nearest Research Station may have paid the village a visit. There is easier transport of produce to the market-town, a better road, a truck instead of pack-animals. The country 'buses run daily, and fairly reliably. Some new and better-type houses may have appeared, a telegraph office or telephone-box where none existed, a postman, a repair-shop. In Turkey and in post-1952 Egypt Village Institutes, a valuable innovation, combine school and dispensary, library and recreation room; these are immense assets to the village. Far more rural schools exist, and with better teachers than ever before, though still far from sufficient; and this degree of education, extended by continuous broadcasts (of whatever quality and content) and sometimes a television set, and relatively easy contact with the near-by town, are forces bound to modify village life slowly or soon wherever they penetrate—and to stimulate the villagers, it may be, to brands of politics varying from progressive to revolutionary, unless, locally, the restraining hold of the landlord or shaikh, agha or sardar, is still effective.

These tribal authorities, just mentioned, lead us on to a consideration of tribalism. The tribe, as a simple, social group living and acting together under some form of patriarchy, is found in many parts of the world and many environments, but nowhere more characteristically, and with more instructive varieties, than in the

Middle East. Tribes exist on a major scale not only in all of the
Arabian peninsula, but throughout the Fertile Crescent. In Egypt
they are present, but in little force and on the outer fringes of the
national life; in the Sudan, they are numerous, important and
various. In Turkey there are today little more than fairly numerous
traces; in Persia the tribes are never Persian, but the Lurish,
Kurdish and Turkish tribes of the country bear famous names, and
are too vital to be ignored.

The tribe is never nothing but a tribe; that is, the households
which constitute it form at the same time an economically viable
group by their own efforts (as graziers, farmers or otherwise), thanks
to skilled use of their environment; they are also, administratively,
subjects of their state and province, and, it may be, politically an
element of some weight within it. The tribal loyalty which binds
them together is habitually the closest and dearest tie of which they
are conscious, far surpassing those of locality or nation; and both
this and the tribe's special interest in uninhibited freedom, and
aversion from 'government interference', result in that reluctant,
imperfect integration of these communities with the rest of the public,
of which governments and non-tribal publics commonly complain.
Their introvert tribal loyalty is derived from their awareness of a
common origin (whether true or mystical) and long inseparable
common fortunes. Some tribes are, or claim to be, literally the
blood-descendants of an eponymous eminent founder, with, obviously, miscellaneous accretions who quickly claim authentic membership. Others derive from a small original body, perhaps military
or migrant from elsewhere or linked to a famous name, and have
multiplied, and attracted incomers, until the tribal form with all its
unifying myth is achieved. Some represent no more than the sedentary inhabitants of a valley or tract whom a leader, indigenous or
immigrant, has come to dominate—or possibly has defended—so
that a self-conscious 'tribe' results. Others are clearly traceable to
the centripetal power of a holy man, or a shrine, around whom or
which have clustered his relations, pilgrims and protection-seekers.
Many groups, including the noblest in tribal estimation, are of great
antiquity and tell ancestral tales of which history can make nothing;
these go back to origins in primitive Arabia and, heedless of present
poverty and fallen fortunes, claim high superiority in the tribal
hierarchy, than which no more rigid yet accepted snobbery exists.

The tribe takes, oecologically, various forms: or rather, tribal
nomenclature, and to an extent its organization, has spread in many

areas from an environment where it was appropriate to one in which it could, to all appearance, be easily dispensed with; and indeed even city-dwellers to whom countryside, and even more mid-desert, life would be unthinkable not infrequently claim, as a social (occasionally a legal) asset, the name and prerogatives of tribesmen. Apart from these, the established classification of Middle Eastern tribes arranges them into four categories. The first is the long-range nomadic camel-owning tribe of Arabia; the second, the mainly migratory cattle-owning tribe, of Persia and Kurdistan and Turkey; thirdly, the largely-settled, agricultural but also, in some sections, sheep-grazing tribe on or near the fringes of the steppe: and fourthly, wholly agricultural village-dwelling communities which use a tribal name and hierarchy, and may be not less sincere in their long-established tribal loyalties.

The pure *badu*, found in true desert and the lightest steppe-country, migrate at all seasons to and between the grazing-grounds and water-holes which are theirs by right of unwritten desert convention. They have no fixed abiding-place, and no houses but their windy, insecure goats-hair tents. Their life is one of hunger, hardship and ignorance. Both food and clothing are simple and scanty, domestic equipment a traditional minimum, water rare and often foul. They live by selling the surplus of their camel-herds—no other animal could survive mid-desert conditions—and by buying grain and coffee and a minimum of cotton-cloth. The less 'noble' *badu* earn a pittance at times by services of carrying or escort. To four-fifths of these nomads contact with the world beyond the desert is not more than annual. Their own amusements are hawking and fireside talk, the pursuit of blood-feuds, and the traditional mutual raiding between hereditary foes. Their expert accomplishment is tracking, their pride is in their pedigree and tribal lore. Their lives are guided by the customs and rules of a millennary tradition, and to a slight degree by those of Islam—but never, if they can help it, those of the government! Their desiderata are the fullest freedom, a sufficiency of water and grass, the give and take of desert hospitality, success in raiding, deference to their status—and enough to eat. Their relations with government, conducted entirely by their shaikh, are as slight and infrequent as they can achieve; attempts by the state to penetrate their deserts and normalize their society are always resisted.

The cattle-migrants, or transhumants, of the hill-country share some features of the camel-nomads' life, but with wide differences. Their migration is six-monthly, to and from their higher mountain pastures and those of the low, warm country where they pass the winter. They move together for lesser distances, by prescribed routes and in formed parties, passing *en route* through settled agricultural country according to an established right which does not, however, exclude numerous quarrels with the crop-growing villagers. Inter-tribal fighting is less common, though hereditary enmities abound; living standards are less abject, tribal pride less immoderate. A part of the tribe-group, certainly including its ruling elements, may own houses and gardens, and often does not migrate; indeed, the propor-tion which moves annually is probably decreasing. These tribes, in Persia, have recovered much, but not all that they lost in lands, numbers and status during the period 1925–1940.

Of the category of sheep-owning but largely sedentary tribes, those on the Upper Euphrates in 'Iraq and Syria are typical. Most of the tribesmen, village-dwelling or housed in semi-permanent wood-built shelters, cultivate permanently on lands by the river-side while specialized sections (each also a sub-tribe within the tribe) graze the sheep of the community on the inlying desert pastures created by the rains, from mid-winter to late spring, or as long as the grazing and water lasts. These are inoffensive folk, ranked in the tribal hierarchy far below the authentic *badu*, exposed to ruin in case of drought, and more raided than raiding; but the tribal organ-ization and chain of command apply, and tribal pride and its mystique are not absent. This applies, with somewhat diminished force (by reason of dilution, and competition from other sources) but still essentially, to our fourth category, the wholly settled communities of villagers, whether in plain or foothill, farmland or mountain, where the structure and attachments of tribalism yet prevail. Here the sense of tribal solidarity can still be dominant, even when the shaikh or agha is also landlord and government agent, and the state has full powers of interference and coercion—and even though the tribal pretentions of the taxed, controlled, laborious villagers would be viewed with curiosity and scorn by 'Aniza or Shammar!

The minimum unit of tribalism is the single group obeying a single headman, who is chosen by majority opinion from the seniors of the community, in most cases from the sons or near relations of the former shaikh. This authority is normally, but without precise formulation, subject to known custom and to prevailing opinion within the tribe; unless of outstanding personality the shaikh can be no dictator, and in case of failure he can and will be replaced. His function is that of protector of all tribal rights and advantages, dispenser of hospitality for the tribe, occasional judge or arbitrator, leader in raids and in defence, policy maker and representative *vis-à-vis* the government, other tribes and the outside world. Upon him rests the cohesion of the tribe, a quality certain, in this region of intense individualism, to vary between the widest limits. Many shaikhs retain their authority for a lifetime, and bequeath it. The formation of groups and confederacies of tribes, with a common consciousness and group-name but composed of many constituent units, is very general; such often furnish, in all territories where tribes exist, the most famous of tribal names—Arab, Kurdish or Turcoman—and may keep their structure and allegiances for decades: indeed for far longer, when the prestige of the name and ruling family provide bonds strong enough to hold the group together in harmony and without (no uncommon event) secession. Every major tribe will prove, on examination, to contain within it, with an accepted order of precedence and distribution of authority, a variety of sub-tribes, themselves probably of differing scales and origins.

The policy of all modern Middle Eastern governments, except perhaps that of the Sa'udi rulers, to tribalism is instructively uniform: it is that of progressive tribe-breaking, with the aim of reducing all tribesmen to the status of normal citizenship. This policy, in force in 'Iraq since the mid-nineteenth century, and notably in Persia in the recent inter-war period, is undoubtedly shared by other concerned governments of today. It is justified by the consideration that tribalism, except in desertic regions scarcely susceptible of normal government, can have little or no future in modern states—as Scotland and other countries have found—because it necessarily, and indeed designedly, detracts from governmental authority; the tribe as such stands openly for conceptions of corporate life and administration inimical to what is nowadays accepted as civilized progress in equity, citizenship, law-enforcement, education and the public services. It is true that procedures of tribe-breaking and resettlement, if they are to be carried out with humanity, and above all to be succesful, call for more intelligent planning, more material aid and imaginative economic thought, more psychological appreciation, than have so far been forthcoming from impatient reformists; but, on a long view, there seems little alternative to such a policy. Its application will be aided by a number of factors affecting tribal life, such as are now visibly operating. These are the increasing sophistication and urbanization of many tribal leaders, with their motor-cars and town houses and amusements, whereby they lose true contact with their followers: the economically serious loss of demand for tribal products: the easier penetrability of desert areas to government transport, and therefore control: the spread of education, through broadcasts if not through schools, leading to a self-critical view of tribalism as archaic and unfashionable: and an increasing realization, by the rank and file of the tribes, that their life is one of hardship and misery from which softer surroundings may one day lure them. Meanwhile the tribes, of every type and scale, are very much alive, represent, at their best, a distinctive form of society, and pose no lack of problems.

CHAPTER TEN

LANDS AND FACTORIES

1. *Agriculture: a general view*

IN its devotion to agriculture, and dependence for livelihood upon it, the region which is our subject suffers—in contrast, it seems, to a general opinion—from serious drawbacks. These include not only its distance from the world's major markets for agricultural produce, but the very high proportion of its land-surface which is uncultivable desert, mountain or marsh; less than 10 per cent of the area is capable of bearing crops. The drawbacks include also the vagaries of a rainfall habitually insufficient for dry farming, and often practically non-existent. They include the prevalence of excessively light soils with inadequate organic content, and a tendency to salinate when habitually irrigated. With all these defects go the prevalence of pests and diseases, including those which afflict and debilitate the peasants: the rural conservatism which, linked to a crippling lack of capital, has perpetuated primitive methods and acquiesced in low productivity and inferior products: and finally, too often, land-tenure systems which deprive the worker of most of the fruits of his labour, and discourage effort and enterprise.

These factors do not, with all their force, prevent the agricultural life from being the favoured (because the only conceivable) livelihood of nearly all our territories. As a source of national income the agricultural industry is exceeded by others only in the oil-states of Arabia, in Israel, and in Lebanon; throughout the Fertile Crescent, in the Nile Valley and the Yemen, Cyprus, Persia and Turkey, the resources of the state, and the livings of from 60 to 80 per cent of the inhabitants, derive directly from the land. And, with all their disadvantages, the farmers of many of our territories have cultures of interest, sometimes of merited fame, to show; such are, as all the world knows, the cotton of Egypt and the Sudan, the dates of 'Iraq, the citrous fruits of Palestine, the coffee of the Yemen, the grapes and fruit of Turkey and the Levant.

Of the serious disadvantages mentioned above, some are manifestly intractable: that is, those deriving from the sheer facts of geography and climate—though, even here, the works of man can, and to some extent do, provide palliatives. Others of the current defects may with time, goodwill and money be partially curable. In any event, so close is the connection between agriculture, actual and potential, and social well-being in the Middle East that some pages must be devoted to these matters. First the basic troubles, almost region-wide, from which agriculture suffers will be more closely considered, together with possible lines of advance: then, a brief survey will be made of the agricultural performance of each territory as it now appears.

The provision of a greater acreage of cultivable land can, in evident cases, be effected by the terracing of mountain-slopes, already a characteristic feature, for long ages past, in the Lebanon, Turkey, the Yemen and Persia: by the costly and long-drawn draining of marshes in, for example, Syria, southern 'Iraq, ultimately the vast *sudd* of the Sudan, and well known localities in Egypt, Turkey and Persia: and, on a far greater scale than these, by the provision of irrigation for lands whose only fault is their aridity. This same method will often replace a precarious rain-cultivation with assured and possibly all-seasonal supply of water, with immediate doubling or trebling of productivity. Irrigation works on a very important scale have in fact been carried out over the last century, but more notably within the last generation, in 'Iraq, Egypt and the Sudan, and less projects have been completed in Turkey, Persia, Syria, Lebanon, Israel, and even the Aden Protectorate. Moreover in all these, and in Cyprus, Sa'udi Arabia, Jordan, and Yemen also, more and more effort has gone into the increased provision of agricultural water by the time-honoured methods of tapped underground channels (the Persian *qanat*, Arab *kahriz*), of captured hill-streams, of wells and channelled springs, of animal and mechanical water-lift. Today major irrigation projects have been drawn up, and are actively in hand, in most of the major countries of our region—notably 'Iraq, Egypt, the Sudan, Turkey and Syria—while almost none of the territories is without one or a number of plans to increase, on an interesting scale, their acreage or its output. The familiar dangers of such projects, even when successfully completed, are those of salination of the soil, for which drainage, and avoidance of over-irrigation, are the cures: and (a more human aspect) failure to complete the unspectacular de-tailed canalization which secures maximum usefulness. And two other aspects of major irrigation-development are notable. One is, that it may lead to immediate social disturbance, by the shifting of popula-tion into the newly developed area and away from an inferior. Another is the economic aspect: that the crops to be grown must needs be such as to pay not only for the probably high cost of the work, but for its upkeep; and this, with only the traditional crops and methods, may be difficult.

For two other curses of Middle Eastern agriculture, inferior light soil with insufficient humus, and the prevalence of pests, one can but leave the solutions to the scientists. In this field, that of research (to be followed, one hopes, by the evolution of practicable techniques, and by popular instruction) the governments of our states are already active (p. 202) according to their lights. Few have failed to realize the present inadequacy of productivity and product-types (with, in consequence, restricted or low-priced demand) due to these causes, and to divert funds and energies to finding cures. Among these is, for example, the increasing number and efficiency of irrigation pumping-engines, the attempt by good landlords to introduce—and, much more difficult, to keep pure—new types of seed, and the now widely extended use of tractors in place of the ancient, infinitely slow, plough-animals. The government research-stations, experimental farms and field-schemes, wherever found, are full of interest and hope; but their entrenched opponents are not only the forces or shortcomings of nature, and the vagaries of plant-disease, blights and locusts, but also the deep conservatism of the peasantry, their ignorance, and their slow acceptance of superior methods which may call, perhaps, for greater effort or for dislocation of time-honoured routines. The inducement of the peasant intelligently to face new methods and conditions can be effected only, in general, as part of his own gradual evolution and education by school and college and all other instructional media; and, in particular, by practical proof, before his eyes, that the new ways demanded are to his own advantage. It is not to be forgotten that the low productivity of Middle Eastern agriculture, per head of workers, is at present a notable adverse factor; it is reckoned, indeed, as one-fourth, or less, of that of European or American workers. The cure for this seems to lie not only in improved methods, equipment and crop-types, but in a progressive improvement in human health and vigour, which better nutrition and living-standards alone could bring.

For the lack of capital which impedes, always and everywhere, the provision of better implements and facilities and the adoption of progressive plans, there appears no rapid cure, unless provided by an oil-enriched government ('Iraq or Persia) able itself to provide what is required, from major irrigation-schemes to tractor-maintenance workshops. The diversion of more capital to agriculture depends in part upon willingness, by the rich, so to invest (and risk) their money: in part, on the slow increase of cultivators' own resources: in part, on direct governmental aid. In this field co-operative societies have, it seems, a leading part to play, once initial suspicions are overcome; and in fact this movement is now well established, and has achieved immediate results, not otherwise conceivable, in Turkey, Persia, Cyprus, the Levant States and the Nile Valley. It permits not only the communal acquisition and maintenance of tractors, harvesters and other costly implements not otherwise within reach, but also co-operative marketing and sometimes management, and even the acquisition of land-holdings by facilitated purchase. This is an important, and relatively new, factor of great value in Middle Eastern society. But, on a wide view, under-financing remains one of the major inhibitive factors in the region's agricultural progress.

Another, yet more serious and not less deeply rooted in the existing social régime, lies in the peculiarity—one might say, the evils—of the land-tenure systems. Not only have these an immediate effect on agricultural efficiency and productivity, but they deeply affect the whole life, morale and happiness of probably two-thirds of the peasantry of the region. In some territories there are areas of small holdings in which, apart from the abiding danger of excessive fragmentation due to inheritance, only minor problems arise; such are Cyprus, Jordan, much of Turkey, small parts of Persia and Syria, and the mountain areas of 'Iraq and Lebanon. There are, elsewhere, large estates, perhaps government-owned or corporation-owned, in which tenant farmers are reasonably well treated and content; and there are districts where peasant small-holding settlement has been, in recent years, carried out by government policy. In countries, or districts thereof, where estates have traditionally been extensive, and privately owned by landlords habitually absentee (as Egypt, Persia, 'Iraq), steps have been taken in late years by the governments to remedy by direct statal action the serious evils of this abused, anti-social and inefficient system: that is, by imposing by law a maximum holding of so-many acres (varying usually as between irrigated and non-irrigated land) per owner, and parcelling out the rest for sale, by instalments, to the ex-tenants. This policy has been adopted for some state-lands in Persia and the ex-royal estates in Egypt, and for part of the excessively large private holdings in Persia, Egypt and 'Iraq—and, in intention at least, in Syria. Such legally enforced redistribution has shown a new willingness to deal with social evils, and has proved encouraging to thousands of new owners, even though it has created also new problems for the cultivators in the field of large-scale canal-management and upkeep, and in the immediate finding of even minimum finance (for seed, animals, and interim existence) by the penniless and now landlord-less new owner. But, morally and practically, the new position is, where it exists, no doubt more hopeful than the old.

No such steps, however, have yet been taken in respect of many other wide private estates in Persia, 'Iraq, Syria and the plain areas of Lebanon. The districts of large-scale absentee landlordism, with inadequate unhelpful supervision, oppressive traditions of the land-lord's rights and dues—but little of his obligations—and chronic insecurity, indebtedness and hopelessness of the tenant-villager, are still all too numerous. With considerable varieties of treatment and of circumstance from country to country, or (as in Persia) from province to province, this type of agricultural organization, an undisplaced remnant of earlier conceptions of human society, still flourishes widely, still precludes even minimal development of the lands concerned, still keeps to their lowest level both agricultural and human standards. But the political 'lobby' which supports it—and is, of course, sup-ported by it—is still powerful and can indicate, not without per-suasiveness, the difficulties which confront any immediate or radical reform. If more and better-distributed capital is one crying need of Middle Eastern agriculture, a more enlightened system of land-tenure is another.

Yet another is, no doubt, a still greater contribution by the State (since there is no other adequate authority) and, for some purposes, perhaps also by concerted inter-statal action, in the field of agri-cultural planning. This might cover, for example, the proportion of each main crop to be grown (as, for instance, between grain and cotton in Egypt), the prohibition of some profitless or damaging cultures, the encouragement of more 'mixed farming' integrated with stock-breeding and its products, the movement progressively from merely subsistence crops to cash-crops, the insistence on drainage, the organization of anti-pest efforts, the expansion of co-operatives, the observance of reputable standards in marketing and export: and many other matters. The part played by governments in this general field (p. 202) is already highly important; it will probably increase, as will their direct provision of more instructors and inspectors, more facilities for trial and experiment, more transport, storage and market-ing organizations. Inter-government consultation could, as in a measure it already does, deal with the apportionment of river-waters

(Euphrates, Nile, Jordan) between neighbouring states: with concerted anti-locust measures: perhaps with the expansion or limitation
of acreage to be devoted to crops regionally in excess or in short
supply. But the success of such consultation would evidently depend
on factors far outside the agricultural sphere.

2. *Agriculture: country by country*

The crops, the methods and problems, the rural circumstances of
our territories as they stand today, only half-way or less on their
journey towards the greater development destined to be theirs,
deserve a closer survey.

In TURKEY, three-quarters of the whole population, it is said,
lives on and from the land, of which, in all, nearly a quarter (a high
proportion for the Middle East) is cultivable. Wheat and other
cereals (barley, rye, maize, millet, oats) are produced on a large scale,
and render the country normally self-sufficient in all but bad years;
indeed in recent times much wheat has been exported. Rice is widely
grown, but without exportable surplus. Excellent fruit, including
citrus, is produced and sent abroad; Turkish raisins, sultanas and
figs are famous, olives are ubiquitous, hazel-nuts a major crop. Part of
the grape-harvest is made into excellent wine, welcomed in foreign
countries. Tea, on the eastern Black Sea coast, is a useful innovation;
experiments in coffee-growing are in progress. Opium poppies are
grown, and, with due authority, their produce is marketed. Turkish
tobacco, of high and characteristic quality, is a renowned product and
in international demand; the main growing areas are those of Izmir
and Samsun. Cotton is grown with increasing success around Izmir,
Antalya, Aydin and Adana, and is now a leading export. Sugar-beet
culture brings self-sufficiency in sugar. Land-tenure problems are
less acute in Turkey than elsewhere; in spite, however, of an impressive increase of tractors and other mechanization in favourable areas,
and development by irrigation in others, the general level of method
and productivity is very low.

In PERSIA dependence on agriculture is equally general, the
environments of its practice not less varied; but here not more than
10 to 15 per cent of the land-surface is cultivable, and a high proportion of this is held in large absentee-owned estates or crown-
lands, with all their habitual evils. Widely grown products are
cereals of every type, sugar-beet, fruit and nuts, rice in the Caspian
provinces, opium (prohibited but still profitably grown), tobacco, and

oil-seeds. Limited quantities of good fruit are gathered, some cotton and a little tea. All the characteristics of Middle Eastern agriculture are exemplified in Persia, including particularly the long and difficult communications, persistently primitive (though in rare localities modernized) methods, and rural poverty at its grimmest. But study, capital and effort are now all being in some degree devoted to agriculture, with emphasis on rural credit (for which a Bank has been founded), on co-operative societies, and on discovering and conserving water-sources. The Shah's personal partition and disposal, in small lots, of the estates amassed by his father is a hopeful feature, not yet imitated by other landowners.

In 'IRAQ, the date crop—three-quarters of the whole world's—picked in the vast date-gardens of the centre and south is the most famous, rice perhaps the most prized by its growers, the winter grains (wheat and barley) the most widespread, of the country's products. A substantial export of dates, cotton, wheat and barley is normal; cotton-growing is well on the increase. All the usual summer grains and vegetables are grown, with small quantities of fruit, and tobacco in Kurdistan. Cultivation is by rain in the north, by controlled canal or pump-irrigation in the centre and south, and by tidal irrigation in the Basra date-gardens. Whatever the contributions of oil-riches and of nascent industries, agriculture and horticulture remain the staple livelihood of the 'Iraqis who, in general terms, seem to possess the greatest agricultural potential of any Middle Eastern state, as well as the necessary capital from other sources (their oil) to help its development. A number of important irrigation and flood-protection projects have been already accomplished (the first in 1912) and others are planned, all on a scale truly impressive and indicative of the extent to which oil-derived Development funds have been so utilized. A multifold increase of cultivated acreage, through new canals and mechanical water-lift, throughout central 'Iraq has been brought about in the last generation, chiefly by private capital and enterprise. Much well-directed governmental effort has been spent in research and instruction, an Agricultural Bank exists, new cultures have been attempted, locust-destruction campaigns conducted, comprehensive anti-salination measures formulated, specialists invoked; nevertheless, the mass of 'Iraqi agriculture is still relatively primitive and wasteful. And the benefits of the redistribution of land, begun in 1930 and reactivated on revolutionary lines in 1958, are as yet but little apparent; some observers feel that it has created more problems than it has solved.

In SYRIA, endowed likewise with abundant cultivable acreage, with Euphrates and Orontes water, and with a normally sufficient rainfall for dry-farming in the north, cultivation has shown striking advances in area since the Second War. Estate-management has here been conducted by owners on enlightened lines, and remarkable strides have been made in profitable cotton-growing; the last-named now produces the most valuable single item of export. The fundamental changes in land-holding made by the law of September 1958, which limited narrowly the area permitted for private holding, were reconsidered, more generously, in 1962, but are still highly restrictive; the new régime, however, has not been universally implemented. Much modernization and mechanization of agriculture has taken place, and private capital has here been made available more, proportionately, than elsewhere. Irrigation works on a considerable scale have been carried out since 1945, nearly doubling the area of irrigable land; others are in progress, and a major utilization of Euphrates water, by flow-canals from a main barrage, is contemplated. The river already serves hundreds of water-lifting pumps. Striking development has been carried out in the Jazira since 1935. The main crops grown in Syria are wheat and barley—with usually, not always, an exportable surplus for needy neighbours—cotton, oil-seeds, sugar-beet (its production increased ten-fold in the last twenty years), grapes and other fruit (olives, figs, apricots, apples), summer grains and vegetables. The tobacoo of Lataqiya is small in quantity, but world-famous.

In LEBANON, about a quarter of the territory is cultivated, a proportion reached only after much effort in drainage, reclamation and terracing; and in a small mountainous country no great further expansion can be possible. In the field of land-tenure, hundreds of holdings in the mountain districts are uneconomically small, those in the plains of the south and north are extensive and often absentee-owned; half the total cultivable land is said to belong to 200 owners. With exceptions, agricultural methods remain primitive. Cereal production is limited, and increasing but little; the population is dependent on imports. Some sugar-beet is grown, and most of the familiar vegetables; onions are a usual export. Lebanese fruit-growing is of more, and characteristic, interest; good apples are grown (though these are not easily marketable outside the country), and the citrus fruits, of excellent quality, furnish an export to Europe. The crop has increased strikingly in late years, and is now nearly half that of Israel. Bananas manage to survive the winter, and indeed to increase in output; the grapes, also an increasing crop, produce a respectable wine. Figs and olives are locally consumed. A little cotton and tobacco are grown. With all this, Lebanon is an agricultural country to a less predominant extent than most in the Middle East; about half its labour-force is so employed, the rest being occupied in industry, commerce, and service activities. Trade, not agriculture, here provides most of the national income.

In CYPRUS, the case is otherwise; the agricultural population is well over half the total, and agriculture the mainstay of its humble economy. Small-holdings are the rule, many too small to be economic. The deficient rainfall makes irrigation desirable for most cultures, and this is achieved wherever possible by a numerous variety of small works—pumping, conservation of flood-water, and minor canalization. About one-sixth of existing cultivable land is or can be irrigated, the rest is exposed to the danger of drought and failure. No major expansion of cultivable area (now some 1,250,000 acres) can be hoped for. In the plain, mechanization by tractors and combine harvesters has made advances. Production costs are relatively high, the income of agricultural workers low, and a drift to urban employment results; agriculture, within Cypriot limits and problems, can barely, or cannot, support the population which successful measures of health-improvement have so greatly increased. The principal crops grown are cereals, grapes from which saleable wines and grape-alcohol are produced, citrous fruit—a considerable export—olives, carobs, potatoes, onions and other vegetables, and some tobacoo.

The agricultural picture in JORDAN is, on the west side of the river, one of poor and largely eroded soil, well cultivated with terraces, trees and vineyards, while on the east lies less eroded and more extensive land still under a primitive and little productive régime of cultivation. The Jordan Valley itself is highly fertile; it is currently the scene of a technically and socially progressive agricultural estate and settlement, admirably organized by an eminent Palestinian on behalf of the Refugees. Otherwise improvement by major irrigation schemes seems not immediately probable, thanks to acute international stresses; none of the schemes for utilization of the Jordan or Yarmuk waters has yet secured the agreement of all concerned. The use of mechanization in farming has made only slight progress. Land-tenure problems, a field in which admirable work of settlement and stabilization was done under the Mandate (1920–1946), are limited to the too exiguous acreage of many of the holdings. The total area now cultivable is of the order of 2,250,000 acreas, of which about 75,000 acres are irrigable from streams flowing east or west to the Jordan, and from springs or wells. There is no likelihood of a serious increase in this acreage, since no source for irrigation water except the Jordan and Yarmuk exists, other than those already in use. Only more laborious and more skilful farming, it seems, can increase production. The crops now principally grown are cereals, especially wheat—but in quantities necessitating the regular import of grain and flour to feed the population—pulses, vegetables and fruit, especially olives which are largely exported.

Of the insistence on land-work in ISRAEL, for both ideological and economic reasons, we have spoken elsewhere (p. 190); and reference has been made also to the forms of agricultural settlement adopted, so different from those found elsewhere in our region. The Israeli community has tackled its agricultural problems with a wealth of energy and science, under the spur of necessity to feed its public and to save the cost of imports; it has enjoyed at the same time, to an extent wholly unknown to its neighbours or to the Palestine of earlier years, the advantage of massive financial help from outside. This has permitted expenditure on settlement-building, irrigation, mechanization, research, etc., on a scale to which the resources of the territory itself could never aspire. Thus supported, the Israeli state has more than doubled the cultivable land which they took over *en bloc* from the previous (Arab) population, and has contrived in addition to irrigate a higher proportion, up to one-third, as well as cultivating it with every scientific refinement.

The draining of the Hula marshes gave an additional 15,000 acres. The cultivable area would be further and materially increased if the plan to divert Jordan waters by conduits to southern Judaea and the Negev were realized; to what extent these plans will prove attainable, by force or diplomacy, remains to be seen. Such cultivation in the Negev, where with irrigation almost everything is growable, would be, one must suppose, uneconomic by normal standards, by reason of the immense cost of the preliminary works and their upkeep; this might, however, in a state so heavily subsidized by its friends abroad, be of secondary importance. Meanwhile, all otherwise available water-sources are in fullest use, to the great benefit of production. Israel, with a notably diversified and increased agricultural production since 1948, is now reported as self-sufficient in vegetables, fodder, and dairy produce, though large imports of grain and meat are still necessary. Citrus fruit-growing (the famous Arab industry of such long standing, based on the inimitable Jaffa orange) has been restored, after a severe recession, to near its pre-1948 level; it provides Israel's most valuable agricultural export. Other fruits grown and in part exported are olives, grapes, apples and bananas. Crops grown on unirrigated land are cereals, pulses, fodder-crops, oil-seeds; on irrigated, cotton, sugar beet, ground nuts, tobacco. As much of all this as possible is processed for export, by the industries established *ad hoc*: by the manufacture, for instance, of wine, sugar, fruit juices and cotton textiles.

The agriculture of EGYPT is of high importance not only for its own sake as the sole support of 70 to 80 per cent of Egyptian lives, and the activity of some of the world's most skilled and industrious cultivators, but as a field also of economic and political problems whose range exceeds that of Egypt herself. The soil of the Nile valley is of unusual fertility; but by reason of the sheer numbers of the population, still growing at a minimum rate of 2 per cent a year, intensive cultivation with two, three, or four crops a year is necessary in the very limited irrigable areas. This has called, and calls, for an agricultural régime radically different from that of any other Middle Eastern country. The intensive use of fertilizers, which must be imported and paid for, is unavoidable, costly and widespread; there are hopes, however, for self-sufficiency through local industry before the end of the present decade. The conversion of earlier 'basin' irrigation (by merely local and temporary capture of the annual flood-water, in confined basins) into perennial irrigation (by vast-scale imprisonment of high-season Nile supplies, by great river barrages) has been proceeding for a century—the first Delta barrage was built in 1843—and now covers almost all areas except those of Upper Egypt; and it has called, and is still inevitably to call, for enormous expense. At the same time the devotion of a high proportion of the restricted acreage to the most financially rewarding crops, notably cotton, cannot but lead to diminished food-growing, and therefore to greater dependence on imports.

In major irrigation works, to those existing at 'Aswan, Isna, Nag Hamadi, 'Asyut and elsewhere is to be added the much-discussed High Dam at 'Aswan (a work separate from the earlier barrage) which has been made possible by the recent (1959) revised Nile Waters agreement with the Sudan. The High Dam, which when complete bids fair to be the greatest man-made construction in the world, depends upon Russian technical and financial aid. The work is already well begun. The resulting reservoir will cover 740 square miles—the evaporation from which, under such a sun, can be imagined!—and will store 130,000 million cubic metres of water. The dam will be 110 metres high, its cost some £E350,000,000. It will, if all goes well, make available an additional 2,000,000 acres under irrigated cultivation, as well as a highly important hydro-electric potential of immense advantage to industry. The increased crop-area will, it is hoped, by providing for the increased population of the country by the time of the work's completion, enable Egyptian standards of living *not to fall below* their present level. The existing 'Aswan Dam is also to be raised, for the fourth time, and another barrage will be constructed at Girga. Of a different type is the current project to develop, with the help of underground water which is believed to exist and to be exploitable, wide areas of desert land in the Western Desert.

The contribution of the Egyptian Government to its agriculture has not been limited to these works. It has embraced agricultural research, experiment, demonstration, control, and a policy, not always capable of implementation, of balancing internal needs against the advantage of added exports. It has embraced also, with social and political as much as agricultural exigencies in view, a radical re-distribution of lands from the hands of the great landowners—sometimes admirable estate-managers, but not infrequently heartless exploiters of poor and indebted tenants—to those of the cultivators themselves. This, under laws of 1952 and 1961, has thus disposed of between 500,000 and 750,000 acres, with important psychological results but without, it seems, serious gains to productivity. Dispossessed landowners, their estates cut down to 100 acres, are to be compensated over the next forty years. Some 4,000 landowners have been, or will be, thus affected, and one of the major scandals of Egyptian society will have been in some measure corrected. But the fragmentation of the smallest holdings, of which hundreds of thousands are less than a single acre, goes on, and many peasants are entirely landless. The minimum subsistence holding is two acres.

The crops grown in Egypt consist of both subsistence and cash crops. Among the former, wheat and maize are necessities for food, rice and sugar cane are important for local consumption and for export. *Barsim* (a clover fodder-crop), vegetables, pulses, dates, barley, millet and ground nuts are other products. Cash crops include citrus, grapes and other fruit, onions for export and, overshadowing all the rest, the famous Egyptian long-staple cotton. This crop, the object of intense care and great skill at every level, gives Egypt the rank of fifth among the world's cotton-producers, and an output of nearly half the world's long-staple cotton. The crop covers about one-fifth of the total cropped area in the country and provides half the national income from agriculture. The dangers of so great a dependence on outside demand and on uncontrollable, fluctuating prices are realized.

The SUDAN is strictly an agricultural country, where efforts are now being made to diversify produce and to lessen dependence on the cotton-crop, at present the country's most highly developed culture. In areas where rain-cultivation is possible, traditional methods still largely prevail, though mechanization has notably increased. The main crops grown on rain are maize and millet, sesame, ground nuts, and short-staple cotton. The characteristic, perhaps unique, method of grain cultivation in these districts is that of *hariq*—that is, by burning the grassy or weedy ground prior to planting. The problems of rainland farming are currently under close study and experiment. On lands irrigated by flood or by controlled gravity, or by human, animal or mechanical water-lift, the extent of which has grown greatly in recent years, most of the same crops are produced, with wheat, pulses and some barley and dates. The outstanding success of irrigated agriculture, and of an imaginative experiment in agricultural organization, has been the Gezira Scheme: a project involving an area of approximately 1,000,000 acres, in the triangle of the Blue and White Niles, irrigated since 1925 from the reservoir created by the Sennar Dam. This has been developed by an admirably managed threefold partnership of government, an *ad hoc* board of management (successor in 1950 to the Sudan Plantations Syndicate), and the cultivators themselves, with careful regard to the rights and functions of each. The area thus developed is henceforward to be extended, as more water becomes available, to a maximum of 5,000,000 acres: the Roseires and Khashm al-Girba dams are designed to assist in this. A major extension of the Gezira estates, southward into the Managil district, was planned in 1957, and completed in 1961, adding some 750,000 acres. The Gezira cotton output—though other crops than this are also grown—is the mainstay of Sudani exports and of the national agricultural income. Other governmentally organized projects are those at 'Abdul Majid, watered by a canal from the Gezira, another in the Gash Delta under a carefully regulated government-tenant partnership, another in the Tokar Delta similarly; others exist in the Nuba Mountains where rain-grown cotton is produced under constructive official control, and in the Rufa' district of the Blue Nile where pumped water irrigates cotton and food-crops.

In no country, it would seem, is a visible agricultural effort being made with more determination or a more prudent adaptation to conditions.

In the ARABIAN PENINSULA, on the other hand, vast as it its area, agriculture plays, with interesting local exceptions, the minor part which alone Nature permits. In the SA'UDI ARABIAN kingdom there are fairly extensive date-gardens at the oases, with small yields of other fruits. A little wheat, maize, millet and lucerne can also be grown in these favoured but limited locations. There are current projects for small irrigation works at two or three places where sub-surface water is believed to exist, following a geological and hydrographical survey which has been carried out in much of the country. At the al-Kharj oasis, south of Riyadh, American initiative has produced, by well-irrigation, a watered estate on a considerable scale, with valuable fruit and vegetable cultures. The Sa'udi authorities are instituting research and instructional centres to foster whatever the best technical help can devise in agricultural enterprise; but this can, by the nature of things, be little. The YEMEN, as we have seen, is more favoured; if the lowlands are mostly uncultivable, except for some dates and a little cotton and oats, highland districts are capable of growing admirably both irrigated and rain-fed crops, to which, and notably to the famous coffee, the moderate level of subsistence prosperity and (by Arabian standards) the dense population are due. Terracing is widespread, and small-scale irrigation works represent a long tradition of skilful husbandry. Among the hill-villages and around the chief towns, varieties of maize and millet are grown, with some barley, sesame and rice; the fruit are dates, grapes, apricots, almonds, citrous fruits, plums and apples. *Qatt* (p. 161) is widely grown, and tobacco on a small scale. The coffee plantations are said to cover 150,000 acres.

The southern and south-eastern districts of Arabia contribute as little to the world's agriculture as almost any inhabited region on earth. The ADEN PROTECTORATE can show a little grain and vegetable cultivation, a very few fruit gardens, a steady export of gum, and some not unpromising attempts at development in the Hadhramaut valley by pump-engine irrigation, the sinking of deep wells, and the culture, for the first time, of citrous and hard fruit. In the Western Protectorate cotton has been introduced and an important scheme has been brought into being at 'Abyan, east of Aden, by a hopeful collaboration between the Protectorate government, the local rulers, and the cultivators. At least two similar projects, respectively

150 miles east and 15 miles north of Aden, have followed. There is, therefore, in this borderland of Happy Arabia some forward activity —and some hope. The OMAN principality can boast its isolated but attractive seaside oasis of Dhufar, where wild vegetation is rich, grain-crops and vegetables sufficient for local use, date- and fruit-gardens a delight to Arabian eyes. In the Jabal Akhdhar dates and fruit abound in the rare but long-established mountain settlements and the deep passes, where grain and fodder crops, rain-grown or irrigated from *qanats*, cater for man and beast. This is true equally of the coast strip of the Batina, from which date-export is, by Omani standards, considerable. Under the current development programme in the Sultanate an agricultural experimental station has been established at Nizwa, deep in the more fertile part of the mountains, and further development will be practicable if and when water-sources, believed to exist, can be exploited. In or depending on the TRUCIAL COAST, agriculture is limited to the few and small inland oases, notably those of the Buraimi group: to a recent experimental project at Ras al Khaima: and to a few hundred scraggy ill-tended date trees. BAHRAIN, as we have seen (p. 170), has its district of attractive and intensive cultivation, with dates and fruit, vegetables, grain and lucerne. QATAR, the two NEUTRAL ZONES, and KUWAIT have, and can have, no agriculture.

3. *Industry*

Factors are not lacking which would seem to favour a major industrial development in the Middle East, even though density of population, a usual motive, is lacking except in Egypt, Israel and perhaps the Lebanon. The local governments favour such expansion for reasons of prestige, industrialization being reckoned progressive and anti-traditional; they hope also to lessen imports, increase exports, and give employment to the un- or underemployed rural and urban proletariat, as well as to the growing ranks of the *évolués* for whom politics or the overcrowded professions seem to be otherwise the only outlet. Governmental encouragement to such enterprise has therefore been freely given, in most of our territories, by fiscal privileges, by government participation, by an *étatiste* policy (as in Turkey, Persia, Israel and Egypt), and by customs-tariffs calculated to exclude competition. At the same time, the public are equally well disposed to the same development, and can point to consider-able private initiative, a modicum of industrial skills, and a local purchasing power increased, in some territories, by the recent and continuing boom in oil prosperity.

Why, then, is it more prudent to treat industry with caution when offered as the panacea of Middle Eastern economic, and perhaps social, troubles?

The reasons, some foreseeable *a priori*, others already demonstrated in practice, are clear enough. Local purchasing power, if higher than of old, is still wretchedly small. Local manufactured products, with very few and special exceptions, can scarcely hope to reach, for some time, competitive international standards; and if forced upon foreign markets (itself no easy task) by sheer lowness of price, they would show little profit. Raw materials exist only in a narrow range, and are of indifferent quality—for example, wool and (save in Egypt) cotton; and they include few ores. Technology is generally backward, individual skills of high quality exist only in rare categories. Capital is notably scarce, the moneyed public is little accustomed to the risks of industrial investment: they prefer to hoard, or to buy real-estate; and foreign capital, a clear necessity for any major development, is more often scared by insecurity and political threats than it is attracted by governmental or promoters' blandishments. Finally, the planning of industrial enterprises, when undertaken on any major scale, as in Turkey, Egypt or Persia, has shown endemic defects of over-optimism, insufficient study, defective financing, uncalculated markets; and even when quick profits have been realized they are all too likely to prove short-lived.

The factors thus enumerated, which are unlikely soon to disappear, make it improbable, or inconceivable, that factory-industry will, for many years, have a dominant part to play in the Middle East. Such it may have in small, highly differentiated communities such as Israel and possibly the Lebanon; it may play an important though always a subsidiary role in Egypt, on a scale almost certainly less than confident Egyptian ministers hope today. It can make a contribution, and valuably diversify national life, in Turkey, Persia, 'Iraq, Syria, Cyprus. It is unlikely to lead more than a marginal existence, which need not, however, exclude all such enterprise, in Jordan, the Sudan, or Arabia.

Of countries today pressing forward in industrialization, only Israel and the Lebanon derive more of their national incomes from that source than from agriculture; next in order would come Turkey, Egypt and Persia, followed by 'Iraq and Syria. In them all, both public (governmental) and private funds have been employed; in all, the state has shown keen interest and helpfulness, most notably in Egypt, Turkey, Persia and 'Iraq. In Israel both statal and para-statal funds as well as copious investment by non-resident supporters have been available. In Syria and the Lebanon private enterprise has borne the main burdens. (The wholly or partly governmental background organization of financial support, in the form of Industrial Banks, Development Boards, Economic Development organizations, Seven Year Plan organizations, and so on, does not here concern us.) The scale of factory construction and organization has varied widely; most plants are small, the great majority employing less than fifty, and few more than five hundred workers. But it should be emphasized that the unfamiliarity of industrial installations in these territories and of the industrial way of life itself, and the interest and hopes (perhaps illusions) excited by their appearance, are far greater than in developed countries, and they therefore represent a more striking social contribution than their scale or economic value would suggest. For better or worse, they proclaim change and progress, and seem to offer an alternative to the age-long, almost static, agricultural life hitherto without rival. The numbers of workers employed in industry may vary from not far less than a million in Turkey, and a not much inferior figure in Egypt, to a very few thousand in Cyprus, still fewer in Jordan or the Sudan, and mere hundreds in the Arabian states.

By reason of lack of metallic ores, and shortage (in most countries) of fuel, and perhaps undemanding domestic markets, heavy industry has so far been attempted only by Turkey, in her Karabuk iron and steel works, soon to be followed by another at Eregli: by Israel, in her small steel-rolling mill at Acre: and by Egypt, with her iron and steel plant at Halwan, supplied from 'Aswan ore. Persia and 'Iraq both have plans for similar enterprises. The manufacture of arms and ammunition is carried on in Turkey, Persia, Egypt and Israel, nowhere on other than a limited scale. The assembly of lorries and cars (to be followed probably in future years by their construction) is in progress in Egypt, Turkey and Israel. And the semi-heavy industries of brick- and tile-making, stone and marble quarrying, and (most widespread of them all) cement-making, are found in almost every territory. That all have their thermal, or rarely hydro-electric, power-stations, constantly growing in scale and numbers according to increasing demand for electricity, needs no insistence.

The wide range of light industries favoured by many or most of our territories can be no more than briefly listed. They include notably textiles—that is, the spinning, weaving, dyeing, etc., of cotton-cloth, usually from local cotton and intended predominantly for the local market. This is on an important scale, and with very few territories excepted; in some the textile industry is the most developed branch of their industrial life, as in Egypt, Syria, Turkey, Persia. Woollen textiles as well as cotton are produced in Egypt, 'Iraq and Persia: jute also in Persia, silk in Turkey, Persia and Lebanon, and rayon in Lebanon and Israel.

The food-processing industries, using raw materials of the country and varying in their product with the local produce available, have established a useful, perhaps a growing, place. Wines, beer and spirits are all produced in diverse grades of excellence and quantity. Tea comes from Turkey and Persia. Vegetable oils are prepared for the market from sesame, cotton seeds, the olive, sunflowers and ground nuts; cattle-cake is a by-product of some of these. Sugar-refining is widespread, and renders much of the region self-sufficient in sugar. Date syrup is exported from south 'Iraq. Fruit- and vegetable-canning occupies dozens of small plants in many countries, with the confection of sweets, jams and cakes. Flour mills, bakeries and biscuit-factories are numerous. Soft drinks and mineral waters cater for the Muslim abstainer from alcohol. With these food-industries may be grouped those (if indeed worthy of a place in the industrial picture) devoted to preparing natural products for export: these are, for example, hides, skins, wool, mohair, incense, gums, oyster shells, liquorice, intestines and dried fish.

Industries connected with building, additional to brick-making, etc., already mentioned, are those of bitumen-preparation, joinery, sheet-metal production, the making of glazed tiles and plate-glass, electrical equipment and refrigerators, woodwork and furniture, ply-wood and plasterboard. These are all widely represented. Less so is the manufacture of explosives, fertilizers and insecticides, refined sulphur, industrial alcohol, and petrochemical products including plastics. These, or some of them, are found in Israel, Egypt, Turkey, Persia, 'Iraq.

A complete census of factories and plants throughout the region would probably reveal that an actual majority of workers and resources was being devoted, if not to the food-processing industries, then to those providing consumer goods, almost wholly from local materials, to the limited local public able to afford them. These include cigarettes and tobacco: footwear, hosiery and clothing: glass ware and ceramics: soap: pots and pans of aluminium and tin: leather goods, paper and matches: buttons and artificial teeth. The last-named, from Israel and Cyprus, is an item designed principally, one may assume, for export: and in this it resembles the diamond-cutting and polishing industry established in Israel, the drugs and toilet preparations in the same country, and, most famous perhaps of all Middle Eastern manufactured articles, the carpets of Persia, prized throughout the world for their design, colour and craftsmanship.

Some of the same factors which operate to limit the export of Middle Eastern products—that is, foreign competition, and changing tastes—have served also to diminish the importance of the home or cottage industries of the region. Many of these, as other pages of this book have mentioned, were for centuries highly prized in the form of local textiles and brocades, carpets, needlework, carved or worked metal, jewellery and painted panels. These, mainly luxury products, and the humbler industries of tribal rug-making, pottery, reed mats and blankets, still survive; but both their output and, one cannot but observe, their quality also have been for some time in decline.

To sum up, the Middle East industrial picture (from which we have reserved the vastly important petroleum industry for separate treatment) is full of interest, of variety, of laudable initiative and confidence. It has a part to play in the development and uplifting of these territories; it can do something to increase national wealth, afford employment, satisfy needs, save foreign exchange, and act in some measure as an educative and modernizing agency. But it would, for reasons already indicated, be an illusion to suppose that the factors are widely present in the Middle East which could enable it to achieve more than a moderate potency in solving economic or social problems in the foreseeable future.

CHAPTER ELEVEN

OIL

1. *Facts and Comparisons*

A RTISTICALLY or ineptly, we have reserved to the last our
region's greatest industry and main source of wealth, and the
outstanding reason for its international significance: its petroleum
resources.

No space need be wasted upon propositions which the writer
holds to be undeniable: that oil is an indispensable commodity in
world-wide demand for a score of essential economic and social, as
well as military, purposes: that the world will, for at least the next
century, require more and more of petroleum products, since none
of the imaginable alternative fuels, including nuclear, is for many
decades at all likely to displace it from its functions, or most of them:
and that Middle Eastern deposits, being by far the richest in the
world, will be called upon ever increasingly to supply these needs.
If the world in 1962 used approximately 1,200,000,000 tons of petroleum and its products, it will probably use 1,750,000,000 in 1970:
if the Middle East supplied in 1962 305,000,000 tons of crude—or
25·7 per cent of the world's output—it is likely to supply 500,000,000
tons in 1970, and perhaps 800,000,000 tons in 1980. In response to
the civilized world's insistent demand, which other regions, on all
present indications, will be unable to meet because fully occupied
with their own and each other's requirements, but which must be
met, the Middle East's contribution is bound to grow in volume,
both absolutely and proportionately, and with all the significance of
sheer indispensability. It has grown already from nothing in 1910
to 7,000,000 tons in 1932, 15,000,000 in 1942, 104,000,000 in 1952,
and 305,000,000 in 1962. These figures, as representing a rate of
increasing output of a major product in a single region, are without
parallel. The region, moreover, was until recent years one in which
such activities—those of maximum-scale industrial organization,
finance, construction, technology, labour-employment—were hitherto completely unknown.

Earlier pages of this book have referred in passing to some effects
of the region's new-found wealth; we pass now to consider these and

others more fully, beginning with some of the present facts and figures of the industry.

Not by coincidence, but in obedience to the basic geological conditions necessary for major oil-accumulation, which are found in unique perfection in the Persian Gulf geosyncline, the principal area of Middle Eastern production is situated in the territories in, and bordering on, that outstanding geological feature. It follows that a number of the Middle Eastern countries other than these—at least as far as yet revealed, and to their own puzzled chagrin—are oil-less. These are CYPRUS, the LEBANON, JORDAN, the SUDAN, and all of ARABIA except a limited area of its eastern flank. In these countries all the processes of exploration and testing have been active for some decades, in vain. The Lebanon, traversed by trunk pipelines (p. 129), which bring her a comfortable revenue, possesses also important loading-terminals (Tripoli and Sidon) and two refineries. Aden Colony has likewise a refinery of much importance. Jordan is crossed by 'Tapline' (p. 137) and by now derelict pipelines from 'Iraq, but has no terminal and only one small refinery. Cyprus and the Sudan have nothing to show.

In a second group of territories oil has, indeed, been discovered, but in quantities of only minor or very moderate significance. The first of these is SYRIA whose deposits, located but not yet in production, may or may not be economically exploitable, being of doubtful quality and situated in the extreme north-east, at maximum distance from the coast. The country, also a toll-taking transit territory for two systems of pipelines (p. 132 f.), has a small refinery of its own, and an export terminal for 'Iraqi oil, at Banyas. ISRAELI production amounted to a mere 130,000 tons in 1962; the country has, by inheritance, refinery capacity above its needs, and this is now supplied with crude no longer from 'Iraq but by pipeline from its own port of Eilat. Long and intensive search has revealed no considerable indigenous crude to add to that of a small field, Heletz, discovered by the 'Iraq Petroleum Company in 1948. EGYPT, with half a dozen small but far from negligible fields on both sides of the Gulf of Suez, yielding poor quality oil not easily produced, enjoyed nevertheless a useful output of more than 4,000,000 tons in 1962; it has its own internal pipeline system, and a refinery capacity almost adequate to its needs. The oil industry is here strictly government-controlled. The importance of the Canal as a highway for tankers needs no emphasis. TURKEY, where Turkish as well as authorized foreign oil-seekers have for forty years spent much effort and treasure in prospecting, has still sadly little to show; less than half a million tons of crude production was obtained in 1961 from a number of small, inferior, ill-situated fields. Its refining capacity however has lately been increased by a new internationally-owned refinery at Mersin, and is soon to be further increased, while the search for crude sources, if slackening, is by no means at an end. BAHRAIN Island, another small producer since 1934 from a single field with a current output of 2,250,000 tons a year, is also a highly important refining centre for its own and Sa'udi crude, and benefits greatly thereby.

None of the ten territories so far mentioned, or all of them together, would give the Middle East its leading importance in the oil-world. That falls instead to three major territories of the Persian Gulf region—'Iraq, Persia and Sa'udi Arabia—and two politically minor states, those of Kuwait and Qatar. These will be considered in turn, in slightly greater detail; but first, two other interesting cases of oil-occurrence must be mentioned. The first of these is the extensive but wholly desertic shaikhdom of ABU DHABI, on the Trucial Coast (p. 167). There is here a discovered mid-sea oil-field in the Gulf, recently placed in production by its British and French concessionaires, and another field (Murban) on dry land, not yet in production, but probably of highly important potential. With these, Abu Dhabi, though not yet among the main producers, will in every probability be so from 1964 onwards. The on-shore rights of Abu Dhabi belong to an 'Iraq Petroleum Company associate.

The second case to be indicated is that of the Kuwaiti-Sa'udi NEUTRAL ZONE (p. 156), the benefits from the oil of which are divisible equally between the two governments who share sovereignty. The Zone is the scene of activity (under concessions from each of the rulers) of two separate but collaborating all-American companies; production in 1962 amounted to 11,500,000 tons, giving each ruler some £12,000,000 as his share from this source. A refinery has been constructed in the Neutral Zone, and may be followed by another. An additional concession, this time for the off-shore area of the Zone, was given by the two rulers in 1957 to a composite Japanese firm, which lost no time in discovering commercially producible oil under the sea, and shipped the first cargoes in 1961. A capacity of at least 8,000,000 tons a year is believed to be available. The Neutral Zone has therefore already reached the rank of a major source of crude oil; it is doubtless the only example in the world of a territory with great riches, in full production—but no inhabitants.

We pass now to the 'Big Five' of Middle Eastern oil producers, the combined output of which approaches 300,000,000 tons a year, or more than a quarter of the whole world's present production.

The industry in 'IRAQ is conducted, under three regional concessions from the government, by an international British-American-French-British/Dutch Company, the 'Iraq Petroleum Company, and its two identical sisters. These operate highly important fields in northern 'Iraq (Kirkuk) and in southern (Rumaila, in the Basra area), exporting from the latter by tanker, from the former by trans-desert pipelines across Syria to the Mediterranean. Lesser fields in both main areas are also in production, and linked by pipeline for export. Production in 1962 was 49,000,000 tons. The 'Iraq Government, which itself undertakes refining and distribution in its territory, and exploits, moreover, a small field of its own (formerly British operated) on the Persian frontier, receives at present about £95,000,000 a year from the I.P.C. and its associates, in royalties and taxes. The establishment of an 'Iraqi National Oil Company, with a wide field of activities, was commenced in the autumn of 1962; but it appeared to be making a slow start.

In PERSIA, operations are divided between, first, the National Iranian Oil Company which represents the Government and intends to produce and sell oil on its own, when it can, from fields it has discovered and proved in central Persia (Qum area): second, two joint companies formed by the N.I.O.C. with American and Italian partners respectively for search and operation in Persian Gulf off-coastal areas, both hoping in the very near future to produce the oil which has been discovered (1961–1962) in both these concessionary areas; and thirdly, and by far the most important, an international Consortium (British-American-British/Dutch-French) as successor, since 1954, to the all-British Anglo-Iranian Oil Company which was, from 1901 onwards, the true pioneer of the whole Middle Eastern oil industry. The Consortium's production from its great fields in the Khuzistan province in the southern Zagros, was in 1962 some 64,000,000 tons a year, bringing about £125,000,000 to the Persian treasury. Recent discovery and development has added to the already great resources of this area and enterprise. The Consortium operates also the very large Abadan refinery, but takes no part in internal distribution or marketing in Persia; these are the concern of N.I.O.C., which is itself also a small-scale refiner. Nor does the Consortium as such export or market oil abroad, this being the function of the Companies who are its constituent elements.

In KUWAIT, the enterprise on land is that of a single joint Anglo-American company, which, after a career of phenomenally rapid success, produced and exported 91,000,000 tons of oil in 1962, and operates also a refinery of some 9,000,000 tons annual capacity, largely for bunkering requirements. Conditions for production in the amirate (other than climatic or scenic!) approach perfection, and every advantage has been taken of these. There is one outstandingly rich and extensive field (Burgan) and others of considerable scale. The industry, and its resulting flood of wealth for the Amir and his people, cannot but completely dominate the Kuwaiti scene and outlook (p. 171). The ruler's direct revenue from the Company is of the order of £185,000,000 a year. An off-shore concession in Kuwait waters was allotted in 1960 to the Shell group, who are prospecting. Of the Kuwaiti Neutral Zone we have spoken above.

The oil-fields in the al-Hasa province of SA'UDI ARABIA, located over a wide area in a variety of desert settings, are on a scale of the greatest magnitude and productivity. The Arabian-American ('Aramco') enterprise, born in 1934, is all-American. A series of major fields, with others in reserve, are under current full-scale exploitation, to the limit of market demand. Production of crude in 1962 amounted to 74,000,000 tons. Export is by tanker from the Sa'udi coast, by submarine pipeline to Bahrain for refining, and by trans-desert pipeline—the famous Tapline, 1,070 miles in length—to the Lebanon for shipment. A large refinery is also operated in Sa'udi Arabia. Every effort is made to develop Sa'udi industries ancillary to Aramco's own enterprise, which is itself the source of hitherto unimaginable revenues, currently about £155,000,000 per annum, paid to the Sa'udi treasury.

In the QATAR peninsula a single field has been in production since 1950, in the hands of an international group identical in all but name with the 'Iraq Petroleum Company. Export is all by tanker from the terminal at Umm Sa'id, constructed ad hoc. Production in 1962 was of 8,500,000 tons. The Shaikh's revenue was in that year of the order of £20,000,000; the resulting revolution in Qatar life has been elsewhere suggested (p. 169). An off-shore concession over waters east of the peninsula, allotted in 1952 to the Shell group, seemed late in 1962 to be on the point of revealing exploitable oil.

More particulars of Middle Eastern crude-oil production, by its constituent countries, is given in Appendix B. The refining capacity of the region was, in 1962, about 80,000,000 tons a year of throughput, to which the largest contributors are Persia (25,000,000 tons, but only two-thirds currently employed), Sa'udi Arabia (12,000,000), Bahrain (10,000,000), Kuwait (9,000,000), Aden (5,000,000), Egypt (4,500,000), Israel (4,000,000, but only one-third used), 'Iraq (3,500,000), Turkey (3,000,000), with lesser plants in the Neutral Zone, Lebanon, Syria and Jordan. But a fuller picture of the industry as visible in the territories must include, in a wide variety of physical surroundings, a fragmented yet interconnected mass of wells and pipelines, storage tanks and multifarious industrial buildings, plants and installations, ports and jetties, stores and offices and laboratories, domestic quarters and clubs, hospitals and schools and training-centres, streets and gardens and sports grounds. These things, and the presence of hundreds of foreign—mainly American and British, sometimes Dutch or French, more rarely Italian or Japanese—experts, managers and technicians, as fellow-workers in the industry at all its levels with its local labour-force and executives, are inevit-ably a leading social influence in the areas of their operation, and far beyond them.

The current offtake from Middle Eastern oil sources has been, and still is, limited to figures, and to a proportion of world supply, far below its immediately available potential. This has been due to its relatively late arrival on the scene of the world oil-trade, and to the already existing flow-channels to (and the integrated companies' interests in) the major markets. But the proved and published reserves of crude available in the Middle East—reserves, that is, existing as a matter of certainty, and recoverable practicably and economically at any time—far exceed those claimed in any other region of the world. Some figures are given in Appendix B. They show that, as at the end of 1961, some 26,000,000,000 tons of liquid petroleum, out of a world total of about 42,000,000,000 (that is, more than 61 per cent) lay buried in Middle Eastern soil. The cor-responding figure for the U.S.A., traditionally the world's greatest oil-producer as well as consumer, does not exceed 5,000,000,000. Middle Eastern reserves are thus five times greater than either those of the United States, or those assigned to the U.S.S.R. Future dis-covery will doubtless reveal, as it is continuously doing, further deposits in one region or another, and these figures must then be revised; but at present, and for some years past, the rate of new discovery in the Middle East has been more rapid than anywhere else, and this is likely to continue.

2. The Nouveaux Riches

It is clear that if the oil industry is merely one among many others in Egypt, Turkey and Israel, and makes not more than a fairly substantial contribution, by way of ton-mile transit dues and terminal loading-fees and payments for services of all kinds, to Syria, Lebanon and Jordan, it is, on the contrary, a vastly important factor in the economies of 'Iraq and Persia and Bahrain, and a completely dominant element in those of Sa'udi Arabia, Kuwait, and Qatar. Since it is in these latter six territories that Middle Eastern oil in its most massive volume is, and for the next century will be, produced, and since in these too the local characteristics of the industry—the services it tenders, the attitudes towards it—are most fully developed, we pass next to study these aspects.

The attitude of the Companies' many thousands of workers to their industry is generally loyal and satisfactory; long and exemplary service is common; the Companies' efforts to be just, generous, considerate employers are not unappreciated; and in fact the oil companies, thanks to their pay-rates, terms of service, offer of hopeful careers, training and miscellaneous benefits, are, without known exception, by far the best employers of labour in all these territories. The general public also is, in normal times, complacent or well-disposed, except in so far as inflamed at times by xenophobic voices among the politicians; and this attitude would seem a natural consequence of the very substantial benefits derived by the local public in any area of oil industry activity, in the diffusion of employees' wages and salaries, the profitable contracts given locally for works and supplies, the extensive purchases from wholesale and retail suppliers, the industrial training freely given, and often the substantial aid offered in many forms to local institutions and amenities. The central governments of the enriched states might be expected, for much the same reasons, to take a similar view, especially since the whole of the new wealth, which has transformed their governments and countries, has been discovered, financed, produced and developed without risk or trouble to them at any level; and further because, beyond all question, the immensely costly tasks of exploration, development, transport, marketing, etc., must at all times have been, and admittedly still are, a whole world beyond the financial, technical, organizational or commercial powers of any local or national body or authority whatsoever. If not for this reason alone, then a favourable governmental attitude to these enterprises might have been expected because of the rapid, fantastic enrichment itself; because the unbroken continuance of the complex of operations to perpetuate the profits now enjoyed by all parties is a clearly shared, indivisible interest of company, public and government: and because this heaven-sent wealth permits the fortunate states not only to achieve an outwardly superior status (in their diplomatic and military establishments, for instance, and in all the 'things that show') but also, and far more important, to develop their countries on lines of benefit to all their inhabitants, whether near or far from the oil-fields—in improving agriculture and extending irrigation, in fostering industry, in perfecting communications, in providing superior public services (schools, hospitals, town-improvement), in achieving a more honest and reliable civil service and judiciary. Every project, every major enterprise and improvement without exception in these six countries depends on the continuance of their income from this single source. Especially since sheer proverty has been the age-long curse of these territories, and a principal factor in inhibiting their upward progress, it is not easy to exaggerate the social and economic benefits, direct and indirect, which this oil-wealth, wisely used, is capable of conferring on them in almost every material—and also, if less directly, cultural—sphere of their lives. The services rendered to these countries by 'the Companies' have, indeed, been of extraordinary value, and could, in practice, have been afforded by no other means; and they have been accompanied by the genuine good-will of the companies' managements and staffs. Nevertheless, the attitude of governments and most, and the most vocal, politicians is habitually hostile to these benefactors. Why should this be?—and does it matter?

This attitude, which is clearly predominant though neither continuous nor universal, 'matters' because it creates a sense, or even a fact, of insecurity directly inimical to further investment and development, and because it can, in some of its phases, physically impede the field-work and export upon which all benefits depend. The attitude, amounting at times and places to a specifically anti-Company policy (as in the 'Iraq of 1961–1962, or the Persia of 1951–1954), is chiefly due not to coolly reasoned considerations but to a complex of emotions. They are those of antipathy to a looming, *foreign* industrial giant in their midst—to envy and dislike of his so evident success: to distrust of the attraction felt by many company's employees and well-wishers to a non-governmental, and foreign, focus of loyalty: to hints or rumours that the Company is 'interfering in politics' (a wildly improbable event); to feelings in some cases that the Company was the beneficiary of an earlier governmental régime, and enjoys too favourable a concession—which ought, therefore, in the eyes of every good patriot, to be unilaterally annulled. Such feelings are normally exacerbated by a widespread inferiority complex *vis-à-vis* prosperous complacent foreigners (suspected always of 'imperialist' or 'colonialist' policies), by the inevitable frictions and minor disagreements in the daily running or relations of the industry, by the government's endless demands for more money (too often regardless of economic considerations, or of future development) and for more direct participation, and by its scant respect, not uncommonly, for bargained, signed and sealed agreements. In the aggregate these feelings have created at times an unquiet or menacing atmosphere in government-company relations which is destructive of confidence in the future of the industry, and, therefore, in the safe continuance of the immediate benefits it confers.

The industry is, if ever one existed, a goose laying golden eggs; and there is proverbial advice as to how not to treat that rare and sensitive bird, which hot-head xenophobic nationalists in the countries concerned would be wise to heed. Present, admittedly foreign, concessionaires and their merits or demerits apart, there seems no alternative currently in sight to the operation by them of the oil industry in these Middle Eastern territories, least of all at a time of global over-supply of petroleum. These great foreign, integrated companies alone possess the capital, the technological and organizational command, and above all the worldwide markets which are indispensable; and they have been and are, as it happens, conducted on reasonable, sympathetic and humane (as well as highly efficient) lines by men of probity and goodwill. The interested observer can but hope that, by the efforts of both sides, present imperfections in the atmosphere as between 'the authorities' and the operating companies can and will be removed, and their immensely important, inter-dependent enterprises will enjoy a favourable environment.

The regrettable government-company relations so far considered arise chiefly when, as in all the earlier and greater concessions given by Middle Eastern governments, the 'blanket concession' method was *faute de mieux* adopted: that is, the grant of oil-rights over very wide areas of territory to a single company for a long term, as was done in Persia, 'Iraq, Sa'udi Arabia, and the Gulf States. Such concessions have, of course, been repeatedly reconsidered, renegotiated and greatly modified, in the states' favour, since their original grant; and in some cases additional outside concessionaires, to cover unallotted or abandoned territory, have additionally been introduced, as in Persia, the Neutral Zone (off-shore), Qatar (marine areas), Abu Dhabi (the same), Kuwait (the same). Elsewhere, as in Turkey, Israel or Egypt, some of the odium of near-monopoly has been avoided by a system of licences given, under a general Petroleum Law equal for all comers, for smaller areas and shorter periods; but, by ill fortune, little oil-discovery has yet eventuated in these cases.

Resentment at the great foreign companies' success and, in some territories, their exclusivity of oil-operation would in a measure be diminished by the undertaking on the part of government itself of an increasing range of activities in this field. Already in most of the Gulf territories, including 'Iraq and Persia, an official corporation carries out refining and local distributing and marketing functions, and, in Persia (henceforward to be followed by 'Iraq) those also of prospecting and production. Most of the governments take a proportion of their agreed royalty in the form of crude oil, which they are free to market or to sell back to the company. It is to be hoped that such active participation in the industry by local governmental or, if possible, private enterprise will increase; it is educative, it affords outlets for the employment, in addition to that offered by the companies, of local technicians, engineers and executives; it helps to destroy the galling picture of 'foreign monopoly', and to substitute a local interest and achievement. The example of the N.I.O.C. might well be widely followed, though the countries' lack of a position in foreign markets, and of available capital on an adequate scale, must prevent them for some years to come from enterprise of the largest magnitude.

We have referred above to some of the social benefits obtainable by the diffusion of the industry's local expenditure, and by country-wide governmental measures thus financed; is, or will be, the local political world—so closely bound to the social—equally a beneficiary? This is more doubtful. Greater wealth, while not conferring greater wisdom or more statesmanlike qualities, must complicate public life and administration, widen the fields of controversy, and make more attractive than ever the rewards of personal success in terms of power and glory. In none of the enriched territories does it appear that their new material circumstances have tended to stabilize or strengthen the constitution, or the body politic, or its leadership;

indeed, the lessons of 'Iraq and Persia tell a very different story, and the precipitate emergence of Sa'udi Arabia, Kuwait and Qatar into the stresses of the modern world, due solely to their respective, prolific, golden-egg-laying geese, will probably tend to threaten rather than to consolidate their patriarchal régimes of government. From this angle, and indeed from that of the rapid multiplication of the literate, but often underemployed and discontented, middle class, whose world is politics, the effects of sudden enrichment can be questionable. Its effect on the morals and manners of the people is unlikely, one may conjecture, to be all in the direction of grace and uplift. This need be no subject of present despair; weaknesses apparent today may prove to be but passing phases, and should be as nothing compared with the undoubted blessings to which oil-derived wealth, wisely used, can and should lead in other and broader fields of living.

CHAPTER TWELVE

CONCLUSION AND PROSPECT

IT will not be easy for the writer, after forty-seven years of close connection with the countries of the Middle East, to select, and to compress into a few paragraphs, what seems to be most worth saying, most likely to be valid for some period at least, of the situation, prospects and hopes of these territories.

The region's geographic situation is, in human terms, unchangeable; its land-surface can be modified only in local detail, by routes, bridges, dams, afforestation or reclamation; its climate, unless by humanly unforeseeable, uncontrollable changes, must remain what it is, even though science, by prophylactic medicine, air-conditioning and other means, can mitigate its severity.

Even with such differences as may be effected by rapid ubiquitous air-travel, closer and instant telecommunication, nuclear weapons and other not-yet-evolved factors, the region cannot but retain more than a little of its central, tri-continental importance, political and strategic. It must continue to command east–west global routes by sea and land; it will remain close to the centres of eastern-hemisphere power and wealth on the one side, and the dozens of weak but aspiring new states of Asia and Africa on the other; its possession of unique reserves of petroleum will give it more, not less, importance with passing decades. The fortunes of its populations will continue to be watched with exceptional keenness by co-religionists and sympathizers throughout the world, and it will continue, no doubt, to be an object of concern, possibly of ambition or cupidity, to stronger powers or blocs. These facts, and the local unease and stresses to which they may conduce, cannot be without consequences in the social and political life of the area. This will never be among the happy regions which have no history.

In spite of factors which might seem to make for closer inter-country relations, perhaps ending with political unity—the sense of Arab brotherhood and (non-political) homogeneity, the common front against 'imperialism' and against Israel—the not less real, and seemingly even more effective, disparities between the Middle Eastern states in their geographic and economic circumstances, stages of evolution, vested interests and foreign contacts, combine still to keep them apart and disunited; nor is it possible, at the time of writing, to see cause to expect any major change in this regard. All, or almost all, of the states of the region are still far from having reached a stage of national development in which they would be willing, unless temporarily and exceptionally, to accept any diminution of their national sovereignty. Pacts and alliances will doubtless be made from time to time between two or more governments, but these may well prove as short-lived as in the recent past. Artificial, or even imposed, 'unions' or confederations of small units, such as those of the Trucial Coast or the Aden Protectorate, may be proclaimed, but can contribute little to the area as a whole unless in diminishing the vulnerability of a single sensitive area. A weak state with a precarious ill-based régime, such as Hashimite Jordan, may imaginably be annexed by a stronger neighbour—Egypt or (improbably) Syria, and the world is aware of the proclaimed ambitions of Persia to annex Bahrain, and of 'Iraq for Kuwait. None of these can be adduced, however, as signs of an increasing movement towards, or toleration of, greater regional unity; far from it! Possibly the present Egyptian conception of some form of bloc of 'democratic' socialist Arab states, feasible only if and when they adopt an equivalent of current Nasirite policies, may prove to be a more centripetal force. In the case of Syria, the attempt failed; in that of Jordan, it may some day be made; in the Yemen it seems, at the moment of writing, likely to be attempted; yet the history of 'Iraq since July 1958 indicates that anti-monarchical revolution need not be synonymous with a move into the Egyptian orbit.

Current world opinion, and the global organization of United Nations, have decreed that these states should face, each by and for itself, the stresses and problems of the most difficult and dangerous of periods through which human society is now passing. Their administrations, central and local, give today, as earlier pages have suggested, some grounds for satisfaction and hope; the governments, here in accord with articulate public opinion, are aiming in every field at higher standards than of old, are using to advantage the improved class of better-educated and more public-spirited officialdom, are providing law and order and social and technical services to the best of their often considerable ability. That in all these fields there will be steady—certainly not rapid or sensational—improvement and expansion can be a confident hope. The less attractive picture is that of the constitution of the state itself, and the world of politics; here, optimism is not easy to achieve.

Most of these countries have still only a small élite class of educated, modern-minded citizens with some real acquaintance with the present-day world, its facts and standards; the masses are still largely illiterate, leading lives scarcely different from those of past centuries and, over wide areas, far from habituated to the processes and standards of law and civil discipline. There are in fact, politically and socially, the two co-existent worlds, medieval and modern, western and eastern, progressive and conservative. Temperamentally, a large majority are highly individualistic—an outstanding feature of the Arab character—emotional, and peculiarly averse from self-submission in any form; and they are fed by their politician-leaders on a diet of phrases and catchwords—independence, imperialism, colonialism, etc.—of, too often, little real content or present relevance: or on self-glorifying myths and promises. At the same time, it is taken for granted, even in the least advanced and least opulent state, that a fully-developed, western, modern-type administration and range of public services is their right, and must be their ambition. The exigencies of a vigorous and competitive political life, where this is permitted, lead to much public denigration of the western foreigner as the traditional oppressor, and thus unnecessarily alienate foreign sympathy.

The rival claims of discipline and liberty, which in all governing régimes are notoriously difficult to satisfy simultaneously, are at their most antagonistic in Middle Eastern administrations; 'discipline' easily takes the form of oppressive dictatorship denying all popular rights, 'liberty' becomes lawless licence. In all the circumstances of the modern Middle East, internal, regional and global, the conduct of a reasonably liberal and secure administration, in any one of the territories, cannot but be a task of quite exceptional difficulty, and one which demands from the outside observer more informed sympathy than scornful criticism. It may be many years—and here perhaps Latin America offers a precedent—before an acceptable stability is achieved; for the present weaknesses of Middle Eastern political and social structure—deplored, needless to say, by their own most enlightened citizens—there is no simple or single cure. They are likely to last for many decades to come, until gradually corrected by the spread of education, enlightenment, experience, and a widely improved standard of living.

Meanwhile, and additionally to the general, region-wide shortcomings in stability and in orderly political-constitutional life, each separate territory, as previous pages of this book have sufficiently suggested, has its particular problems, to few of which an easy solution appears. In Persia, much power still resides in the rich landowning class who distrust 'progress', much corruption flourishes in the public service, the army is or may become doubtfully loyal, the monarchy has many discontented critics. In Turkey, the economy has for years been overstrained, and indeed sacrificed for party-political ends; a stable form of government and administration, acceptable to a solid majority of Turks, still awaits realization. In Cyprus there is a continuance of inter-community rancour, and sur-viving aspiration for Enosis. In 'Iraq a dictatorship combining an unintelligent rigour with inefficiency has deprived the territory of all political and much personal liberty, and has painfully lowered the good name of the country abroad; today the restoration of con-fidence, sound administration and a tolerable pattern of public life is the country's pressing requirement: but to come from where? In Syria, where much ability and goodwill are devoted to public affairs, there is, with a marked regionalism, a singularly restless and divided public life with sharply differing objectives; it remains to be seen whether a form of representative government worthy of the name can be established and maintained. Lebanon, of the Arab states the least devoted to international Arabism, has found no shared basis on which to achieve a true national unity, and remains an unstable congeries of its Christian and Muslim communities. Jordan is a weak and indigent state, united only within its monarchi-cally-minded minority, and dependent for its livelihood and its sur-vival on foreign friends. Israel, feared and detested by all its neighbours, will survive as long as the remittances from abroad to pay its bills and finance its development continue to arrive in their present abundance—and/or as long as the Jewish pressure-groups of North America and Europe possess their present formidable power. Egypt is facing its gravely difficult economic and demographic situ-ation with vigour and, with however inadequate an administrative machine and with whatever deficiencies of justice and prudence, is seriously attempting to improve its people's standard of life. In the Sudan the comparatively mild but politically repressive dictatorship will perhaps before long permit some revival of political life and use more of its available talent, and there seems no reason why this should prove disastrous; there is here a tradition of, and a general preference for, good administration: but the absorption of the non-

Muslim south in a Sudani nation poses a task demanding much patience and high-mindedness. The Sa'udi Arabian theocratic monarchy will probably be able to maintain itself for a further period, thanks to its prestige and its monopoly of the only wealth in the territory; but, as long as it does so, any general enlightenment or improvement in the conditions of the Sa'udi population can scarcely be looked for; the régime's most dangerous enemy will probably prove to be not popular discontent, but dissidence, with foreign support, in the royal family itself, or in the army. The future of the Yemen is, at the time of writing, quite uncertain: even if a modern-type (which may here mean a Nasir-type) government establishes itself in replacement of the Imamate, it must be many years before the country, with its present almost total lack of an educated class or a modern infra-structure for official and public life, can play any significant part even in Arabian affairs. The petty states and village-kingdoms of southern and south-eastern Arabia continue to present the seemingly insoluble problem of—what to do with them! Only in the cases of Abu Dhabi, Qatar, Bahrain and Kuwait is the problem, on the contrary, that of—what to do with the money? Means, it appears, must be found to distribute a proportion of the available wealth (that is, the oil-revenues) of the region so as to benefit the poor and deprived, and to move towards freely accepted closer asso-ciations between the tiny, traditional units now so embarrassingly anachronistic. Such steps cannot be conditional on the consent of the present rulers of the 'have' communities; they could properly be a task for the Arab League, if only this were a wise and effective body.

The social as well as the political development of the Middle East must depend in considerable measure on its economics: which means on the actual wealth which the countries are able to produce and to devote to intelligent development and beneficent services. After centuries of grim poverty, the need for rapid economic uplift is paramount: not only are there pressing needs of every kind in each country's affairs and services, but the mere equipment of the terri-tories with adequate works and buildings, housing and institutions, routes and facilities—the whole complex of national fixed assets upon which developed nations have been spending their money for centuries past—must call for expenditure of a magnitude at present far out of reach. Ignoring for this purpose such lesser sources as the tourist traffic, entrepôt and commercial services, and remittances from abroad, the possible production of greatly increased national wealth can, within the domestic purview, be envisaged only as coming from agriculture, from natural (mineral or other) resources, or from industry. Of these, agriculture will certainly remain the greatest subsistence-occupation of the region; but, as we have shown, it seems unlikely, in any one of the states, even after much greater development and specialization than at present, to do more than contribute moderately to the Treasury or to private wealth. Industry has and will have, it is believed (pp. 247–51), a helpful and useful but never a dominant place in the future of the region. Of natural resources, only petroleum is of really major importance, and the substantial wealth from this source, already in process of full realization, provides (except in the Gulf statelets) no superabundance even for the happy possessors. The essential seems here to be, firstly, that there should be no interruption of the working of the oil industry such as to jeopardize its output of wealth; secondly, that some machinery should be devised whereby the 'haves' should, willingly, aid the development of the 'have nots'. This is no new idea, and it is realizable on commercial lines, given reasonable inter-country amity and confidence. Of one other possible fertilizing source of wealth for the region, material aid to be offered by other countries or by world organizations, it must be realized that, important as such aid can be locally and temporarily, and considerable as may be the part it plays —and, on every ground of humanitarianism and policy, ought to play—it cannot take the place of (nor could it ever be relied upon with as much confidence as) wealth produced and developed by the recipient country itself. Nor, it must be confessed, have ways yet been devised whereby both giver and receiver of such 'aid' can be counted upon to emerge cordial and satisfied from the deal; experience, hitherto, has been sadly otherwise.

The economic resurgence of the Middle East is, it seems, likely to be slow rather than rapid, and lack of wealth will long remain a chief and resented factor restrictive of progress.

Enough has been said elsewhere (pp. 201, 216 ff.) of the considerable changes in the urban—and, not negligibly, in the rural—social life of these countries. These developments will certainly continue until they spread to remoter parts and to all strata, and progressively modify the dominant, traditional ways of life everywhere: in literacy, in housing and clothing, in private and public amenities, in social habit and intercourse. Much that is, to foreign eyes, pleasant and gracious may be lost in the process; an old-time way of life will disappear from the world: much in the new, westernized scene may seem characterless or merely imitative. But such changes will, on the whole, benefit those who form, under the ancient social régime, the most depressed classes of the populations, and will be part of the modern tendencies and forces capable of offering them a less depressed, narrow, insecure existence.

What the region may prove able to bring to the world in the form of cultural output, in its narrower sense, cannot be foreseen. The likelihood of a more valuable contribution will increase with the wider spread of education, power of expression, broader appreciation of the world and humanity at large. The Middle Eastern populations are gifted with an exceptional degree of natural intelligence and sensitivity, and they contain—indeed, have never not contained—an élite fully capable, as their past and present output has shown, of artistic and literary achievement. This, it is certain, will increase; and it will form another link, of which there are now too few, between these confident, aspiring—if also puzzled and unstable—national societies in the Middle East, and their many friends and well-wishers elsewhere in the world.

STATES OF THE ADEN PROTECTORATE, AND THE TRUCIAL COAST

(i) *Western Aden Protectorate*

The sultanates, amirates and shaikhdoms of the 'Abdali[2] (with Lahaj), Amiri[1] (with Dhala), Fadhili,[1] Upper Yafa'i, Lower Yafa'i,[1] Haushabi, Mausatta, Dhubi, Maflahi, Hadhrami, Shaib, Qutaibi, 'Alawi, 'Aqrabi,[3] Upper Aulaqi[1] (sultanate) (with Nisab), Upper Aulaqi[1] (shaikhdom), Lower Aulaqi (with Ahwar), Audhali, Baihan,[1] and Dathina.[3]

(ii) *Eastern Aden Protectorate*

State of Shihr and Makalla (Qu'aiti), with H.Q. at Makalla. State of Sayyun (Kathiri), H.Q. Sayyun. State of Qishin and Socotra (Mahri), H.Q. Socotra and Saihut. State of Balhaf and Bir'Ali (Wahidi), H.Q. Maif'a.

(iii) *Trucial Coast Shaikhdoms*

Abu Dhabi, Dubai, Sharja (with Kalba, previously independent), 'Ajman, Umm al Qaiwain, Ras al-Khaima, Fujaira (independent since 1952).

[1] Formed the Federation in February 1959.
[2] Joined the Federation in October 1959.
[3] Joined the Federation in February 1960.

(i) *The Growth of Middle Eastern Oil Production (in million long-tons)*

Country	1911	1915	1920	1925	1930	1935	1940	1945	1950	1955	1960	1962
Egypt . .	0·003	0·03	0·16	0·18	0·28	0·17	0·91	1·30	2·31	1·76	3·30	4·25
Persia . .	—	0·38	1·38	4·33	5·94	7·49	8·62	16·84	31·75	15·95	51·30	64·00
'Iraq . .	—	—	—	—	0·12	3·66	2·65	4·62	6·50	33·11	47·00	48·00
Bahrain .	—	—	—	—	—	0·17	0·94	0·95	1·51	1·50	2·25	2·22
Sa'udi Arabia1	—	—	—	—	—	—	0·68	2·84	25·90	46·78	60·50	74·00
Turkey .	—	—	—	—	—	—	—	—	0·01	0·20	0·35	0·53
Qatar . .	—	—	—	—	—	—	—	—	1·62	5·36	8·20	8·00
Kuwait2 .	—	—	—	—	—	—	—	—	17·00	53·90	82·50	92·00
Neutral Zone	—	—	—	—	—	—	—	—	—	1·34	6·90	11·50
Israel . .	—	—	—	—	—	—	—	—	—	—	0·14	0·13
Syria3 . .	—	—	—	—	—	—	—	—	—	—	—	—
Abu Dhabi4 .	—	—	—	—	—	—	—	—	—	—	—	0·80
MIDDLE EAST .	0·003	0·41	1·54	4·51	6·34	11·49	13·80	26·55	86·60	159·90	262·44	305·43
WORLD . .	47	59	95	148	195	225	289	356	518	763	1,035	1208·00

Notes. (1) and (2), *excluding* their share (one half) of Neutral Zone production (shown separately).
(3) Small oil deposits located (far inland), but not yet in production.
(4) Production from off-shore location; probably bigger discovered deposits, on shore, will be exploited from 1964.

(ii) *'Proved Reserves' of Liquid Petroleum (in millions of tons)*, 1961

Caribbean area (including Venezuela)	2,500
Far East	1,300
Africa (including Algeria, Libya, etc.)	1,100
Communist bloc	4,300
Canada	700
U.S.A.	4,700
Other Regions	1,200
Middle East	25,760

(Kuwait, 8,500; Sa'udi Arabia, 7,000; Persia, 4,700; 'Iraq, 3,500; Neutral Zone, 900; Qatar, 360; other Middle East, 800)

The World 41,560

APPENDIX C

SOME BOOKS FOR FURTHER READING

With no attempt at even a partial bibliography of the Middle East, which would necessarily fill volumes, a few suggestions are here offered as to recent, accessible books in English, with which some reader may care to extend his knowledge. With rare exceptions, historical and political works are omitted.

GENERAL FOR THE MIDDLE EAST

(a) Books of reference

Bullard, R. W. (ed.), *The Middle East*, 3rd ed., London, 1958.
Fisher, W. B., *The Middle East: a physical, social and regional geography*, 3rd ed., London, 1957.
Hogarth, D. G., *The Nearer East*, London, 1905.
Statesman's Year Book, London, 1962.
The Middle East, 9th ed., Europa Publications, London, 1962.
United Nations (Dept. of Econ. Affairs), *Economic conditions in the Middle East*, New York, 1951.

(b) Other general works

Antonius, G., *The Arab Awakening*, London, 1947.
Atiyah, E., *The Arabs*, London, 1955.
Berger, M., *The Arab World Today*, N.Y., 1962.
Bullard, R. W., *Britain and the Middle East*, London, 1950; *The camels must go*, London, 1961.
Cantwell-Smith, W., *Islam in modern history*, N.Y., 1957.
Childers, E., *Common sense about the Arab world*, London, 1960.
Fisher, S. N. (ed.), *Social forces in the Middle East*, Ithaca, N.Y., 1955.
Gibb, H. A. R., *Mohammadanism*, 2nd ed., London, 1953.
Hourani, A., *Minorities in the Arab world*, London, 1947.
Ionides, M. G., *Divide and lose*, London, 1960.
Izzedin, N., *The Arab world*, Chicago, 1953.
Kirk, G., *Short history of the Middle East*, 6th ed., London, 1961.
Laqueur, W. Z., *Communism and Nationalism in the Middle East*, London, 1956; *The Soviet Union and the Middle East*, London, 1959.
Lenzowski, G., *Oil and State in the Middle East*, Ithaca, N.Y., 1960.
Lewis, B., *The Arabs in History*, London, 1954.
Longrigg, S. H., *Oil in the Middle East*, 2nd ed., London, 1961.

Morris, J., *The Hashemite Kings*, London, 1959; *The Market of Seleucia*, London, 1957.
Nuseibeh, H. Z., *The Ideas of Arab Nationalism*, Ithaca, N.Y., 1956.
Partner, P., *A Short political guide to the Arab world*, London, 1960.
Rondot, P., *The destiny of the Middle East*, London, 1960.
Stark, F., *East is West*, London, 1945.
Warriner, D., *Land reform and development in the Middle East*, 2nd ed., London, 1962.

CYPRUS

Arnold, P., *Cyprus Challenge*, London, 1956.
Balfour, P. (Kinross, Lord), *The Orphaned Realm*, London, 1951.
Barclays Bank D.C.O., *Cyprus, an economic survey*, London, 1960.
Durrell, L., *Bitter Lemons*, London, 1957.
Foot, S., *Emergency Exit*, London, 1960.
Hume, G., *Cyprus then and now*, London, 1960.
Mayes, S., *Cyprus and Makarios*, London, 1960.

EGYPT

Hussein, T., *The stream of days* (tr.), London, 1948.
Issawi, C., *Egypt at mid-century*, London, 1954.
Lacouture, J. and M., *Egypt in transition*, London, 1958.
Little, T., *Egypt*, London, 1959.
Marlowe, J., *Anglo-Egyptian Relations*, London, 1954.
Robichon, C. and Varille, A. (edd.), *External Egypt*. London, 1955.
Stewart, D. S., *Young Egypt*, London, 1958.
U.A.R. Handbook for 1960, Cairo, 1961.
Watt, D. C., *Britain and the Suez Canal*, London, 1956.
Wynn, W., *Nasser of Egypt*, London, 1960.

IRAN : *see* PERSIA

IRAQ

Caractacus, *Revolution in Iraq*, London, 1959.
Edmonds, C. J., *Kurds, Turks and Arabs*, London, 1957.
Fulanain, *Haji Rikkan*, London, 1927.
Harris, G. L. (ed.), *Iraq, its people, etc.*, New Haven, 1958.
Ionides, M. G., *The Régime of the Rivers Euphrates and Tigris*, London, 1937.
Khadduri, M., *Independent Iraq, 1932–58*, London, 2nd ed., 1960.
Langley, K. M., *The Industrialisation of Iraq*, Cambridge, Mass., 1961.
Lloyd, S. F. H., *Twin Rivers*, London, 2nd ed., 1947.
Longrigg, S. H., *'Iraq 1900 to 1950*, London, 1953; (with Stoakes, F.), *'Iraq*, London, 1958.
Maxwell, G., *A reed shaken by the wind*, London, 1957.

Salter, Lord, *The development of Iraq*, London, 1955.
Stark, F., *Baghdad Sketches*, London, 1939; *Beyond Euphrates*, London, 1951.
Stevens, E. S., *Folk Tales of Iraq*, Oxford, 1931; *The Mandaeans*, Oxford, 1937.
Stewart, S., and Haylock, J., *New Babylon*, London, 1956.

ISRAEL

Barbour, N., *Nisi Dominus*, London, 1946.
Ben Gurion, D., *Rebirth and Destiny of Israel* (tr.), N.Y., 1954.
Bentwich, N., *Israel Resurgent*, London, 1960.
Bernadotte, F., *To Jerusalem*, London, 1951.
Eisenstadt, S. N., *The absorption of immigrants*, London, 1954.
Eytan, W., *The first ten years*, London, 1958.
Halperin, H., *Changing Patterns in Israel Agriculture*, London, 1957.
Hyamson, A. M., *Palestine under the Mandate*, London, 1950.
Parkes, J., *End of an Exile*, London, 1954.
Peretz, D., *Israel and the Palestine Arabs*, Washington, 1959.
Rubner, A., *The Economy of Israel*, London, 1960.
Statistical abstract of Israel, Jerusalem, annually.
Schwarz, W., *The Arabs in Israel*, London, 1959.
Tavener, L. E., *The revival of Israel*, London, 1961.
Weizmann, C., *Trial and Error*, London, 1949.
Williams, L. F. W., *The State of Israel*, London, 1958.

JORDAN

Abdullah, H.M. King, *Memoirs* (tr.), London, 1950.
Dearden, A., *Jordan*, London, 1958.
Glubb, J. B., *A Soldier with the Arabs*, London, 1957; *The Story of the Arab Legion*, London, 1948.
Harris, G. C. (ed.), *Jordan, its people . . . etc.*, New Haven, 1958.
Hussein, H.M. King, *Uneasy lies the Head*, London, 1962.
Kirkbride, A. S., *A crackle of thorns*, London, 1956.
Patai, R. (ed.), *The Kingdom of Jordan*, Princeton, 1958.
Shwadran, B. Jordan, *A State of Tension*; Baltimore, 1957.

LEBANON, *see* SYRIA and LEBANON

PERSIA

Arberry, A. J. (ed.), *The Legacy of Persia*, London, 1953.
Carroll, M. A., *From a Persian Teahouse*, London, 1960.
Edwards, A. Cecil, *The Persian Carpet*. London, 1953.
Frye, R. N., *Iran*, London, 1954.

Groseclose, E., *Introduction to Iran*, N.Y., 1947.
Haas, W. S., *Iran*, N.Y., 1946.
Lambton, A. K. S., *Landlord and peasant in Persia*, London, 1956.
Lockhart, L., *Famous Cities of Iran*, London, 1939.
Mohammed Riza Shah, *Mission for my Country*, London, 1961.
Stevens, R. B., *The Land of the Great Sophy*, London, 1962.
Sykes, P. M., *History of Persia*, London, 3rd ed., 2 vols., 1930.
Vreeland, H. H. (ed.), *Iran*, New Haven, 1957.
Wilber, D. N., *Iran past and present*, Princeton, 1955.

ARAB STATES of the PERSIAN GULF

Adamiyat, F., *Bahrain Islands*, N.Y., 1955.
Belgrave, C. D., *Personal column*, London, 1960.
Dickson, H. R. P., *Kuwait and her neighbours*, London, 1956.
Faroughy, A., *The Bahrain Islands*, N.Y., 1951.
Freeth, Z., *Kuwait was my home*, London, 1955.
Hay, R., *The Persian Gulf States*, Washington, 1959.
Kuwait Oil Co., *The Story of Kuwait*, London, 1957.
Marlowe, J., *The Persian Gulf in the twentieth century*, London, 1962.
Owen, R., *The golden bubble*, London, 1957.
Shamma, S., *The oil of Kuwait*, Beirut, 1959.
Wilson, A. T., *The Persian Gulf*, London, 1928.

SA'UDI ARABIA

Butler, G., *Kings and camels*, N.Y., 1960.
Cheney, S. C., *Big oilman from Arabia*, London, 1958.
Dickson, H. R. P., *The Arab of the Desert*, London, 1949.
Hogarth, D. G., *History of Arabia*, Oxford, 1922.
Lebkicher, R., Rentz, G., and Steineke, M., *Sa'udi Arabia*, New Haven, 1952.
Lipsky, G. A. (and others), *Sa'udi Arabia*, New Haven, 1959.
Philby, H. St J. B., *A pilgrim in Arabia*, London, 1946; *Arabian Jubilee*, London, 1952; *Sa'udi Arabia*, London, 1955.
Sanger, R., *The Arabian peninsula*, Ithaca, N.Y., 1954.
Twitchell, K. S., *Sa'udi Arabia*, Princeton, 2nd ed., 1953.
Williams, K., *Ibn Sa'ud*, London, 1933.

SUDAN

'Abbas., Mekki, *The Sudan Question*, London, 1952.
Sudan Almanac for 1962, Khartum, 1962.
Barbour, K. Q., *The Republic of the Sudan*, London, 1961.
Duncan, J. S. R., *The Sudan*, Edinburgh, 1952; *The Sudan's Path to Independence*, London, 1957.
s*

Gaitskell, A., *Gezira*, London, 1959.
Hamilton, J. A. de C. (ed.), *The Anglo-Egyptian Sudan from within*, London, 1935.
Henderson, K. D., *The Making of the Modern Sudan* (Letters of Sir D. Newbold), London, 1953.
Holt, P. M., *A modern history of the Sudan*, London, 1961.
Jackson, H. C., *Behind the Modern Sudan*, London, 1956.
Langley, M., *No woman's country*, N.Y., 1951.
Macmichael, H. A., *The Sudan*, London, 1954.
Mann, A., *Where God laughed*, London, 1954.
Shibeika, M., *The independent Sudan*, N.Y., 1960.

SYRIA and LEBANON

Atiyah, E., *An Arab tells his story*, London, 1946.
Fedden, R., *Syria*, London, 1946.
Gulick, J., *Social structure and culture change in a Lebanese village*, N.Y., 1955.
Haddad, J., *Fifty years of modern Syria and Lebanon*, Beirut, 1950.
Hitti, C. K., *History of Syria*, London, 1951; *The Lebanon in History*, London, 1957.
Hourani, A. K., *Syria and Lebanon*, 2nd ed., London, 1954.
Longrigg, S. H., *Syria and Lebanon under French mandate*, London, 1958.
Stewart, D., *Trouble in Beirut*, London, 1959.
World Bank (IBRD), *The Economic Development of Syria*, Baltimore, 1955.
Ziadeh, N., *Syria and Lebanon*, London, 1957.
[*N.B. The great bulk of the (European) literature of these two countries is, of course, in French.*]

TURKEY

Bisbee, E., *The New Turks*, Philadelphia, 1951.
Bridge, A., *The failure in flight*, N.Y., 1951; *The Dark Moment*, N.Y., 1952.
Gabriel, A. (ed.), *Turkey in Pictures*. London, 1962.
Heyd, W., *Foundations of Turkish Nationalism*, London, 1950.
Karpat, K., *Turkey's Politics*, Princeton, 1959.
Kinross, Lord, *Turkey*, London, 1959; *Within the Taurus*, London, 1954.
Lewis, B., *Turkey today*, London, 1940; *The emergence of modern Turkey*, London, 1961.
Lewis, G. L., *Turkey*, London, 1955.
Luke, H., *The old Turkey and the new*, London, 1955.
O.E.E.C., *Economic conditions in Turkey*, Paris, 1957.
Orga, I., *Portrait of a Turkish family*, London, 1950.
Salter, C., *Introducing Turkey*, London, 1961.
Stark, F., *Ionia*, London, 1954; *Lycian shore*, London, 1956; *Riding to the Tigris*, London, 1959.

World Bank (IBRD), *The economy of Turkey*, Baltimore, 1951.
Yalman, A. E., *Turkey in my time*, Oklahoma, 1956.

YEMEN, ADEN, OMAN

Bethmann, E. W., *Yemen on the threshold*, Washington, 1960.
Colonial Office, *Aden and the Yemen*, London, 1960.
Faroughy, A., *Introducing Yemen*, N.Y., 1947.
Fayein, C., *A French Doctor in the Yemen*, London, 1957.
Hamilton, R. A. B., *The Kingdom of Melchior*, London, 1949; (as Lord Belhaven) *The uneven road*, London, 1955.
Helfritz, H., *The Yemen, a secret journey*, London, 1958.
Hickinbotham, Sir T., *Aden*, London, 1959.
Ingrams, D., *Survey of the social and economic condition of the Aden Protectorate*, Asmara, 1949.
Ingrams, W. H., *Arabia and the Isles*, London (2nd ed.), 1952; *Report on social, etc., conditions in the Hadhramaut*, London, 1936.
Morris, J., *Sultan in Oman*, London, 1957.
Scott, H., *In the High Yemen*, London, 1942.
Stark, F., *The Southern Gates of Arabia*, London, 1936; *A Winter in Arabia*, London, 1940; *Seen in the Hadhramaut*, London, 1940.
Thesiger, W., *Arabian sands*, London, 1959.

	Agronomy	Area: Population	Climate: Topography	Communications	History	Industry
ADEN	162 f., 234, 246	162 ff.	19 f., 162 ff.	163	74 ff., 86	163
CYPRUS	18, 233 ff., 241	185 f.	185 f.	187	29, 40, 60, 66, 70, 76 ff.	248 ff.
EGYPT (U.A.R.)	18, 144, 233 ff., 243 ff.	139 f.	20, 142	146	29–68, 72 f., 76, 83 f.	144, 247 ff.
'IRAQ	18, 234 ff., 239	123 f.	15, 17 f., 19 f., 123 ff.	126 f.	28–69, 72, 76, 79 f., 87	125 f., 248 ff.
ISRAEL	233, 242 f.	188	15, 188 f.	192	35 ff., 40 ff., 72, 76, 82 ff., 137	247 ff.
JORDAN	135 f., 234, 236	134 ff.	15, 17 f., 134 f.	136 f.	35, 40, 76, 81 f., 137	136, 249 ff.
LEBANON	233 f., 236, 240 f.	127 ff.	15, 17, 127	129	13, 69, 72, 76, 80 f.	247 ff.
MUSKAT AND OMAN	165, 247		16, 162 ff.		55, 69, 74 f., 86	
PERSIA (IRAN)	18, 175 ff., 233 ff., 238 f.	172 f.	15, 17, 19 f., 172 f.	178 f.	27–70, 75, 78 f.	247 ff.
PERSIAN GULF STATES	166, 247	166 ff.	15, 20, 166	167 ff.	69, 86 f.	
SA'UDI ARABIA	18, 157, 234, 245	154, 156	15 ff., 19 f., 154 ff., 162	158	47–64, 66, 68 f., 73 f., 76, 85	
SUDAN	149, 234, 245	148, 150 f.	148 ff.	152 f.	44, 73, 83 f., 85, 147	248 f.
SYRIA	18, 132, 234 ff., 240	130 f.	15, 17, 19, 130 f.	133	29–69, 72, 76, 80 f.	248 f.
TURKEY	18, 179 ff., 233 ff., 238	179 f.	15, 17, 19 f., 179 f.	184 f.	29–60, 66–77, 104, 106	247 ff.
YEMEN	18, 233 ff.	159 f.	16 f., 20, 159 f.	161 f.	46, 53, 55, 66, 68 f., 73 f., 85 f.	

INDEX

Abadan, 173, 179, 255
"Abana and Pharpar", 130
'Abbas, Shah, the Great, 70
'Abbas, al-, 50
'Abbasids, 50 ff., 55 ff., 66, 93
'Abdul 'Aziz ibn Sa'ud, King, 85 f., 157
'Abdul Hamid II, Sultan, 71 f., 157
'Abdul Kuri, islands, 162
'Abdul Majid (lands), 245
'Abdul Malik, 50
'Abdullah, Amir, later King, 81, 138
'Abbud, General Ibrahim, 85
Abha, 154
Abu Dhabi, see Persian Gulf States,
    pp. 278–9; also, 167, 254, 261, 267
Abu Kamal (Kemal), 131
'Abyan, 246
Achaemenid (dynasty), 38 f., 40, 42,
    45, 175
Acre ('Akka), 72, 188, 249
Actium, battle of, 40
Adana, 181, 183, 238
Adapazari, 181
Aden, Colony, see pp. 278–9: also, 13,
    19, 74, 97, 102, 109, 153, 159, 163,
    189, 200
Aden Airways, 163
Aden Protectorate, see pp. 278–9: also,
    13 f., 74, 97, 154, 159, 161, 164, 208,
    234, 246 f., 264
Adiaman, 120
Aegean Sea, 11, 13, 15, 17, 30, 38, 179,
    181
Aegean peoples, 27
Afghanistan, Afghans, 11, 14, 54, 70,
    75, 118, 172, 175, 189
Africa, passim.
Africa, east, 83, 94, 163
Africa, north, 47, 52, 54, 61, 63, 70, 95
Africa, west, 96, 103, 108, 151
Afshar (tribe), 70, 115
Afyonkarahisar, 180
'Afula, 192
Agha Khan, the, 94
Agha Muhammad, Shah, 70
Agri, province, 120
Agriculture, see pp. 278–9: also, 202,
    226 ff., 232–47
Ahmad, the Imam, (of Yemen), 86
Ahuramazda, 39
Ahwaz, 173, 178 f.
'Ajlun, district, 136
Akhdhar, Jabal, 16, 165, 247

Akhisar, 181
Akkad, 29
Alamut, 55
'Alawi (or Nusairi) sect, 94, 101, 131,
    208
Albania(ns), 72, 116
Aleppo (Halab), 13, 19, 55, 72, 102, 118,
    131, 133
Aleppo button, the, 21
Alexander the Great, 39 ff.
Alexandretta, 77, 133
Alexandria, 39 f., 105 f., 142, 146, 203
Algeria(ns), 16, 70
'Ali (the Prophet's son-in-law), 51, 65,
    93
'Alids, 52
Alp Arslan, 55
Alpine Man, 25 f.
Alps, the, 15
Altaic languages, 111
'Amara, 125
America, Americans, 11, 72, 78, 82,
    108 f., 128, 133, 136 f., 157 ff., 161,
    169, 171, 177 f., 183 f., 186, 200, 202,
    213, 224, 235, 246, 254 ff., 266
America, Latin, 98, 265
America, South, 108, 213
'Amman, 135
Amir Ghani (Mirghani), sect and family,
    95
Amorites, 30, 33 f., 36
'Amra, 160
Amraphael, 32
'Anaiza (oasis), 155
Anatolia, see Asia Minor
Anglican Church, 107, 177
Anglo-Persian (Anglo-Iranian) Oil Co.,
    255
Angora, see Ankara
Angora goats, 183
'Aniza (tribe), 69, 230
Ankara (Ancyra, Angora), 20, 41, 77,
    115, 180, 183, 203, 223, 225
Ansariya, Jabal, 130
Antalya (Adalia), 181, 238
Anti-Lebanon, 127, 130
Antioch (Antakiya), 40, 77, 105
'Aqaba, port, 18, 136, 188
'Aqaba, Gulf of, 134 f., 154, 188,
    191 f.
Arab Confederation (of 'Iraq-Jordan),
    81
Arab Refugees, see Palestine Refugees